THE RITUAL YEARBOOK

365 SIMPLE DAILY PRACTICES TO BOOST HAPPINESS & FULFILMENT

The Sunday Times Bestselling Author
THERESA CHEUNG

THE RITUAL YEARBOOK
365 Simple Daily Practices
to Boost Happiness & Fulfilment
By Theresa Cheung
First published in the UK and USA in 2019 by
Watkins, an imprint of Watkins Media Limited
Unit 11, Shepperton House, 83–93 Shepperton
Road, London N1 3DF

enquiries@watkinspublishing.com

Design and typography copyright © Watkins
Media Limited 2019
Text copyright © Theresa Cheung 2019
Artwork copyright © Watkins2019

The right of Theresa Cheung to be identified
as the Author of this text has been asserted
in accordance with the Copyright, Designs
and Patents Act of 1988.

Commissioning Editor: Jo Lal
Managing Editor: Daniel Culver
Head of Design: Georgina Hewitt
Designer: Karen Smith
Production: Uzma Taj

A CIP record for this book is available from
the British Library

ISBN: 978-1-78678-207-6

10 9 8 7 6 5 4 3 2 1

Typeset in Interstate and Harman
Printed in the United Kingdom

www.watkinspublishing.com

ACKNOWLEDGEMENTS

Sincere gratitude to my publisher, Jo Lal,
for being the inspiration behind this ritual
book series and to her invaluable help with
final editing. Thanks to Etan Ilfield for his
support and his vision. Thanks also to Ingrid
Court-Jones for her wonderful input and
much needed help at copy edit, to Daniel
Culver for his fantastic work at proof stage,
to Vikki Hartley for her joyful promotion,
to Jenna Brown for her magic with foreign
rights and to everyone at Watkins involved
in the publication and promotion of this
book. I am forever honoured to be given the
opportunity to write books for a publisher
that has such an incredible history and
esteemed reputation in the world of mind,
body, spirit.
   Heartfelt thanks to my brilliant publicist
Lyndsey Mayhew (www.lyndseymayhew.
com) and my wise agent Jane Graham Maw
(www.grahammawchristie.com). Credit also
to Ruthie Cheung for her research efforts
and her help with proofreading. And last,
but by no means least, deepest love and
gratitude to Ray, Robert and Ruthie, as I
immersed myself in the blissful ritual of
writing this book.

ABOUT THE AUTHOR

Theresa Cheung was born into a family of spiritualists. Since leaving King's College, Cambridge with a Masters in Theology and English, she has written numerous bestselling mind, body, spirit books, including two *Sunday Times* Top-10 bestsellers. She has sold over half a million books and her titles have been translated into more than 30 different languages and become international bestsellers, with *21 Rituals to Change Your Life* (Watkins) translated into 13 different languages. She has written features for personal growth and spiritual development for magazines and national newspapers, and her radio and TV work include an interview about spirituality with Piers Morgan on *GMTV* and Russell Brand's *Under the Skin*. She works closely with scientists studying consciousness and is collaborating with The Institute of Noetic Sciences (IONS), who awarded her readers this landing page: http://noetic.org/Theresa-Cheung/. Theresa has a thriving author page on Facebook and her website is www.theresacheung.com.

CONTENTS

INTRODUCTION: TIME TO WAKE UP

"You are what you repeatedly do"
ARISTOTLE

Relying on the power of positive thinking to change your life is like choosing the blue pill - to reference that iconic *Matrix* movie scene, where Neo is offered a choice between taking a red or a blue pill. Choose the blue pill and he will remain blissfully unaware of his destiny. Choose the red pill and he will see things as they really are. Choosing rituals is taking the red pill. It's waking up to the reality that if you want your life to change, positive thinking just isn't enough. You need to take meaningful action. You need daily rituals.

THE REAL SECRET

We've grown accustomed to thinking that intention, or the power of positive thinking, is everything when it comes to attracting good things into our life. But just as we eventually learn to trust a person by their actions and not their words, perhaps that's the same for the law of attraction. What if the universe responds not so much to our thoughts but to our actions? What if our daily actions signal to the universe that we are someone worth trusting and investing in? What if our daily actions are the real secret to a rewarding life? What if the universe is only interested in supporting someone whose actions match their intentions?

Seen in this clear light, we are not what we *think* but what we repeatedly *do*. Repeat an action often enough and it becomes a habit, but habits can't ignite change because they are mindless. They lack personal meaning. For actions to create lasting change they need to be filled to the brim with meaning. They need to be **ritualized**. This book will help you become aware of the meaning and significance of specific actions, so you can transform them into empowering rituals. You'll be encouraged to perform daily rituals for a year and, during the course of that year, to watch all areas of your life improve.

THE SCIENCE OF RITUAL

Rituals are repeatable actions performed with mindfulness, feeling and intention. Rituals give our lives meaning. They bring an element of the sacred into our lives or an awareness of something higher or greater than ourselves. Not surprisingly they are often associated with religion, but you don't need to be religious, pagan or even to believe in their power. Rituals, like spirituality, are universal and for everyone regardless of culture or individual belief.

Research[1] backs up the life-changing power of rituals. Numerous studies show that your brain is led more by your daily actions than by your thoughts. Change starts with what you repeatedly do – your small

1 Neal, D., *et al*: 'How do people adhere to goals when willpower is low?: The profits and pitfalls of strong habits', *American Journal of Personality and Social Psychology*, Jun 2013; 104(6): 959-75: doi 10.1037/ a0032626

Hobson, N. M. *et al*. 'Rituals decrease the neural response to performance failure', 2017; PeerJ, e3363, doi: 10.7717/peerj.3363

Brooks, A., *et al*: 'Don't stop believing: Rituals improve performance by decreasing anxiety', Harvard Business School, Jan 2017: http://faculty.chicagobooth.edu/jane.risen/research/Don't_stop_believing_rituals.pdf

Norton, M. and Hino, F.: 'Rituals alleviate grieving for loved ones, loves and lotteries', *Journal of Experimental Psychology*, Feb 2014; 143(1): 266-72: doi:10.1037/ a0031772. Epub 11 Feb 2013;

Conman, A.: 'Designing personal grief rituals: An analysis of symbolic objects and actions', Lancaster University Research portal, *Death Studies*, 19 June 2016: www.research.lancs. ac.uk/portal/en/publications/designing-personal-griefrituals (6f440948-5f38-45aa-bad1-9573ecfad1c3).html

everyday actions – regardless of what you are thinking. If you've ever felt your mood boosted after a brisk walk, you will already know the truth of this. It's how rituals work. The power lies in actually doing them and how they can focus your concentration on the present moment. These rituals may feel like small actions, trivial even, but you will find the transformative impact comes from repeating them. Daily rituals really can evolve into life-changing results.

Intention, or belief in the power of a ritual, is helpful but intriguingly new research[2] shows that you don't need to believe in the power of a ritual for it to work. The ritual just needs to have personal meaning for you, so you understand the reason you are repeatedly doing it. It also doesn't seem to matter what the actual ritual is, as other studies[3] suggest simply having personal rituals in your life is the key, regardless of what they are.

Most of the rituals are backed up by solid research and throughout this book you will find extensive footnotes[4] so that you can find the source of that research. When there is evidence of the benefits of a certain ritual, you will find it here, which will help you understand why you are being asked to do it. But it won't always be possible to provide evidence. Sometimes you will be asked to take a leap of faith and perform rituals inspired by influential thinkers. This lack of scientific evidence is not because the benefits aren't real, but because the real power of rituals is unseen. Science isn't yet ready to fully acknowledge the power of the unseen in our lives – although as you work through this book you will see that the gap between science and spirituality is closing.

2 www.scientificamerican.com/article/why-ritualswork/; www.bakadesuyo.com/2015/10/ritual/

3 F. Bryant, 'Savouring: A New Model of Positive Experience, NJ Lawrence Eribaum Associates, 2007; Vohs, K., et al.: 'Rituals enhance consumption', Association for Psychological Science, 2013; 24(9) F. Gino, Sidetracked: Why Our Decisions Get Derailed and How We Can Stick to the Plan, Harvard Business Review Press, 2013

4 As much as possible I have tried to provide footnotes to studies and references used for each ritual. However, please be aware that scientific research changes over time and it's possible that ideas or research may be connected to incorrect or out-of-date sources and/or credit not given when it should be. If you feel either to be the case please do email me at angeltalk710@aol.com and I will do my best to correct the issue.

All the recommendations for each day are inspired by rituals, or daily actions, that people do and which have been proven to have transformative benefits. Many may seem relatively small or trivial and you may feel that if you want to change your life you need to make big, dramatic changes. But transformation comes from the cumulative impact of numerous small rituals that keep you productive and on track.

Don't worry if you don't yet believe that rituals can empower your life. Just let this book help you understand the meaning of the rituals you will be asked to perform on a daily basis. Then perform them and allow them to prove their life-changing power to you in the days, weeks and months ahead. Above all, let rituals teach you the ultimate life hack, which is that the path to happiness is in your own hands. Fulfilment can't be found outside yourself in other people, money, a fabulous body, your career or status. It is something you make happen for yourself by what you choose to repeatedly do every day of your life.

HOW TO USE THIS BOOK

There are 365 rituals in this book. The 21 Foundation rituals should be repeated every day of the year and every ritual following on from those is also designed to be repeatable, in that you can do it on a daily basis if you choose to. However, they can also stand alone or be repeated for shorter periods - for example, seven days - or as often as you choose. Indeed, every ritual in this book should be an activity you choose to do repeatedly because you know that it will improve your life, not because it is something you feel you should do.

You don't need to start at the beginning of the calendar year. You can start today, right now, and seize the power of the present moment. All 365 rituals are simple, fun and easy to do. No additional equipment except a pen and paper and/or a couple of notebooks is required, and you may want to get into the routine of writing down or documenting your reactions after each ritual and charting your progress. There are 16 Power rituals scattered throughout the book, so-called because they consolidate or reinforce previous rituals in their section.

The recommendation is to work through the ritual year chronologically.

During that year you will work through a series of rituals that cover all areas of your life, making this a book dedicated to your holistic wellbeing. Start with the Foundation rituals and then move through the Body, Mind, Success, Spirit and Heart sections, performing one new ritual a day. Complete your year with the Closing rituals.

Although the chronological approach is highly recommended, this book also serves a multi-purpose function. The Foundation rituals must be completed first, but after that you can choose to dive right into the section that you feel is most relevant to you. For example, if feelings, relationships and low self-esteem (because the most important relationship you have is with yourself) are the areas of your life that you want to focus on first, you should start with the Heart section. If physical health is your priority, you may want to begin with the Body rituals. To banish negative thinking and discover greater focus, seek out the Mind rituals; for deeper meaning go to the Spirit rituals first; and if you want to focus on immediately boosting your productivity, try the Success section. Be aware the first three Closing rituals are for special days in the year: your birthday, an anniversary and holidays. You can jump to one of these when it's a special day, but afterwards do revert back to the section you were previously working through. It goes without saying that the Closing rituals should only be performed at the end of your ritual year.

To recap: the chronological approach is highly recommended but, with the exception of the 21 Foundation rituals, which should be approached first (as they lay the foundations for all the remaining rituals), and the Closing rituals, which should only be performed at the end of your ritual year (because they are all about the power of letting go, reflection and reinforcement of what you have learned during the year), there really is no right or wrong way to work through the rest of the sections in this book. Just aim to perform rituals every day for a year. This may sound daunting, but it is far easier than you think once you have completed the first three weeks and rituals have started to become a way of life.

To help you stay on target with your daily rituals, I've created a free ritual tracker and several other free resources to accompany your work through this book. You can download them at www.theresacheung.com where you will find a special page dedicated to rituals. You may want to head over there now to check it out.

LET YOUR NEW YEAR
OF RITUAL BEGIN

Before you begin your ritual year, find a pen and a blank piece of paper and write down how you would like to feel about yourself and your life one year from today. Write a few paragraphs or one short sentence, as much or as little as you like. Then fold that note, seal it in an envelope and hide it in a drawer or safe place where no one but you can find it. Commit to not looking at this note until a year from now when the Closing rituals in this book will remind you to revisit it.

Each day that you incorporate rituals into your life increases your chances of happiness and fulfilment, but you won't likely see clear signs of improvements until you've been doing them for at least three to four weeks. This is the period of time research[5] suggests it takes for neuropathways to form in your brain and for there to be a noticeable change in how you think, feel and act. So, commit yourself initially to working through this book for a minimum of 21 days and then hopefully your increased wellbeing will motivate you to keep going with your ritual programme for the entire year. You can also pick any three rituals in this book and just choose to repeat them for a minimum of 21 days, to see and feel the benefits.

You won't regret it. I have never felt happier and more fulfilled than on my ritual-a-day programme. I'm living proof of the difference a year of daily ritual can make. After decades of subscribing to the positive-thinking mantra – and feeling like a failure because however hard I tried to think positive, my life still sucked – a year ago I shifted my focus from affirmations to rituals, from thinking to doing. Three hundred and sixty-five ritual days later I've got energy and focus. I've purged toxic relationships from my life. My work is thriving. I'm filled with creativity and wake up each morning with a contented glow, eager to start a meaningful new day. Rituals have become such an important and empowering element of my life now, I can't imagine living without them.

5 Lally, P.: 'How are habits formed: Modelling habit formation in the real world', *European Journal of Social Psychology*, Oct 2010; 40(6): 998-1009

If you had told me a year ago that this level of personal transformation was possible using the power of daily rituals to wake up to the wonder of my life, I would not have believed you. Chances are you don't believe me right now either. I don't blame you. The only thing that can convince you is your own direct personal experience. So, without further ado, I'd like you to turn over the page and begin your year of life-changing rituals immediately, so you can discover for yourself the meaning and joy they can bring into your life. Let's take action. The right time for you to wake up is now.

Get in touch: please feel free to get in touch with me at any point during your year of ritual to discuss your progress or ask me any questions. You can email me at angeltalk710@aol.com or via my website www.theresacheung.com or contact me via my Theresa Cheung author page on Facebook and Instagram. You are also welcome to enrol at the Watkins Academy and take my Rituals and Spells for Every Day course there as a complement to this book.

Disclaimer: If you are wheelchair bound, on medication, injured, ill or pregnant you are advised to skip any rituals that require a full range of bodily movement. Move onto the next ritual or replace them with suitable exercise alternatives in consultation with your doctor.

21 *Foundation* RITUALS

The first 21 rituals are the foundation stone for your year of ritual

Unlike the other rituals in this book, which you can choose to make stand alone or repeatable, these 21 Foundation rituals need to be done every single day of your ritual year. The first 10 rituals should ideally be performed in the morning, Rituals 11 to 16 in the day time and Rituals 17 to 21 in the evening.

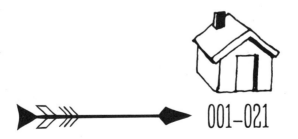

001–021

Once you have completed 21 days - learning one new ritual a day and cumulatively adding that new ritual to the other rituals learned the previous days - it won't be difficult to keep doing them every day because all 21 Foundation rituals are inspired by simple actions or tasks you already do. You will simply be shown how to assign personal meaning to these everyday actions and in the process **ritualize** them. Remember, the most effective and powerful rituals are not associated with religion, paganism or any tradition, but with your heart and your heart alone. It's the personal meaning combined with performing the action itself that gives the ritual its tremendous power.

21 AGAIN!

Consciously creating ritual acts that mean something deep to you will open you to an expanded version of yourself and help you attract good things into your life. However, for rituals to truly impact your life, you need to commit to doing them daily for at least three weeks, which is the minimum amount of time for an activity to imprint itself on your brain and become a catalyst for change. Hence the emphasis here on 21 rituals established over a period of 21 days being the foundation stone for your new year of ritual.

After 21 days you can choose to continue with your daily ritual programme or not. Chances are you will continue because you will already be feeling their benefits, but your conscious mind needs to be given the opportunity to make a choice at the three-week mark. If you tell your conscious mind on Day 1 you are going to commit to an entire year, it may well rebel because it hasn't yet experienced the benefits. Allow these Foundation rituals to prove to your conscious mind that the benefits are real and it is in your best interests to keep going for the entire year.

MORNING FOUNDATION RITUAL
#1: MAKE YOUR BED

If you want to change your life,
begin by making your bed

Making your bed every day when you get up can change your life.[1] It gives you a sense of pride, organization and motivation and can trigger a chain of good decisions during the day. It also turns your attention to the importance of little things in life. Last, but by no means least, it is a sign that you care about yourself and your environment, feeling cared for boosts mood.

It's very easy not to bother to make your bed and to come up with all sorts of excuses, but it's also very easy to do it and start your day – and the rest of your life – the right way. Making your bed every morning is perhaps the most common, simple and easy thing you can do to boost your chances of happiness. So, what are you waiting for?

Every day from now on commit to making your bed. If you already do this routinely, turn that routine into a **ritual**. As you plump your pillows, smooth your sheets and/or duvet, focus your thoughts on why accomplishing this first task of the day matters. Remind yourself that the simple ritual of making your bed sets the tone for the rest of your day. It can also provide you with comfort and satisfaction at bedtime. After all, few things match the pleasure of climbing into a well-made bed after a busy day.

1 William H. McRaven, *Make Your Bed*, Michael Joseph, 2017
Gretchen Rubin, *The Happiness Project*, Harper, 2011

MORNING FOUNDATION RITUAL
#2: RISE AND SHINE

Waking up early increases your chances of success in life, so become an early riser

Productive and successful people don't lie in. They wake up early, sometimes as early as five in the morning to plan their day and give themselves a head start. Many of them call this time of day their preparation or power time when they are at their most peaceful and creative. There[2] is a strong connection between early rising and success so, if you find it hard to get up in the morning, making a commitment to getting up earlier and sticking to that waking up time each day so your body clock adjusts, is a simple but extremely effective way to boost your productivity, health and positivity.

Treat waking up earlier and getting out of bed as a sacred gift to yourself that you know will give you the head start, energy and focus to begin living the life of your dreams. Make waking up each morning a **ritual** by congratulating yourself and filling those first waking moments of every new day with sacred meaning.

If you think you aren't a morning person, give waking up earlier a try for a few weeks to see if all the research is right, and you feel and work better. Just awaken to the day earlier than you normally would, even if only by half an hour. (Bear in mind, between six and nine hours of sleep each night is considered optimum.) If your work schedule makes it hard for you to greet the dawn, simply get up earlier at the appropriate time of day for you.

2 www.entrepeneur.com/article/289823
www.medicalnewstoday.com/articles/322159.php
3 Time.com/4737286/multitasking-mental-health-stress-texting-depression
Shakya, *H., et al.*: 'Association of Facebook use with compromised well-being: A longitudinal study', *American Journal of Epidemiology*, 1 February 2017; 185(3) 203-211. doi.org/10.1093/aje/kww189;
www.scientificamerican.com/article/mental-downtime

MORNING FOUNDATION RITUAL
#3: UNPLUGGING

*Make unplugging from screens and technology
a sacred part of your daily routine*

Most of us have our eyes glued to screens these days. Texts, emails, messages, updates bombard us. The digital world is addictive and we fear we will miss out if we aren't constantly scrolling. The opposite is true,[3] as there is a link between depression and too much screen time and social media use.

If you are worried about missing out, don't be. Relying on technology every moment of the day is unhealthy and taking regular time away from screens and social media will ease stress, boost your mood and help you focus and sleep better. Very little that we think is urgent actually is. The goings on or opinions of others won't change or improve your life; but giving yourself regular time to unplug and put the focus firmly back on yourself will.

Make a commitment to yourself to have at least one hour a day when you unplug. The ideal time is first thing in the morning when you wake up because what you do then will set the tone for the rest of the day. If you reach for your phone first thing, the message you send the universe at the start of the day is that the needs and opinions of others matter more than your own. Doing this ritual when you get up in the morning is highly recommended but, whatever time of day you choose, stick to it and make your unplugging hour a daily **ritual** of sacred time. It doesn't matter what you do in that hour either - you may decide to meditate, exercise, walk, tidy up, journal, sing or dance - as long as it doesn't involve a phone or screen of any kind, it's perfect.

MORNING FOUNDATION RITUAL
#4: POWER POSE

Stand tall and physically project your confidence in yourself and your life

Stretching is a sure-fire way to feel better. It[4] can increase flexibility, improve circulation, stimulate brain function and ease stress – it can also give you a wonderful shot of confidence. You are telling your mind, body and the universe that you matter. You are putting yourself centre stage in your own life.

Stretching and making yourself as big as possible sounds easy, but it isn't as easy as you might think, especially if you've got into the habit of minimizing yourself with closed postures. Many of us linger too long in the foetal position when we wake up or hunch over our phones or screens during the day, but our mind is led by our actions. If you diminish yourself physically this will diminish your thinking.

Stretching yourself as big as possible first thing in the morning is a daily **ritual** that sets the tone for the rest of your day. When you get out of bed, reach for the skies with an enormous stretch, perhaps accompanied by a loud battle cry as you remind yourself that your thoughts are led by your actions. You need to do something at this time that encourages your thinking to be expansive and shows you are worth all the blessings the universe can bestow. Later in the day when you need to make an important decision, use the power of this ritual again by striking a confident open superhero pose with hands on hips, elbows bent and legs spread apart. Pose and project your power.

4 uk.businessinsider.com/amy-cuddy-advice-waking-up-right-2016-1?r=US&IR=T
www.sciencefocus.com/qa/why-do-we-stretch-when-we-wake

MORNING FOUNDATION RITUAL
#5: DRINK UP
Drink in the benefits of water

Your body is around 60 per cent water. Drinking[5] sufficient water is essential for optimum brain function, hormonal balance, weight management and for your health and wellbeing in general. Water has incredible healing and purifying benefits. If you want to think, feel and look your best and get a better night's sleep, the message is clear: drink enough water.

Many of us grab coffee, tea, sodas and sugary drinks to keep us going during the day, but nothing beats a simple glass of water for giving you renewed energy and focus. Experts recommend around 2.8 to 3 litres or 8 glasses of water a day. That sounds rather a lot but it can be done easily if you drink a glass of water when you wake up, before going to sleep and before each main meal and snack.

Creating a daily **ritual** of drinking a glass of water first thing when you get up and before you dress or eat breakfast will help you make sure you drink enough during the day. As you drink it, pay attention to how refreshing and energizing water is. Remind yourself how essential water is for your health and how knowing all the benefits of drinking enough water improves its taste. You truly can't live without water, as every cell, tissue and organ in your body needs it – that is why this ritual is a foundation one.

5 www.healthline.com/nutrition/7-health-benefits-of-water
www.sciencedaily.com/releases/2016/03/ 160301174759.htm

MORNING FOUNDATION RITUAL
#6: THE POWER OF THREE

Writing down three things you are grateful for every day is a powerful happiness booster.

If you write down three things you are grateful for every day, this will dramatically increase your chances of happiness.[6] Not only can an attitude of gratitude increase your willpower and calm anxiety, it can also make you feel more positive. It seems that your brain has a gratitude "muscle" and the more you flex it by expressing gratitude, the more it adapts to an optimistic mindset.

If you are facing heartbreak, setbacks or loss, it can feel very hard to cultivate a grateful mindset. But paying attention to the good things we so often take for granted has been scientifically proven to boost mood. This ritual is something practical you can do to help yourself that actually works.

At the start of your day make a point of thinking about or, better still, writing down or typing three things that you feel grateful for in your life. Writing them down is better as the action of putting pen to paper empowers and transforms this exercise into a life-changing ritual. As you write down your three things to be grateful for, calm your thoughts and sense how performing this **ritual** is actually changing your brain. It can be gratitude for the sun shining, the support of loved ones or something trivial like the chocolate sprinkles you enjoy on your cappuccino. Doesn't really matter what you are feeling grateful for, just count to three and flex that gratitude muscle first thing every day. It's a genuine game changer that can attract success by changing the way you think, feel and act.

6 Siew, Tim, *et al.*: 'The three good things – the effects of gratitude on wellbeing: a randomised controlled trial', *Health Psychology*, March, 2017; 26(1)

MORNING FOUNDATION RITUAL
#7: LEAD WITH YOUR BREATH

*A small change in your breathing
can make a big difference to your life.*

Deep breathing[7] has astonishing health and happiness benefits. It oxygenates your cells, eases stress, boosts energy and clears your mind. In short, your body and mind follow your breath, so lead the way forward today and every day with a few moments of deep breathing.

Deep breathing feels unnatural at first because most of us have got used to taking small breaths. The problem is that shallow or "chest" breathing doesn't oxygenate your body and increases risk of poor health and stress. Given the proven health benefits of deep breathing, it simply doesn't make sense for a person who wants to change their lives for the better to not incorporate deep breathing into their daily lives.

Make a conscious decision to focus on your breathing for a few minutes. Breathe in through your nose from your belly (not your lungs) for about three seconds and allow your lungs to fill completely with air. Hold for a second or two and then exhale slowly, pushing all the air out of your lungs through your mouth. Repeat this cycle for a minimum of five inhales and five exhales. Use this exercise to remind yourself that this is about so much more than breathing – it is a **ritual** that will help boost your holistic health and wellbeing. The ideal time for this ritual is first thing in the morning as it will set the tone for the rest of the day, but doing it at any time is beneficial. The more you focus on deep breathing, the more naturally you will do it.

7 www.health.harvard.edu/mind-and-mood/relaxation-techniques-breath-control-helps-quell-errant-stress-response

MORNING FOUNDATION RITUAL
#8: IMPRESS YOURSELF

Look in the mirror and make a great impression on yourself

Smiling at yourself when you look at your reflection in the mirror first thing in the morning will significantly boost your mood, even if your smile is fake. The more you smile the more positive you will feel. Smiling[8] can generate positive emotions because it changes your brain activity. An added bonus is that smiling can also lift the mood of others because if one person sees another person smiling, mirror neurons in that person's brain activate as if they were smiling themselves.

There are many reasons not to smile, especially when life isn't going your way, but even a fake smile can make you feel a whole lot better. Research shows that a big smile involving muscle activity around the eyes triggers a change in your brain activity and mood. The action of smiling, even if that smile is with your teeth rather than your heart, is what matters here.

The next time you look at yourself in the mirror, take a moment to greet yourself with a big smile. This **ritual** of smiling will remind you that your relationship with yourself is the most important and sacred relationship in your life. We often look at our reflection in such a tense or serious way. From now on smile at yourself in the mirror as if you were meeting someone you really love or admire, or want to impress. Light yourself up with your beautiful smile.

8 socialpsychonline.com/2017/05/smile-psychology-science/
www.forbes.com/sites/rogerdooley/2013/02/26/fake-smile/#245862d73676

MORNING FOUNDATION RITUAL
#9: JUST SAY OM

Chant and infuse your life with joy

Chanting[9] has been shown to ease stress, lower blood pressure, improve focus and concentration, calm the mind and lead to improved wellbeing, peace and joy. It seems that the sound vibration you create when you chant really can make you feel happier, more energized and focused.

Chanting is associated with religion, but you don't need to be religious to enjoy its benefits. You may feel faintly ridiculous when you first try, but remind yourself that chanting is no different to humming, which many people do to help them relax and concentrate. Nobody considers humming odd. If you feel embarrassed, the recommendation is to chant when you are alone so you aren't influenced by the reactions of others. Indeed, doing your chanting when you are alone is beneficial as regular time alone is highly therapeutic.

Spend a few moments each morning before you begin your day doing some **ritual** chanting. As you chant, know that you are drawing good things into your life with every sound you make. If you don't know what to chant, you can simply use the most famous and ancient mantra of them all – *Om*, which is pronounced A-u-m. This primordial sound vibration is both calming and invigorating. You can also research specific mantras or you can make up your own. It doesn't matter what or how you chant, as long as you use chanting to infuse your life with joy.

9 www.theguardian.com/education/2010/may/03/repetitive-physics-om-improbable-research
Kalyani, B., et al.: 'Neurohemodynamic correlates of 'OM' chanting: A pilot functional magnetic resonance imaging study', *International Journal of Yoga*, 2011, Jan–Jun; 4(1): 3–6.

25

MORNING FOUNDATION RITUAL
#10: MORE UPBEAT

Power your day (and your life) with an upbeat track

Cheerful music lifts your spirits and can transform even the most mundane tasks into fun ones. Upbeat music[10] has the power to reduce stress, help you pay attention and give you all-day-long good vibes. If you believe music is a distraction and won't help you concentrate or feel better you are wrong. Studies show music plays a beneficial role in cognitive function, social skills and boosting mood, as long as we don't play the music too loud. As we get older many of us listen to music less and less, but this is your year of transformation and it's time to let more fun back into your life.

Before you begin your work or day be sure to put your headphones on and listen to a few minutes of energizing music. If you feel like singing along, all the better as singing also has therapeutic effects. Transform listening to your song into a **ritual** by focusing on nothing but that song and feeling the good vibes. Make this a sacred moment of joy in your day. You can choose a new tune each day or stick to the same one if it never fails to energize you. It doesn't matter what song or track you listen to, just make sure it is upbeat and makes you want to dance. Here are some that are guaranteed to make you smile instantly: "Dancing Queen" by Abba, "Hey Ya" by Outkast, 'Walking on Sunshine' by Katrina and the Waves, "Heaven on Earth" by Belinda Carlisle, "Happy" by Pharrell Williams.

10 psychcentral.com/news/2013/05/16/upbeat-music-helps-improve-mood/54898.html
Ferguson, Y., *et al.*: 'Trying to be happier really can work: Two experimental studies', *The Journal of Positive Psychology*. 2013; 8(1)

DAYTIME FOUNDATION RITUAL
#11: BACK TO EARTH
Get your daily nature fix

Science[11] is now clearly indicating what we intuitively know: a daily dose of nature is good for you. A cluster of recent studies have linked depression, obesity, aggression, ADHD and other health conditions and psychological disorders to a disconnection from nature. Nothing helps boost wellbeing more than a simple walk in the woods or the park. The problem is that the message is so simple it just isn't getting across effectively and millions of us aren't taking those walks in nature.

If your life and work is indoor focused, and you don't live near the countryside or a park, this isn't an excuse. There are ways you can incorporate a return to nature into your daily routine. It can be something as simple as leaning against a tree, walking barefoot on the grass, buying a potted plant or just getting more fresh air.

As a society we are increasingly dislocated from the outdoors due to reliance on technology and urban-based living, but the fastest way to boost mood and focus is to step outside. So, incorporate into your day a nature **ritual** where you simply appreciate, for a minimum of ten minutes, the wonders of the natural world. A walk in the woods or a park is obviously ideal but, if that's not possible, just head outdoors and seek out the nearest green space or garden. If going outdoors isn't an option, open your window, drink in the fresh air and watch the clouds drift or the stars sparkle. The more time you spend in green spaces or outside and make nature a part of your daily life, the happier you will feel.

11 www.bbc.co.uk/earth/story/20160420-how-nature-is-good-for-our-health-and-happiness
www.psychologytoday.com/us/blog/people-in-nature/200901/no-more-nature-deficit-disorder

DAYTIME FOUNDATION RITUAL
#12: USE YOUR EARS

Benefit from the sacred power of listening when you want to talk.

Constant communication is an unavoidable part of life today. The problem is that many of us listen selectively. We push our own agendas and don't actually listen to what other people say to us and in the process may miss out on learning something important. You will be surprised how much you can learn if you listen when you want to talk. Listening[12] is a key ingredient for success in life. The most effective leaders are those who listen to their colleagues, and the happiest relationships involve partners who listen to each other.

You may think that listening places the spotlight on someone else rather than yourself when this book is all about focusing more on yourself, but the only time active listening becomes toxic is if your voice is not heard or respected at all and you should avoid such one-sided dialogues and relationships. Balance is key. Have your say but when it comes time for someone else to speak, actively listen. Give someone the gift of your undivided attention. Don't check your phone, think about what you are going to say next or listen to find fault. Listen to understand.

Turn at least one conversation each day into a listening **ritual**. Remind yourself as you talk that there is sacred power in listening. Become aware of how paying attention positively impacts the person you are speaking to. It will have a beneficial effect on you, too. If you make other people feel significant because you really listen to them, they are more likely to want to listen to you.

DAYTIME FOUNDATION RITUAL
#13: BE MESS FREE

Tidying one thing every day will create positive change in your life

Less truly is more. The moment you start tidying up your living spaces, ridding yourself of mess and material clutter, is the moment you start resetting your life. Regular decluttering[13] is incredibly beneficial. It saves you time as you know where to find things and it eases stress because living mess-free encourages calm, organized thinking.

Clutter and mess can often feel overwhelming if you haven't been diligent for a while, but don't feel you have to do a time-consuming purge or spring-clean right away. Start small with the simple act of making sure your bag and your coat or jacket pockets are emptied out and tidied every day. Make tidying your bag and coat pockets a **ritual** by focusing on how being organized and tidy increases your chances of inner calm. Let this ritual inspire you to tackle other small tidying-up tasks during the day, such as sorting out your sock drawer or cleaning your bathroom sink, or donating items you don't need any more to charity, or even simply washing up your mug or cup rather than leaving it on your desk or in the sink. It doesn't have to be anything major. Small acts of tidiness can all help you experience the life-changing magic of living clutter-free.

12 www.wright.edu/~scott.williams/LeaderLetter/listening.htm
www.huffingtonpost.com/entry/the-power-of-listening-what-it-means-and-why-it-matters_
us_58129614e4b08301d33e079b
13 www.sharecare.com/health/stress-reduction/article/the-health-benefits-of-declutterng
McMains, S., *et al.*: 'Interactions of top down and bottom up mechanisms in human visual cortex', *Journal of Neuroscience*, Jan 2011; 31 (2): 587-97

DAYTIME FOUNDATION RITUAL
#14: CULTIVATE A BEGINNER'S MIND

Live on purpose by bringing your full attention back to the familiar

There is a reason why mindfulness has recently become a buzz word in the personal transformation movement and that reason is simple - it transforms lives. Mindfulness[14] can change how our brains work. It can help us stay focused, make better decisions and become more emotionally resilient. If you want to think and feel better, incorporating a mindfulness activity into your daily life makes absolute sense. If you think mindfulness sounds complicated, it really isn't. In fact, all the daily rituals you have performed so far have encouraged you to practise mindfulness without you even realizing it, because mindfulness is simply being fully present. It is being aware of what you are doing and not overly distracted by what is going on around you. It is focusing on something you are doing completely and on purpose. If your attention wanders, gently bring it back to the task.

Although every ritual in this book requires you to perform it with awareness, today's **ritual** encourages you to turn the spotlight on one task you typically do each day on autopilot and transform it into a powerful mindfulness ritual. It can be brushing your teeth, washing your hands, showering, cleaning or any activity that involves repetitive activity. It doesn't matter what that task is, just don't think about anything else but that action while you are performing it. Approach the task as if it was the first time you were doing it and give everything you see, hear, feel, smell and sense while you perform it your undivided attention.

14 www.forbes.com/sites/jeenacho/2016/07/14/10-scientifically-proven-benefits-of-mindfulness-and-meditation/
www.apa.org/monitor/ 2012/07-08/ce-corner.aspx
15 www.sciencedaily.com/ releases/2017/03/ 170307155214.htm
https://psychcentral.com/blog/10-health-benefits-of-daily-exercise/

DAYTIME FOUNDATION RITUAL
#15: WORK IT OUT
Exercise is a ritual most successful people do every day

Exercise[15] is an essential ingredient for a healthier, happier and longer life. There is no right or wrong exercise and it doesn't have to be anything complicated – a brisk walk will do. The key thing is to decide what form of exercise you enjoy doing, whether that be walking, running, cycling, swimming, dancing or sport and so on, and then just make sure you do it every day, without fail.

It's easy to make excuses to avoid exercise (and the "no time" one is the one many of us use), but if you are serious about changing your life for the better, daily exercise is non-negotiable. It releases feel-good hormones and boosts health and self-discipline and makes all the other rituals in this book stronger.

Today, make a sacred commitment to yourself to schedule regular exercise into your life every day for a minimum of 20 minutes. The health benefits are undeniable and you simply can't afford not to. Treat your daily exercise as a **ritual** from now on and, as you exercise, remind yourself just how good flexing your muscles, stretching and boosting your circulation is for you. Morning is potentially the best time to exercise as it can energize you for the day ahead. But it doesn't matter when you decide to exercise – just drop the tired excuses and do it. If you can exercise outdoors in natural daylight every day that's ideal, because lack of natural daylight can negatively impact your mood and ability to concentrate and sleep well at night.

There are many other powerful rituals that can dramatically boost your physical health. If you often feel tired, or your health just isn't as good as you would like it to be, the Body section is where you may want to head first after you've completed your 21 Foundation rituals.

DAYTIME FOUNDATION RITUAL
#16: MAKE SOMEONE'S DAY

Be the change you want to see in the world

It is all too easy to allow the negative opinions or behaviour of others to derail us. This book rightly puts the focus on you – and how you can attract happiness and success through the power of **ritual** – but research[16] shows one of the best ways to break free from the negative impact of others is to help them. Helping others can enhance your mood, ease stress and give you a confidence boost.

It isn't easy if you feel unhappy, but you will be amazed what a lift it gives you when you do something kind for someone else. It doesn't have to be anything big: something as simple as a smile or holding the door open or offering up your seat is enough. The only time helping becomes toxic is if you are giving at the expense of your own happiness or others take advantage and, if that's the case, you need to visit the Heart section of this book after completing the 21 Foundation rituals.

There's a third-party effect to helping others because there is strong evidence to suggest that if anyone sees or hears about someone being kind, it inspires them to do the same. So, one good deed really can start a chain reaction that makes the world a better place. It can all start with you. So today, and every day, make a point of being kind to someone. Notice the "helper's high" that you experience and tell yourself you are changing the world one small step at a time. In this way you are giving your daily act of kindness profound meaning. You are ritualizing it.

16 www.randomactsofkindness.org/the-science-of-kindness
https://helix.northwestern.edu/article/kindness-contagious-new-study-finds
17 www.forbes.com/sites/ellevate/ 2014/04/08/why-you-should-be-writing-down-your-goals/#4a839e733397
Brady, E., *et al.*: 'Journal writing among older adults', *Educational Gerontology*, 29: 151-63, 2003

EVENING FOUNDATION RITUAL
#17: WRITE UP

Writing about your goals and dreams every day increases your chances of achieving them

Psychologists[17] have proved that recording your goals and dreams in a journal on a regular basis can have a big impact on whether or not you transform what you are thinking about into reality. Journalling brings a clarity to your dreams that just thinking about them can't. In short, you are more likely to make your dreams come true if you commit to them to writing.

You may think something as simple as recording your goals won't make a difference, but it does because thinking activates the creative part of your brain and writing activates the logic-based part. With both parts of your brain fully engaged, you signal to yourself and the universe that you are absolutely committed and serious about changing your life for the better.

Journalling is a **ritual** that has deep personal meaning. It connects you to what is within you and what you want to do with your life. It helps you grow in self-awareness, as well as significantly increasing your chances of success. You don't need to be a writer to journal, just purchase a blank notebook or open up a document on your computer and commit to the ritual of journalling about yourself and what you want for your life every day. You can write as much or as little as you want but be sure to write something. The ideal time to journal is in the evening before you go to bed but it doesn't matter when, just be sure to do it. Write down your dreams and your goals for your health, your relationships, your career and your happiness every single day.

EVENING FOUNDATION RITUAL #18: ALL ABOUT THE NIGHT BEFORE

A rewarding day begins the night before

Planning your day by writing a to-do list the night before will drastically improve your productivity. You will wake up knowing what you want to achieve that day and there's nothing more satisfying at the end of the day to see items ticked off. Successful people[18] plan ahead or set out a framework for what they want to achieve each day.

You may feel by the evening that you want to switch off thinking about what needs to be done. While it is important to wind down at the end of the day (and to give yourself regular breaks in the daytime when you do nothing but daydream), if you give yourself a framework for the coming day the night before, you will be surprised how much more your productivity soars.

This evening, and every evening from now on, spend a few minutes planning for the next day. Give this planning time your full attention and transform it into a **ritual** that you know will attract success. Begin by laying out the clothes you will wear. See yourself wearing them tomorrow and having a productive day. Then sit down and give your undivided attention to planning ahead. You can schedule your day precisely, write a to-do list or simply create a framework that can be adjusted. It doesn't matter how you plan, just remove some of the guesswork so you have a sense of what needs to be done tomorrow and when. Be aware that the first few hours when you get up are often crucial for setting the tone of the day, so try to plan to do your essential tasks then.

For other rituals to increase your chances of productivity after completing your 21 Foundation rituals, you may want to refer to the Success section.

EVENING FOUNDATION RITUAL
#19: A CHAPTER A DAY

Daily reading will expand your mind and make you more productive

Reading every day has many benefits.[19] It keeps you mentally stimulated, boosts your vocabulary and memory, and improves your focus and concentration. It can also ease stress, promote empathy and keep you better informed. Knowledge is power and well-read people are often better equipped to deal with life's challenges. Last, but by no means least, reading is fun. Most of us watch box sets, films and documentaries online when we have free time or want to relax and have fun or learn something new. Nevertheless, however intelligent and well-made online productions might be, they can't beat the brain-boosting benefits of setting aside regular time to read a good book, a newspaper or a magazine. If you suffer from eye strain, the benefits are similar if you listen to audio books.

Make reading a **ritual**, the thing you do when you want to relax or to be entertained or informed. Set aside 15 minutes to half an hour each day, ideally before you go to bed, as your sacred time for focused reading. It doesn't matter whether you read fiction or non-fiction, just be gently aware that what you absorb or learn while reading can help make you smarter. Set yourself a target of reading one chapter a day to keep you on track.

Be sure to complete all the sections in this book but, if boosting your concentration and focus is a priority for you right now, after you have completed Rituals 20 and 21, you may want to head over directly to the Mind section.

18 www.lifehack.org/327177/8-ways-highly-successful-people-plan-their-time
www.success.com/5-daily-habits-of-highly-successful-people/
19 www.lifehack.org/articles/lifestyle/10-benefits-reading-why-you-should-read-everyday.html
www.theguardian.com/books/2014/jan/23/can-reading-make-you-smarter

EVENING FOUNDATION RITUAL
#20: SHARPEN YOUR NIGHT VISION

Dreams are like your internal therapist – listen to their wisdom

Scientific research[20] supports the notion that dreams are a source of intuitive insight that can improve problem-solving, self-awareness and creativity. Many of us don't pay enough attention to our dreams and are missing out on a wealth of untapped wisdom that can guide our waking lives.

If you struggle to recall your dreams, it doesn't mean you don't dream. We all dream during periods of REM (rapid eye movement) sleep. The issue is you can't remember them. The solution is to write them down immediately when you wake up. Don't wait until you have got up because, if you do, your brain will be distracted and the dream will vanish from your memory. If you still can't recall your dreams, don't give up. Research shows that the more you think about dreams and whether or not you will have them, the more likely you are to have them.

This **ritual** starts the night before when you are preparing to go to bed. Put a pen and notepad by your bed and, as you drift off to sleep, tell yourself you will remember your dreams upon awakening. Then, when you wake up, recall your dreams or the feelings and images associated with them, and write them down. Later in the day refer back to your dream journal. Don't force things to make sense, simply thank your dreaming mind for sending you nocturnal wisdom. Your dreams speak to you in the language of symbols and what those symbols mean to you. Everything in your dream is about you or an aspect of you which makes each dream an opportunity for personal growth. If you make a daily ritual of recalling dreams over time, you will find they can become a life-changing source of wisdom and inspiration.

20 Page, I. J., *et al.*: 'Creativity and dreaming: Correlation of reported dream incorporation into waking behaviour with level and type of creative interest', *Creativity Research Journal*, 15 199-205, (2003)

EVENING FOUNDATION RITUAL
#21: PRAY OUT LOUD
Say what you want and totally believe in it

It isn't clear why but science[21] shows that if you focus on something with great passion and positivity, it is more likely to happen – perhaps because if you truly believe in and feel passionate about something, you are more likely to take action to make it happen. When you focus positively in this way, you may not realize it but you are praying.

You don't need to be religious to pray. All you need to do is set your intentions and truly believe they can happen. There is no right or wrong way to pray. The only recommendation is that you do it, preferably in peace and quiet, and feel and believe in it with all your heart.

This daily **ritual** uses the power of prayer to bring about positive change in your life. Before you get into bed this evening, concentrate your mind and your energy on what you want to manifest in your life and then kneel down and say it out loud. You could write down a prayer and then repeat it every single day. The reason you need to kneel and say it out loud is that this action takes your intention from the unreal world of thoughts into the world of reality. You are talking to yourself and humbly asking the universe for what you want and you need both your conscious mind and the universe to hear you loud and clear. The Spirit section of this book will further help you connect to a power higher than yourself and, if discovering meaning and purpose is your priority, you may want to head over there ahead of working through the other sections in this book. Congratulations on completing your 21 Foundation rituals. You've reached a milestone and will soon be feeling the benefits. The recommendation now is to turn the page and begin your programme of Body rituals.

21 www.scientificamerican. com/article/scientists-find-one-source-of-prayers-power/ https://upliftconnect.com/the-science-of-intention/

𝓑ody RITUALS

Rituals for a healthier and more energetic you

Good health is the foundation stone
of any personal transformation
programme and one that is all too
often overlooked, because it is so
simple and obvious. But if you want
to live a fulfilling life, you need to
take the very best care of your body -
treat it as the sacred temple of
your mind, heart and spirit.

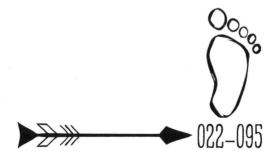

022-095

Scientists have identified the key things you can do every day to stay physically healthy for as long as possible. Problem is, the life-changing potential of what scientists have discovered is all too often hidden in scientific journals. This section takes their findings and packages them in scientifically proven activities presented as daily rituals. These Body rituals all complement your 21 Foundation ritual programme and should be performed one new ritual a day, over a period of 74 days. Each new ritual builds on the previous ones given. Once you have performed a new daily ritual, and understood and hopefully also felt the benefits, you then have a choice: you can continue to repeat it daily or simply whenever you feel it will benefit you the most.

To make it easier for you to perform the rituals in the order given, they are organized into the following categories: Get Moving, Healthy Eating, Sleeping Well, Body Image, Energy Boosting and Stress Reduction.

HOW BODY RITUALS CAN HELP YOU

If your physical health isn't as good as it could be, or you simply want to have more energy, this section is for you. It will help you make a sacred commitment to your body to take better care of it every single day. The hope is that by performing all 74 rituals you will be inspired to make permanent changes in your lifestyle so you continue to experience their incredible health benefits for the rest of your life.

Individually, all the body rituals here will give you an instant pick-me-up. Collectively, they are the golden key to long-term good health. There's a reason why people say that if you haven't got good health, you haven't got anything, so don't be tempted to skip this section thinking it is going to be the same old tedious "eat well, exercise more, blah, blah" advice you've heard a million times before. Some of the rituals here will surprise you, while others may seem like nothing more than common sense advice repackaged in ritual form. Whether unfamiliar or familiar, understanding the reasons why each action is good for your health and then performing that action mindfully with respect and gratitude (so it is **ritualized**) will help you feel nourished, energized, full of natural good health and, most important of all, zest for this wonderful life.

GET MOVING BODY RITUAL
#22: SKIP AWAY

Rediscover the lost art of skipping

Your first 12 days of Body rituals encourage you to incorporate regular exercise into your life. Let's begin by going back in time. Can you recall the last time you skipped? Probably not.

If you exercise regularly, this is great news for your health. But it isn't just regular exercise that makes a difference. It is how you spend the rest of your day. There's an abundance of evidence[1] to show that people who move more during the day are healthier.

At some point today break from your work or daily routine and spend a couple of minutes skipping. You can skip with a skipping rope or simply skip instead of walking. If you feel embarrassed, skip when you are alone and no one is looking. It doesn't matter when or where you do it, just give it a try. If skipping isn't physically possible, do something equally liberating and fun, like waving your arms in the air or stamping your feet. **Ritualize** your skipping by noticing how it makes you feel young and alive. Let your skipping ritual encourage you to make regular movement breaks a part of each day.

1 http://science.sciencemag.org/content/283/5399/212

GET MOVING BODY RITUAL
#23: FIDGET
Don't sit still

Time to dismiss all that advice you were given as a child to stop fidgeting – fidgeting[2] is good for you. Many of us spend extended periods sitting down and this increases the likelihood of weight gain and blood pressure problems. The obvious answer is to move more when you can (*see* Body Ritual 1) but, if you are driving, working at your desk or stuck in a meeting, this may not be possible, so the advice from doctors is to fidget.

When you are required to sit for an extended period of time today, tap your toes, bop your feet and shake your legs. Just keep your lower body in motion and, if anyone notices, tell them it's good for your health. Similarly, if your day involves extended periods of standing, fidget with your posture. The best posture is one that constantly changes, so keep changing it. Whether standing or sitting, **ritualize** your fidgeting by feeling grateful that something so natural and simple is a health-boosting gift you can give yourself anytime, anywhere.

2 www.physiology.org/doi/full/10.1152/ajpheart.00297.2016

GET MOVING BODY RITUAL
#24: ON THE EDGE OF YOUR SEAT

Perform a yoga chair pose

Even though yoga is perhaps one of the best overall health gifts we can give our bodies[3], many of us are still reluctant to commit to it. Perhaps there are mobility issues or we don't have the space or time. If this is the case, there are yoga exercises that take just a few moments, which you can do sitting in a chair without anyone noticing.

Today's ritual requires you to perform a sitting-down yoga pose called Cows and Cats. **Ritualize** by being fully aware of what your body is doing and the deep sense of overall wellbeing this pose is gifting your body. Sit at the front edge of the chair, place your hands on your thighs and keep your spine straight. Inhale and slowly and carefully arch your back, pushing your chest forward. Hold for a few beats. Then exhale and curve your stomach slowly into a "C" shape with your chin on your chest. Repeat. Notice how good this simple stretch pose feels. Let it inspire you to research other sitting yoga poses you can do.

3 www.healthline.com/nutrition/13-benefits-of-yoga

GET MOVING BODY RITUAL
#25: SIT ON IT
Try this D-I-Y yoga exercise

Yoga[4] is a wonderful form of health-boosting exercise. There are a number of simple basic yoga poses you can safely do by yourself.

Today's ritual is called the Chair pose. Stand with your feet hip-width apart and pointing forward. Take a deep breath and raise your arms in front of you shoulder height with the palms facing down. Relax your shoulders. Then with your arms still raised in front of you, bend your knees and gently push your pelvis down as far as you can comfortably, as if sitting in an imaginary chair. "Sit" there for five deep breaths before returning to standing again. Repeat. **Ritualize** your yoga pose by focusing only on the action of performing it, noticing your breathing and reminding yourself that this simple exercise is helping to strengthen your back and legs, and tone your entire body. (If mobility is a problem, *see* Body Ritual 3.)

4 Woodyard, C.: 'Exploring the therapeutic effects of yoga and its ability to increase quality of life', *International Journal of Yoga*, 2011; 4(2): 49-54.
doi: 10.4103/0973-6131.85485.

GET MOVING BODY RITUAL
#26: WALK OUT

Walk away and then back to it all today

Going for a daily walk[5] is brilliant therapy for your mind and your body.

Find 20 minutes today to go for a walk outside and take time off from the routines and pressures of your everyday life. Don't walk because you know it can help you keep fit, walk for the pure joy of walking. Let your mood set the pace. If you want to walk slowly, walk slowly. If you want to walk briskly, walk briskly. **Ritualize** your walk by noticing your breathing and how it perfectly coordinates with your walking. Pay attention to the pace of your walk and the way your arms gently swing without any conscious instruction from your mind. There's no effort or struggle. Walking is something you simply do.

As you walk and your breathing becomes deeper and fuller, feel your mind expanding too. You are giving your logical left brain a rest and your creative right brain an opportunity to shine, so you can return to your day with a new perspective.

5 www.health.harvard.edu/staying-healthy/5-surprising-benefits-of-walking

GET MOVING BODY RITUAL
#27: STEP UP
Take the stairs instead of the elevator

The health and mood-boosting benefits[6] of climbing stairs are well known. Your ritual today is to take the stairs instead of an elevator, whenever you get the chance.

As you climb up, **ritualize** the action by noticing how wide awake you feel. If you notice any fatigue or strain, pay attention to that and take it easy. You are using different leg muscles from the ones you use when walking. Enjoy the feeling of using those neglected muscles, as they are designed to be used. Remind yourself that you are strengthening your heart and boosting your circulation. You are climbing your way to better health. Hopefully, this stair ritual and its energizing benefits will motivate you to habitually use the stairs instead of the lift when there is a choice.

6 www.health.harvard.edu/staying-healthy/fast-way-to-improve-heart-and-muscle-fitness

GET MOVING BODY RITUAL
#28: CLIMB A MOUNTAIN

Grow in stature today

Spending[7] just a few minutes a day in a simple yoga pose can be great for your body's health. Today's ritual helps improve posture and balance, and eases stress. It's called Mountain pose. If you perform it with deep breathing, intention and presence, you **ritualize** it.

Stand up as tall as you can with your feet hip-width apart and your shoulders relaxed and down. Look straight ahead and gently focus your eyes on a spot ahead of you to keep your balance. Bring your hands together as if praying, with your elbows raised to the sides, and breathe deeply. Stay in this position for a few minutes, focusing only on your breath and how empowered it makes you feel. Imagine there is a thread attached to the top of your head pulling you upward. It might seem you are simply standing there but, when you try it, you will find that this is a very active and physical pose.

7 www.nhs.uk/live-well/exercise/guide-to-yoga/

GET MOVING BODY RITUAL
#29: KNEES TO CHEST

Lie down and think of your back

Today's ritual is a simple yoga pose[8] called *Apanasana*, which is therapeutic for your entire body, especially your back.

Lie down on your back with your legs stretched out, heels together, knees bent and arms resting at your sides. Exhale as you slowly move your knees to your body and hold them there as close to your chest as you can without straining. Keep breathing slowly and deeply, pressing your lower back into the floor. If you feel comfortable you can slowly and gently rock side to side to massage your back. Then, breathe out while you release your knees and place them back on the floor. Rest for 15 seconds before repeating again. **Ritualize** by doing everything in a slow and deliberate manner and by reminding yourself that you are doing this to stretch your lower back, tone up your abdomen, improve your posture and digestion, and boost your overall health. If you can't bring both knees to your chest, try doing one leg at a time.

Note: If you are unable to lie on the floor, try doing this ritual seated. Lock your hands underneath one thigh and bring it as close to your chest as you can, with your bottom pressing down into your seat, pulling up through your body to stretch your back. Repeat with the other leg.

8 www.ncbi.nlm.nih.gov/pubmed/26029093

GET MOVING BODY RITUAL
#30: DOMESTIC BLISS

Welcome housework as an opportunity to exercise

Housework is good exercise[9]. All that lifting, bending and reaching is a health-boosting workout and far cheaper than going to the gym.
Today think of housework not as an unpleasant chore you want to put off, but as an opportunity to work out. Set aside 30 minutes or more for some essential chores, like hoovering or cleaning surfaces and windows, which you may have been dreading doing because they require a burst of sustained, vigorous energy. This will help you burn calories, tone your muscles, improve your circulation and boost your energy, all at the same time. **Ritualize** your chore time by switching off entirely from the cares and concerns of your day and feel gratitude for the opportunity to move your body and do a free workout. Relish the fact that you can combine the benefits of exercise with the stress-busting power of decluttering. Reframe your attitude to housework. It's good for your body and mind.

9 www.independent.co.uk/life-style/housework-good-health-gym-workout-physical-study-training-body-a7960706.html

GET MOVING BODY RITUAL
#31: STAR JUMPS
Take a leap today

Jumping[10] like a child is great for your health. You don't need to buy a trampoline or a rebounder to experience the health benefits of jumping. Simply jumping on the spot for a few minutes can increase your heart rate, boost your energy and help strengthen your bones.

Your ritual for today is to set aside five minutes to do some gentle star jumps or jumping on the spot. **Ritualize** this by taking a moment before you start to be fully present. Then, do ten star jumps and rest for 30 seconds before you repeat. During your 30-second break, breathe deeply and notice how jumping makes you feel. Perhaps it reconnects you to your childhood when jumping was something you did just for the fun of it. You don't have to jump high or vigorously, simply jump on the spot and feel the impact. If you feel energized, you may want to consider buying a rebounder and making regular star-jumping breaks a fun part of each day.

Note: If jumping isn't possible for health reasons, do the low-impact version one leg at a time, reaching out to the sides with your arms, then reaching them over your head.

10 www.ncbi.nlm.nih.gov/pubmed/24460005

GET MOVING BODY RITUAL
#32: DANCE WITH YOUR ENDORPHINS

Say "yes" to good health with dance today

Dance therapy[11] has been shown to have encouraging health benefits. Moving to music is something you can do anytime, anywhere, and you don't need training or to join a class unless you want to. If you feel embarrassed, you can do it in the privacy of your own home when no one is watching.

Begin your ritual by preparing yourself to dance with a nod, as nodding can impact your mood positively. Lower your head right to your chest and then roll it back so your eyes are staring at the ceiling. Do this slowly and carefully five times and then make your whole body nod "yes" by rolling your upper body forward as far as you can and then slowly and carefully unfurling to an upright standing position again. **Ritualize** by focusing on how empowering it feels to signal a great big yes to the universe, not just with your head but with your entire body. Then put on some music you love and dance freely for a minimum of five minutes. Just let the music and the feel-good exercise endorphins guide you.

11 www.berkeleywellness.com/fitness/active-lifestyle/article/many-health-benefits-dancing

GET MOVING POWER RITUAL
#33: MOVE WITH GRACE
Treat your body to some Tai Chi

If you are used to a sedentary lifestyle, it can be hard to find the motivation to exercise even though you know exercise is good for your body. That is where ritualizing your exercise schedule (*see* How Much box opposite) can help because rituals bring a higher or deeper meaning to what you do, making you more likely to commit. Today's ritual is a **power ritual** because it reinforces the idea that exercise is about more than boosting the health of your body. It requires you to try a little Tai Chi. There is plenty of evidence[12] to suggest that Tai Chi has tremendous holistic health benefits.

Dating back to 13th-century China, where it was first developed as a non-combative martial art, Tai Chi is now practised all over the world. It is a form of gentle exercise that combines the benefits of deep breathing and meditation with flowing, graceful movements. It's a mistake to perform Tai Chi purely as exercise, as it's a way of moving that needs to be felt internally, and that is what makes it an ideal Body ritual.

The best way to learn Tai Chi is to sign up to a beginners' class with a trained instructor but, if that is not for you, Google Tai Chi movements and you will find many instructional videos. (The "Wave Hands Like Clouds" movement is a beautiful and calming exercise for beginners that you may want to search for first online.) Don't forget that Tai Chi can be performed anytime, anywhere, although the recommendation is always to

12 www.health.harvard.edu/staying-healthy/the-health-benefits-of-tai-chi
13 www.mayoclinic.org/healthy-lifestyle/fitness/expert-answers/exercise/faq-20057916

THE RITUAL YEARBOOK

do it outside, preferably barefoot on some grass, so you get the feel-good benefits of fresh air and nature, too.

Here's a simple D-I-Y, ankle-tapping Tai Chi warm-up exercise for today's ritual.

1 Stand tall and place your hands on your hips. Keep your knees slightly bent.

2 Put your left foot a little forward, and tap the ground in front with your heel.

3 Next, with your foot still forward, slowly tap the toes to the floor. Then tap with your heel. Do this three times in slow motion before returning your foot to the starting position. Repeat with your right foot.

Remember to **ritualize** this exercise by focusing on your breathing and noticing with full awareness not just what your ankle feels, but what your entire body feels, even the minutest sensations.

HOW MUCH?
EXERCISE

The recommendation[13] for adults is to aim for two and a half hours of moderate aerobic exercise each week. This is the kind of exercise that is continuous, so you get a little out of breath and are moving fast enough to raise your heart rate and breathe faster. Great examples are brisk walking, cycling, jogging and swimming. In addition, you should also aim to move as much as possible in your everyday life. Avoid sitting down for long periods and build regular stretching and muscle-strengthening work into your lifestyle.

HEALTHY EATING BODY RITUAL
#34: A MELLOW MEAL
Try a little slow listening and eating

The next 15 Body rituals will turn the spotlight on eating for good health. Let's begin by focusing not on *what* you eat but *how* you eat.

Busy people live their lives fast. But when it comes to eating, fast isn't better. It takes a while for your brain to register that your stomach is full so, if you eat fast, by the time your stomach is full you will already have overeaten. If you constantly overeat this will lead to poor digestion, fatigue and weight gain. The solution is to slow down when you eat. One way to do this is to play some slow classical music,[14] as this will help set an appropriate pace.

The ideal time to try a little slow eating is your evening meal. Choose some slow, mellow music to listen to while you eat. Beethoven's *Moonlight Sonata, first movement*, is absolutely perfect, but the music you choose is up to you – just make sure it is really relaxing. **Ritualize** your meal by mindfully savouring each mouthful in time to the slow music. Notice when you are full and need to stop eating. Set the intention to carry your newfound awareness of the importance of slow eating into your life.

14 www.sciencedirect.com/science/article/pii/S0195666306003849

HEALTHY EATING BODY RITUAL
#35: MAKE LEMONADE
Treat your body to lemon water first thing

Regularly drinking a glass of lemon juice[15] diluted with water first thing in the morning may have a whole range of health benefits. Lemon is high in anti-ageing antioxidants and nutrients that boost metabolism and immunity.

Start your day by squeezing some lemon juice into a glass of room-temperature water. Then sit quietly and drink the lemon water slowly, don't gulp it down. **Ritualize** as you drink by savouring the taste and reflecting on the health benefits, which have been noticed and revered from ancient Egyptian times to the present day. If you don't have any lemons handy, bear in mind that drinking a glass of water when you wake up may be almost as beneficial (*see* Foundation Ritual 5, page 21.) When you drink lemon water first thing, be sure it is on an empty stomach to help flush out toxins. Always rinse your mouth out afterwards and avoid brushing your teeth for 20 minutes, as too much acid isn't good for your teeth.

15 Theresa Cheung, with foreword by Dr Marilyn Glenville, *The Lemon Juice Diet*, Random House, 2008

HEALTHY EATING BODY RITUAL
#36: KICK START YOUR DAY
Breakfast energizes your entire day

Eating a healthy breakfast has been linked[16] to good health. When you wake up, your blood sugar is low, and breakfast replenishes it so you can get things done.

Your ritual today is to make sure you take time to prepare and eat a healthy breakfast. Many people skip breakfast as they are always in such a rush, but if you do that you are more likely to snack on unhealthy sugary foods to give you an energy boost. You need food in your stomach before you head out of the door. You don't need to eat a large meal – something small will do, like a bowl of porridge or a slice of wholemeal toast. The ideal healthy breakfast is wholegrain cereal with low fat milk and fruit, or a breakfast smoothie made from low-fat yogurt, fruit and a teaspoon of oats. Nuts and wholegrain granola are also delicious options. **Ritualize** eating breakfast today by sitting down and savouring it. Don't go on your phone as you eat, concentrate on the fuel replenishing you. Your body loves breakfast, so let this ritual incentivize you to treat your body to a healthy kick-start every day.

16 www.bath.ac.uk/research/news/2014/06/05/bath-breakfast-study/

HEALTHY EATING BODY RITUAL
#37: FUEL YOURSELF

Eat well today and create a healthier tomorrow

It's common knowledge[17] that you are what you eat, but far too many of us still don't make that crucial link between good health and diet. Your ritual today is to take a moment before each meal to truly think about what you are going to put into your body. **Ritualize** this by thinking of your body as an expensive car, like a Porsche or a Lamborghini. If you owned (or, lucky you, own) an expensive car, would you put low grade fuel in it? No, you would only give it premium fuel. The design and structure of your body is even more sophisticated and exclusive than any Porsche or Lamborghini, so treat your incredible body with respect and only give it the very best. Focus not on calories but on quality food.

Be fully aware in those sacred moments before you eat, that food is fuel. If you fill up on poor quality fuel you won't run efficiently. What you eat today determines how you will feel tomorrow. Make a solemn promise to yourself to choose your food wisely.

- - - - - - - - - - -

17 www.hsph.harvard.edu/nutritionsource/healthy-weight/best-diet-quality-counts/

HEALTHY EATING BODY RITUAL
#38: EAT A RAINBOW
Munch on colourful fruits and vegetables

Nutritionists[18] recommend eating a wide selection of different coloured fruits and vegetables to ensure you get a greater variety of health-boosting nutrients. It also seems that seeing coloured foods on your plate makes you less likely to overeat. Colour sends more potent signals to your brain than taste and smell – which is why foods with artificial colouring are bad news.

Ensure that you have a rainbow of natural colour on your plate today. **Ritualize** by focusing your thoughts on the health benefits, as you chew colourful foods and savour the taste. Here's a starting point:

★ RED: (apples, cherries, tomatoes and red peppers) contain lycopene, which has potent antioxidant, anti-ageing benefits.
★ ORANGE: (oranges, mangoes, sweet potatoes) contain beta carotene for eye health and hormonal balance.
★ YELLOW: (lemons, papaya, sweetcorn, butternut squash) contain both beta carotene and antioxidants.
★ BLUE/PURPLE: (grapes, blackcurrants, aubergines, beetroot) contain powerful antioxidants.
★ GREEN: (apples, peas, spinach, leafy green veg) contain antioxidants and superstar nutrients like sulforaphane, found in broccoli, which may protect heart health.
★ WHITE: (bananas, parsnips, mushrooms) are a good source of potassium, which is important for healthy heart and muscle function.

HEALTHY EATING BODY RITUAL
#39: TALK TO YOUR STOMACH

Before you eat, listen to your gut

Comfort eating[19] when you feel stressed or bored can result in excess weight and poor health.

Ritualize your hunger pangs by gently patting your stomach and then your head whenever they strike today. Let this gentle patting be a reminder to you not to instantly obey what your stomach is saying. Give your hunger your full attention. Study it. Question it. Ask yourself if you are physically hungry or if you are using eating to hide from your true feelings and fill the gnawing space inside. What are you really hungry and thirsty for? Sometimes it is hard to know but here's a clue. Emotional hunger tends to come on suddenly and can only be satisfied with the food you crave. Real hunger builds gradually and doesn't tend to be as specific in its food choices. Also bear in mind that often when we think we are hungry we are thirsty. If you do get a sudden food craving, drink some water and try other ways to comfort yourself. Read. Walk. Talk. Stretch. Meditate. Laugh. Paint. Do something else that helps you feel better.

18 www.bhf.org.uk/informationsupport/heart-matters-magazine/nutrition/5-a-day/colourful-foods
19 www.ncbi.nlm.nih.gov/pmc/articles/PMC4214609/

HEALTHY EATING BODY RITUAL #40: FOLLOW THE 80-PERCENT RULE

Stop eating before you feel full

If you consistently eat more food than your body needs, this will lead to weight gain and your health could suffer. Fortunately, there is a very simple way[20] to get back on track and that is to stop eating before you feel totally full.

Today's ritual asks you to apply the 80-per cent satiety rule to your main meal of the day. Prepare your meal and when you start eating, ritualize it by taking your time to chew thoroughly and ensure you put your knife and fork down between bites. Focus on the taste experience and savour your food. As you eat in this mindful way, pay close attention to what your stomach is telling you after each bite. As soon as you feel satisfied, stop, even if there is plenty of food still left on your plate. Forget what you may have been told about "waste not, want not" and throw the food your body doesn't need away. Become familiar with the feeling of being 80-percent rather than completely full. Feel gratitude for the satiety signal your body has sent you, because now you can recognize it each time you eat and stop overeating for good.

20 www.ncbi.nlm.nih.gov/pmc/articles/PMC4586540/

HEALTHY EATING BODY RITUAL
#41: BECOME A FOOD WRITER
Make your food journal a healthy eating inspiration

Keeping a food diary[21] can encourage you to make healthy food choices. Writing down what you eat is also a great weight-management tool.

Your ritual today starts as soon as you eat breakfast and ends after you have eaten your last meal and/or snack of the day. **Ritualize** by writing down what you have eaten and drunk immediately after you have consumed it. Then, in the evening when you are ready for bed, read your food journal. Understand that your food journal is encouraging you to eat mindfully rather than mindlessly. You will find that knowing you have to write down anything you eat will make you much more careful with your choices. It will deter overeating, encourage you to choose healthy food and also make you think about whether you are hungry or not when you eat. Be sure to record everything you eat during the day and don't omit anything, even if you feel guilty about it. If this ritual helps keep your food choices healthier, you may want to consider becoming your own food writer every day.

21 www.webmd.com/diet/news/20080708/keeping-food-diary-helps-lose-weight

HEALTHY EATING BODY RITUAL
#42: SEE RED
Include tomatoes in your diet

Including tomatoes or tomato sauce in your diet can have an incredibly beneficial impact on your physical health. Scientists[22] have linked the lycopene (the component that turns tomatoes red) to a reduced risk of heart disease and poor health.

Make sure you eat tomatoes and tomato sauce today. Most fruits and vegetables are best eaten raw, but the beauty of tomatoes is that even when they are cooked or made into a sauce, they keep their nutritional value. **Ritualize** eating them by savouring the delicious taste and reflecting on their multiple health benefits. Tomatoes are consistently ranked among the world's healthiest foods for a reason, so let today's ritual incentivize you to see red on your plate at least five times a week, preferably every day.

22 www.cambridge.org/core/journals/british-journal-of-nutrition/article/relationship-of-lycopene-intake-and-consumption-of-tomato-products-to-incident-cvd/56D38B7C2C9CF1D9C267CAE83AE92 BFF

HEALTHY EATING BODY RITUAL
#43: VITAMIN C TODAY

Enjoy the sensory experience of eating an orange

Vitamin C[23] boosts health and the best way to get it is not through supplements but in your diet. Oranges are a fantastic source.

Eat an orange as a snack between meals today, so you can take your time with this ritual and put all the focus on the full experience. One of the main reasons people are reluctant to eat oranges is because they can be messy to prepare, so have some kitchen paper to hand to clean yourself with and a knife to help you cut and peel the fruit. **Ritualize** your orange by taking your time to skilfully peel and cut it. Feel its texture and savour the taste of the sweet juice and flesh. Be sure to revel in any mess it might make on your hands and face, knowing it is a small price to pay for the incredible nutritional benefits. You may wish to wash your hands afterwards.

Eating an orange today will kickstart you snacking healthily, and you can ring the changes by exploring other fruits rich in vitamin C, like grapefruit, pineapple, kiwis, mangoes and guavas, which all make delicious daily alternatives for this ritual.

23 Moser, M., *et al.*: 'Vitamin C and heart health: A review based on findings from epidemiologic studies', *International Journal of Molecular Sciences*, 2016 Aug; 17(8): 1328.

HEALTHY EATING BODY RITUAL
#44: GET YOUR OMEGA-3 FIX
Take back control of your food choices

Deficiency in omega-3 fatty acids[24] can cause weight gain by triggering cravings for unhealthy foods, cigarettes and alcohol.

Today's ritual encourages you to eat some omega-3 essential fats, in the form of a handful of ground flaxseeds or a portion of oily fish, like salmon or fresh tuna. **Ritualize** your omega-3 fix by chewing slowly and savouring the taste. Think about how you are beating unhealthy cravings with a source of nutrient-dense food that is of the very highest quality. Relish how satisfying omega-3 rich food is. Let it incentivize you to make sure you eat oily fish or flaxseeds every day.

Note: You may want to consider buying an omega-3 supplement. It is always preferable to get your nutrients from the food you eat (as the body digests it better) but omega-3 is such an important food for physical and mental health that in this case you can make an exception.

24 www.ncbi.nlm.nih.gov/pmc/articles/PMC4150387/

HEALTHY EATING BODY RITUAL
#45: TAKE A BITE

An apple a day really can keep the doctor away

The rumours are true – apples are one of the world's healthiest foods. Numerous studies[25] have confirmed their health benefits. They are nutritional superstars packed with good-for-you anti-aging, immunity-boosting vitamins, minerals, antioxidants, water and fibre. Every time you eat an apple you can rest assured that you are giving your body premium fuel.

Choose an apple today with a colour and taste that you know is going to appeal to you. Some apples are more bitter than others, with red apples tending to be sweeter than green ones. **Ritualize** by eating your apple mindfully. Pause for a few moments before you eat to appreciate all the health benefits you know this apple is going to give your body. Then when you are ready take a bite slowly. Really savour the flavour. Chew thoroughly and don't take another bite until you have completely swallowed the previous bite. Each time you swallow feel grateful for the premium nourishment this apple is giving you.

25 www.medicalnewstoday.com/articles/267290.php

HEALTHY EATING BODY RITUAL
#46: GET YOUR OATS
Seek out a little oatmeal today

One of the best ways to boost your health is to ensure your diet contains the superfoods that science[26] has consistently proven to be packed with nutrients that are good for you. And there is no better superfood to start off with than oats.

Your ritual today is to get some oats. (If you are intolerant to oats, try quinoa instead.) Oats are rich in feel-full fibre, so can help you manage your weight and encourage healthy digestion. A bowl of oatmeal at breakfast is ideal, but you can also add a little oatmeal to smoothies, yogurt, bread, biscuits, cookie or snacks during the day. **Ritualize** by truly savouring the comforting taste and reminding yourself that foods often fall in and out of favour as far as health trends go, but not oatmeal. It has remained constant. It's a whole grain, feel-good, powerhouse health food that has the backing of solid research; your body will love you for all the oats you feed it.

26 Fulgoni, V. L., *et al.*: 'Oatmeal consumption is associated with better diet quality and lower body mass index in adults: the National Health and Nutrition Examination Survey (NHANES)', 2001–2010. *Nutrition Research*, Volume 35, Issue 12, December 2015, pp. 1052–1059.

HEALTHY EATING BODY RITUAL
#47: POWER UP YOUR DIET

Make spinach your energy-boosting food of choice

Popeye's power food really is as close as you can get to a superfood for heroes because of its proven abilities to restore energy, increase vitality and improve the quality of the blood. Spinach[27] is rich in iron, which helps increase the production of energy-producing mitochondria within your red blood cells. It also contains vitamin K, which is essential for bone health and is an elusive vitamin most of us need to eat more of.

Ensure you eat a cup of cooked spinach or include some spinach leaves in your meals or snacks today. **Ritualize** by paying full and grateful attention to what you are cooking, chewing and digesting. Fully appreciate the powerful energy you are gifting your body and be aware of the support you are also offering to your bones. Other sources of vitamin K (and to a lesser extent, iron) include broccoli, kale and green cabbage, so you can repeat this power-up ritual with them, too. Feel yourself growing in strength every day you cook and digest these nutritional powerhouses.

---

27 www.bbcgoodfood.com/howto/guide/ingredient-focus-spinach

HEALTH EATING BODY RITUAL
#48: CHOOSE BLUE
Incorporate blueberries into your diet

There is a superfood[28] out there, which can help protect your heart health and ward off inflammation, the key driver of disease. That superfood is the humble blueberry. It's packed with fibre and a range of powerful nutrients that can protect your heart, bones and skin, boost your immune system and improve your memory and mood.

Ensure you eat some blueberries today. You can add them to smoothies or to your breakfast cereal. They make a great addition to salads and all kinds of desserts. A handful of blueberries is also a delicious and nutritious snack. **Ritualize** by holding the berries in your hand before you eat or add them to your food. Feel their texture. Notice how light they are but how heavy they are in goodness. Then, when you eat them, think about all those nutrients flowing into your body, improving your mood and protecting your heart and your health. Be grateful for all that these nutritional superstars can do to benefit your body.

28 www.ncbi.nlm.nih.gov/pmc/articles/PMC3068482/

HEALTHY EATING BODY RITUAL
#49: SAVOUR YOUR PLEASURE
Indulge yourself today

One consistent theme among healthy centenarians[29] is that they allow themselves to indulge in things normally considered unhealthy. The secret is they indulge in moderation.

Your ritual today is to fully savour a treat that is typically considered unhealthy, be that your morning vanilla latte, your afternoon bar of chocolate, your evening beer or your after-dinner ice cream, sugary mint or cigar. Ditch your guilt entirely for this ritual. If it works for people who live healthy lives to reach 100 and over, a small treat isn't going to harm you. **Ritualize** your "naughty" pleasure by sitting down so you can really take your time to enjoy it. Remind yourself that it is overindulgence that is unhealthy and a little of what you love every day is good for you. The healthiest diet isn't one that excludes indulgent foods entirely, it's one that allows you to enjoy a wide variety of foods in moderation.

29 www.thenewamerican.com/culture/item/29234-wanna-live-to-100-eat-bacon-and-chocolate-smoke-and-drink-booze

HEALTHY EATING POWER RITUAL
#50: AMAZING GRACE

Give thanks before eating your main meal

In a world where some people still go hungry, it makes sense for the lucky ones who have more than enough to eat to show gratitude. Today's ritual is a **power ritual** because it consolidates all the previous ones that have turned the spotlight on food.

The ritual of giving thanks or saying grace before a meal is one of the oldest in the world. It is also one ritual we are most likely to hold onto when others fade away.[30] Be sure today to mindfully give thanks, either out loud or silently with your thoughts and heart, before your evening meal. **Ritualize** those moments by bringing gratitude and a sense of reverence to the table and put your hands together as if you were about to say a traditional prayer. Or, if you prefer, just sit with your back straight and your hands resting gently on your lap (rather than holding your knife and fork), close your eyes and give sincere thanks for what you are about to receive.

You can choose a traditional spiritual or religious blessing, or make up your own. It can be as simple as "Thank you" or *"Bon appétit"* or drawn from sources that inspire you, such as this beautiful Zen blessing: "In this plate of food I see the entire universe supporting my existence." It doesn't matter what you say, it is the grateful intention behind it that counts.

Bear in mind there are other rituals that can bring sacredness to your meals. You can light a candle or create a beautiful centre piece for your table, such as a vase of flowers. Whatever ritual you choose, ensure that it is deeply meaningful for you, brings a sense of reverence and gratitude and helps ensure that your main meal of the day is as nutritious, nourishing and as sacred as possible.

30 www.beliefnet.com/ wellness/health/2002/07/ bless-this-food.aspx

And now that you know just how linked your health is to your diet, start educating yourself more about the nutritional value of all the food you eat. (*see the What Counts? box below*). Get curious. Treat every meal and snack from this moment onward as a sacred gift to your body.

WHAT COUNTS?
CALORIES

According to research[31] the healthiest diet is a high-fibre one. It should also be balanced and provide your body with all the nutrients it needs to function optimally. You should ideally get most of your calories from unprocessed natural or "real" foods, such as vegetables, fruits, wholegrains, legumes, nuts and lean proteins. Consume oils and dairy products sparingly and also limit your consumption of empty calories from sugary, fatty and processed foods. Depending on activity levels, adult women generally require under 2,400 calories a day and men around 3,000 a day, but you need to experiment to find what calorie intake is optimum for your own weight management.

31 www.theatlantic.com/health/archive/2014/03/science-compared-every-diet-and-the-winner-is-real-food/284595/

www.heraldscotland.com/news/17349827.lancet-study-finds-highest-fibre-diets-linked-to-dramatic-reduction-in-mortality-and-disease/?ref=rss

For more detailed guidelines on eating a healthy diet visit:

www.who.int/news-room/fact-sheets/detail/healthy-diet

SLEEP WELL BODY RITUAL
#51: GOOD-NIGHT STORY
Power down to get your beauty sleep.

For the next five days your rituals will focus on the importance of getting a good night's sleep. Lack of sleep sets you up for fatigue, depression and poor health. There are specific activities[32] that can increase your chances of having a good night's sleep and one of those is to establish a regular winding-down routine. When you were a child you probably had a routine to induce sleep and this likely included a good-night story, a warm bath and a glass of milk. Having a familiar routine worked then and it can work again now.

Establish your own grown-up bedtime routine. One hour before you go to bed, avoid stimulating activities like eating a large meal or using your computer. Reading is an ideal bedtime activity but, if that's not your first choice, listen to classical music, take a bath, stretch, enjoy a cup of herbal tea or do some meditation, journaling, chatting to loved ones or whatever relaxes you most. Before you begin your power-down time, **ritualize** by taking a moment to stand or sit still. Pause and acknowledge the need to start preparing for bed. Be crystal clear in your intention. You are deliberately choosing to wind down, so you can prepare yourself for a good night's sleep.

32 www.sciencedaily.com/releases/2015/05/150507114316.htm

SLEEP WELL BODY RITUAL
#52: TAKE A NAP IN TIME

Shut your eyes for a few minutes

Sleep experts[33] recommend a short nap during the day to promote overall well-being and boost energy and concentration. It's important to set an alarm though, as taking a long nap - 30 minutes or more - isn't good news for your health.

Set aside 20 minutes to nap today, preferably in the early afternoon. **Ritualize** by stopping what you are doing and finding somewhere you can sit or lie down in relative peace and quiet. Be clear in your intention. You are going to recharge your batteries. Notice how you feel before the nap and feel grateful for the shift in your energy levels when you get up. If you haven't got 20 minutes, shorten it to six minutes. Even just lying down on your back with your knees bent and your lower back pressed into the floor for a couple of minutes can significantly push up your energy levels. If you can't lie down, sit and close your eyes. (If you are a contact lens wearer, closing your eyes lightly but not fully for a few minutes is the best alternative.)

33 Sara, C., *et al.*: 'Comparing the benefits of caffeine, naps and placebo on verbal, motor and perceptual memory', *Behavioural Brain Research*, Volume 193, Issue 1, 3 November 2008, pp. 79–86
https://io9.gizmodo.com/the-science-behind-power-naps-and-why-theyre-so-damne-1401366016

SLEEP WELL BODY RITUAL
#53: PAY OFF YOUR SLEEP DEBT
Have an early night

Sleep deficit can lead to poor productivity and can damage your health. Between six and nine hours' sleep a night is considered optimum. If you feel tired during the day, the chances are you have accrued a sleep debt[34] – the accumulated sleep you've lost due to poor sleeping habits.

Today's ritual encourages you to try turning in 15 minutes to half an hour earlier than usual. You might think getting up later is the best way to catch up on sleep, but this can be harmful because it confuses your body clock and makes it harder to fall asleep the next night. **Ritualize** tonight by being fully aware of the importance of going to bed a little earlier to pay back your sleep debt. Decide on your earlier bed time and then, about 30 minutes before, consciously begin to wind down. Write down the time you go to sleep, so you can start keeping a record of how much sleep you need to wake up feeling refreshed.

34 www.sleepfoundation.org/how-sleep-works/how-much-sleep-do-we-really-need

SLEEP WELL BODY RITUAL #54: GOOD-NIGHT DRINK

Have a soothing warm drink before bedtime

Sleeping well is essential for good health and a warm drink[35] before you go to bed has been shown to significantly improve your chances of falling and staying asleep.

Body Ritual 51 encouraged you to stick to a regular bedtime routine. Today's ritual turns the spotlight on making a warm drink an established part of that routine. Chances are when you were a child you were encouraged to drink a glass of warm milk before bedtime. There was wisdom in that advice as milk contains tryptophan, an amino acid that can induce sleep. But if you can't tolerate milk, or fancy something different, try chamomile or passion fruit herbal teas instead, as both may be even more effective at inducing sleep than milk. **Ritualize** by focusing mindfully on your drink and how it will help you sleep like a baby. Let all other thoughts and stresses go. Notice the smell of your drink, watch how it steams and relish the taste. Feel the warm glow settle your stomach ever so gently for the night.

35 Janmejai, K., *et al.*: 'Chamomile: A herbal medicine of the past with a bright future', published in final edited form as: *Molecular Medicine Report*, 2010 Nov 1; 3(6): 895–901. doi: 10.3892/mmr.2010.377

SLEEP WELL POWER RITUAL
#55: BEDROOM REFLECTION

Choose your bedroom placement carefully

Getting enough quality sleep is essential for your health (*see* What Counts? - Sleep box, opposite). Today's ritual is a **power ritual** because it enhances the four previous ones, which focused on getting quality sleep. It encourages you to establish order and calm in your bedroom, so that your chances of sleeping well are dramatically increased. It is inspired by Feng Shui, an ancient Chinese art and science[36] that considers how the placement of objects in relation to yourself in a room impacts your health and all areas of your life. It seeks to rearrange objects so that their combined energies encourage an environment of harmony and balance.

   To begin, sit quietly in your bedroom and really look at the room you spend your precious sleeping hours in. Look at it with curiosity as if you were seeing it for the first time. Then, when you are ready, review the following Feng Shui bedroom tips slowly.

★ **Don't sleep with your head underneath a window. If moving your bed is impossible, invest in some sturdy draft protection.**

★ **Remove work-related devices from your bedroom, so it is only associated with sleep and relaxation.**

★ **Remove as many electrical devices from your bedroom as possible and aim to let in as much natural light as you can during the day. (Opening your windows during the day is a great way to remove stagnant energy. Or you can try "smudging" – the ancient practice of burning sage to clear out toxins.)**

★ **If you have pictures on your wall, ensure they are ones that are positive and calming.**

★ **Remove and/or tidy as much clutter as you can from your bedroom and especially keep the space under your bed clear and tidy, as sleeping over clutter and chaos will drain your energy.**

★ The best bedroom colour is the one you like best, but all skin tones from porcelain to dark brown are recommended because they create an energy similar to an embrace.

Whether or not you believe in the principles of Feng Shui, **ritualize** your bedroom reflection time by doing a simple sketch of the ideal layout on a piece of paper. This will encourage you to truly observe and sense whether your bedroom is a place of love, good health and safety and if there are things you would like to change or reorganize. Ask yourself if you feel happy and nourished in your bedroom. If you don't feel calm in your bedroom, let this ritual incentivize you to make some much needed changes.

Sweet dreams!

WHAT COUNTS? SLEEP

If you stick to a consistent sleeping and waking cycle, your body clock starts to work for you and anticipate events, like getting sleepy at bedtime. Bearing in mind you need between six and nine[37] hours of sleep a night and getting up earlier is one of your foundation rituals, choose a regular bedtime that works best for you. If you would like some guidance, sleep experts generally agree that 10:30pm is a healthy bedtime and waking up before 7:30am is ideal.

36 *Academic Journal of Feng Shui* http://ajofengshui.co.nf/
37 www.sleephealthjournal.org/article/S2352-7218%2815%2900015-7/fulltext

BODY IMAGE RITUAL
#56: PERFORM A BODY SCAN

Give your body some mindful attention

The more you love your body and feel in tune with it, the more likely you are to take good care of it and your physical health. Sadly, most of us don't love our body enough or take the time to understand and connect to it properly. That's why the next three weeks of daily rituals are going to focus on things you can do to reconnect with your body and improve your body image. Let's begin by performing a body scan.

Our bodies try to send us messages about the state of our health all the time, but most of us are too busy to tune in. A body scan is a health-boosting mindfulness technique[38] that can help you tune into your body's wisdom.

Lie down or sit on a chair. Close your eyes and **ritualize** by focusing all your attention first on your forehead. (You will probably notice that you are frowning without even realizing it, so gently relax your forehead and face.) Then, move your mindful scan to your neck and shoulders and gently relax them, too. Turn your present attention to your arms and hands and then to your torso before shifting your awareness to your lower body, legs and feet. Check in with each body part as you go until you have noticed without judgement how every part of your body feels. What sensations and tensions can you detect?

Open your eyes. Write down what each part of your body is trying to tell you.

38 Querstret, D., *et al.*: 'Mindfulness, The effects of an online mindfulness intervention on perceived stress, depression and anxiety in a non-clinical sample: A randomised waitlist control trial', (2018) 9: 1825. https://doi.org/10.1007/s12671-018-0925-0
www.ncbi.nlm.nih.gov/pubmed/26186434

BODY IMAGE RITUAL
#57: INSIDE OUT
Fill your body with love and light

Finding inner peace can help chase away feelings of body dissatisfaction.[39]

Today's ritual will help you make peace with your body. **Ritualize** by taking a few minutes out of your day to sit somewhere quiet. Close your eyes and be fully present in the moment and crystal clear in your intention: you are going to meditate for a few minutes to improve your body confidence. Now, focus on your breathing. After a few moments ask your body what it has done for you lately. Feel grateful for this and all the pleasure it brings. Focus on the positive thoughts but if negative ones appear, just notice where in your body you feel negativity. This negativity might be about appearance or about function. As you observe the areas of tension, imagine a warm, golden light filled with love flowing into those body parts.

Concentrate again on your breath and breathe out any judgements, negativity and tension. Breathe in only light and love.

39 Albertson, E. R., *et al.*: Self-compassion and body dissatisfaction in women: A randomized controlled trial of a brief meditation intervention', *Mindfulness* (2015) 6: 444. https://doi.org/10.1007/s12671-014-0277-3

BODY IMAGE RITUAL
#58: REFLECTION TIME
Look at yourself with love today

A healthy body image is vital for good health.[40] Today's ritual is going to help you fight any inclination to dislike your body. All you need is a mirror or, if you can't find one, your phone camera will do. Look deeply into your own eyes and say out loud the following:

I (your name), love and value the body I live in.

Don't be surprised if you feel odd talking to yourself out loud in this loving way, especially if the internal dialogue you have with yourself is often negative and critical. **Ritualize** by meaning it when you speak these words but, if you don't mean it, just pretend you do, as mirror neurons in your brain will take note of what you say. Notice how talking to your body in a loving way helps shift your energy. Congratulate yourself. Today you are on your way to accepting and appreciating your body.

40 Grogan, S., *et al.*:'Body image and health: Contemporary perspectives', *Journal of Health Psychology* 11(4):523-530 · August 2006

BODY IMAGE RITUAL
#59: REFRESH YOUR WARDROBE

Clear out clothes you never wear today

Clothes you keep in your wardrobe but never wear are sending you a negative message about your body as it is right now.[41]

Look through your wardrobe today. If there is an item there that you haven't worn for ages, donate it to a charity store. If it's something you are saving for a special occasion, put it out to wear tomorrow to ensure tomorrow is a special day, as often those special days never come. **Ritualize** emptying out your wardrobe by reminding yourself that hanging onto items you don't ever wear is like hanging onto the past. It's time for you to look forward. If you are waiting to "grow back" into smaller clothes, this isn't healthy for your body image, because you always deserve to look your best. Clear out any clothes that are holding you back from living fully in the present.

41 Professor Karen Pine, *Mind What You Wear: The Psychology of Fashion*, Amazon books, 2014
www.dailymail.co.uk/sciencetech/article-2644076/You-DRESS-Clothing-significant-effect-self-esteem-confidence-claims-expert.html

BODY IMAGE RITUAL
#60: BRUSH IT OFF
Energize and detox your entire body

Dry skin-brushing is believed to stimulate our skin and lymphatic system, and help our body detox. It may also help distribute fat deposits and improve muscle tone.[42]

Experts recommend skin-brushing for a few minutes before you shower or wash in the morning because of its energizing benefits. For this ritual you may want to invest in a medium to soft skin brush. If you don't have a brush, a dry (not soft) flannel makes a less effective substitute. Avoid using hard brushes, as they may damage your skin. **Ritualize** by focusing all your attention on your brushing action. Think about how you are helping your entire body to detox and encouraging your skin to glow. Brush dry skin in long gentle strokes toward your heart. Start with the soles of your feet and work up your legs, over your lower back and abdomen and then move onto your arms, neck, (avoid face) to your chest (avoid nipples), shoulders and back.

42 https://onlinelibrary.wiley.com/doi/pdf/10.1111/j.1468-3083.2009.03355.x

BODY IMAGE RITUAL
#61: HEADS UP

Massaging your head is great for your hair and your health

Today's ritual is the first of several in this section to help you see every part of your body in a loving, new light. Let's start at the top with your head. Head massage[43] has been shown to ease stress, boost circulation, relieve tension and improve mood.

Try massaging your own head. **Ritualize** by paying attention to how therapeutic the massage action feels. Appreciate the miracle of your head, how it protects your brain and allows you to see, hear, taste and talk. Begin by placing your thumbs on your temples and let the fingers of both hands rest on your forehead. Apply pressure and then release that pressure in a circular massaging movement. Keeping your fingers and thumbs in position, slide your hands up your forehead toward your hairline, keeping the circular movement going. Once you reach the top of your head, apply firm pressure to it and then release. Move down the back of your scalp, and continue the circular pressure and release process as before, with your thumbs and fingers. When you get to the bottom or base of your head, you can repeat the massage starting from the base and moving toward the front of your head.

43 Howard, V., *et al.*: 'Using Indian head massage to aid recovery', *Nursing Times*; 109: 25, 14-16 (2013)

BODY IMAGE RITUAL #62: SCRATCH BENEATH THE SURFACE

Check your nails and your health

Doctors[44] can tell how healthy someone is by the texture, shape, colour and state of their nails. For example, pale and easily broken nails can be a sign of malnutrition or even heart problems, whereas bumps and ridges may indicate arthritis. Take a moment today to notice your finger nails. If your nails are painted, chances are that nail care is already a priority, but you can still benefit from spending time reflecting on how strong your nails look and what your choice of nail colour projects to the world about you.

Ritualize your nail appreciation by washing your hands today and then setting aside some time to examine your nails. Remind yourself how essential nails are for gripping things, scratching and performing all your daily tasks. If your nails aren't in the best condition, groom them mindfully and make a commitment to book a manicure if they are really out of condition. Remind yourself that everyone sees your nails and their condition will make a silent statement about you. Well-groomed nails suggest a person who takes pride in their appearance.

44 www.telegraph.co.uk/news/health/news/10851785/How-doctors-can-tell-if-you-are-healthy-by-your-nails.html

BODY IMAGE RITUAL
#63: HEALING HANDS

Pamper your hands and fingers

During times of stress a hand massage[45] can help you stay calm and relaxed. Today's ritual requires you to activate your self-soothing system with a hand massage.

Ritualize your hand massage today by appreciating just how hard your hands work for you every day, especially if you spend a lot of time typing. Your hands need pampering. Start your massage concentrating on one hand first. Pinch the tip of each finger and thumb gently with the fingers of your other hand. Then massage each finger in turn from knuckle to tip before slowly pulling outward on each finger in the same direction. Firmly massage the skin in between each finger and massage the back of your hand with your thumb working in between the knuckles. Then turn your hand over and massage your inner wrist and the palm of your hand with the thumb and knuckles of your other hand. Repeat the entire process with your other hand. (Alternatively, you can simply moisturize your hands for longer than normal.)

45 Mobini, M., *et al.*: 'The effect of hand reflexology on anxiety in patients undergoing coronary angiography: A single-blind randomized controlled trial', *Complementary Therapies in Clinical Practice*, Volume 27, May 2017, pp. 31-36

BODY IMAGE RITUAL
#64: HUG YOURSELF
Show your body how much you care

One of the most beautiful and healing things your arms and hands can do is hug. Scientists[46] have shown that hugging can lower blood pressure, ease stress and lift spirits. It seems that a 20-second hug encourages the release of serotonin - the happiness hormone. It isn't always possible to ask other people to hug us, but it is always possible to hug yourself.

If you think hugging yourself sounds weird just try it. The more you love your body, the more likely you are to take better care of it and enjoy the health benefits of that self-care but, just as it's not enough to tell someone you love them, sometimes you need to physically show it. The action of self-hugging is demonstrating to your body that you love and appreciate it. Simply wrap your arms around yourself, squeeze tight and hold for 20 seconds. Walk your fingers around your back to deepen the stretch. Ritualize your self-hug by telling your body how grateful you are for all that it does on your behalf. Marvel at what a unique miracle of DNA it is. There truly is no body like yours. Don't just tell your body you care, show it. Embrace yourself today.

46 http://time.com/5413957/hugs-are-good-for-you/
47 https://news.northwestern.edu/stories/2018/january/facial-exercises-help-middle-aged-women-appear-more-youthful/

BODY IMAGE RITUAL
#65: GIVE YOURSELF A FACE LIFT

Keep your fingers on your face

Today's ritual turns the spotlight on your beautiful face. Facial massage is a popular beauty treatment[47] believed to boost blood flow and help skin look younger and healthier. We often carry tension in our faces, so today's ritual is to give yourself a two-minute face massage. The ideal time is when you clean and moisturize your face, but you can do it anytime as long as you ensure your hands are clean.

Ritualize your D-I-Y face massage by focusing your awareness on the action and feeling of your fingers, as they gently touch and massage your face. Be proud of any wrinkles gained, because they are a sign of a life fully lived. Ignore all advice to keep your fingers away from your face. Touch your face with love, gentleness and tenderness. Use small clockwise circles on the following pressure points:

1 The centre of your chin, just below the bottom lip
2 Outside each corner of the mouth
3 Underneath each nostril, above the upper lip
4 On either side of the bridge of the nose
5 On the outside corners of your eyes
6 Under your eyes, pressing your way down to the centre of your cheeks
7 At the inside corners of the eyes, against the bridge of the nose
8 On the length of your eyebrows, pressing as you go
9 Your temples

BODY IMAGE RITUAL
#66: OIL YOUR TEETH

Give your teeth and gums a super clean

Clean, white teeth are good news for your heart health and your self-esteem, so the recommendation today is to try some oil pulling, an ancient Ayurvedic practice for oral hygiene[48] that may be highly beneficial.

Just put a teaspoon of oil, such as coconut, sesame or sunflower oil, in your mouth and swish it around for at least five minutes. **Ritualize** your oil pulling by sitting down and relaxing as you rinse your teeth, focusing all your attention on the smooth sensation of the oil in your mouth and how it is cleaning your teeth and your mouth by activating enzymes that can help flush out toxins. Be careful not to swallow any of the oil and dispose of it in your bin so that your sink does not block. Then, wash your hands and with your first finger gently massage your gums and teeth.

Note: Another Ayurvedic recommendation for oral hygiene is tongue-scraping or -brushing to remove unhealthy toxins and lingering odours. You can simply brush your tongue when you brush your teeth.

48 www.ncbi.nlm.nih.gov/pmc/articles/PMC3131773/

BODY IMAGE RITUAL
#67: HEAR YOUR OWN VOICE
How you talk tells your story

There is growing evidence49 to suggest that the sound and tone of your voice can express a great deal about your physical health. For example, certain conditions can make you slur your words, elongate sounds or speak nasally.

We all believe our voices are much deeper and richer than they are. This is because when we hear our own voice, the sound does not travel along the bone-conducting pathway, distorting the sound we hear. Today's ritual will help you appreciate the sound of your own voice. Begin by recording yourself reading out this paragraph. Then, play the recording back and listen carefully. **Ritualize** by focusing all your attention on the sound of your own voice. Don't concentrate on what you find jarring about it, but on what you like about it. Listen to the unique sound the world hears every day from you. What story does your voice tell? It goes without saying that if you hear yourself slurring or sounding less than healthy, a medical check-up is advised.

49 www.scientificamerican.com/article/the-sound-of-your-voice-may-diagnose-disease/

BODY IMAGE RITUAL
#68: LISTEN, DON'T JUST HEAR
Use your ears today

Things that are good for your body are also good for your hearing. One of those things is meditation,[50] which can improve hearing by increasing blood flow to your ears and impacting the way your brain codes and stores this auditory information.

Today's ritual requires you to do a simple five-minute meditation that is not only good for your body and your mind but for your hearing, too. Take a moment now to pause your day. Set a timer for three minutes and use that precious time to just listen. **Ritualize** by noticing all the sounds going on around you and how they appear and disappear. Don't analyse the sounds or attach any emotions to them, as that is merely hearing. This is not about just hearing but about mindful listening. Simply be aware of the sounds in your environment and let those sounds be. As soon as your mind wanders to stories, images or thoughts connected to the sounds, notice this and bring your awareness back to the sounds themselves. Feel gratitude for the wonderful gift of hearing and listening.

50 www.hearingreview.com/2016/04/research-suggests-enhanced-auditory-cognitive-skills-meditators/?ref=fr-img

BODY IMAGE RITUAL
#69: IN THE EYE OF THE BEHOLDER

Your eyes are a window to your health

It's often said that your eyes are the window to your soul but they can also be a window to your health.[51] Your eyes are often trying to tell you about the state of your health, but most of us don't pay attention to the signals they send us.

Ritualize by taking a good, long, close-up look at your eyes in a mirror today. Then, lose yourself in your eyes and get to know them intimately. There are so many subtle shades and tones of eye colour and all of them are absolutely beautiful. Appreciate the unique beauty and wonder of your own eyes. Notice, too, if they don't look as healthy as they could do and take immediate steps to correct that. (Red or bloodshot eyes suggest eye strain and lack of sleep; dry and puffy eyes point toward dehydration and poor diet; and if the whites of your eyes are discoloured, visit your doctor, as it could be a sign of an underlying disorder.)

---

51 www.webmd.com/eye-health/features/what-your-eyes-say-about-your-health#1

BODY IMAGE RITUAL
#70: MAKE IT 20/20/20
Look far ahead of yourself today

The human eye is not meant to be glued to one image for extended periods of time. If you spend a lot of time online or working at your desk staring at the same object, the 20/20/20 rule[52] will help you minimize the risk of dry eyes, eye strain and accompanying headaches and blurred vision.

Today's ritual requires you to do a simple eye exercise. It will help with eye strain and refresh your vision. At some point today when you find yourself staring closely at a screen or an object for a sustained period of time, refocus your eyes by looking at something in the distance, at least 20 feet (6 metres) away for about 20 seconds. Then return to your work. **Ritualize** your 20-second vision break by being fully present and noticing how thoroughly therapeutic refocusing your eyes feels. You may want to make this a 20/20/20 rule by repeating it every 20 minutes to keep the risk of eye strain at bay.

52 www.webmd.com/eye-health/eye-fatigue-causes-symptoms-treatment#2

BODY IMAGE RITUAL
#71: STAND TALL
Stand with purpose today

Good posture doesn't just project a more assertive image to others and increase feelings of self-esteem, it is also vital for good health. It reduces the risk of back problems and is essential for balance, coordination, breathing and digestion.

The ritual today is to become fully aware of your standing posture. When confidence is low, we tend to droop our shoulders, lower our eyes and let our entire body slump. It's as if we want to disappear. With your new-found knowledge of the proven power of an action to change your mind, set aside a few moments today to practise standing tall. Many of us favour one foot over the other. Rather than leaning or slouching to one side, stand tall with your feet parallel and about 5 inches (13cm) apart. Notice how this immediately makes you feel more stable and grounded. Straighten your back and relax your shoulders. Tuck your buttocks underneath you and gently pull your stomach inward. **Ritualize** your posture correction by focusing on how good it feels for your body to stand with purpose.

BODY IMAGE RITUAL
#72: SIT UP
Elevate yourself today in your chair

Slouching when you sit can wreak havoc on your wellbeing[53]. It can cause neck, back and shoulder pain, and contribute to fatigue, depression and constipation.

When you sit down today make a point of sitting toward the end of your chair first. Then, roll your shoulders and neck forward and deliberately slouch. Next, pull your head and shoulders up into a tall sitting position. **Ritualize** sitting tall by noticing first how unfamiliar but elevating this action feels compared to how you normally sit. Then, focus on how uplifting sitting tall feels. Stay in that position and relish the confident feeling it brings, then slowly release your posture.

Let today's ritual inspire you to check your sitting posture every 30 minutes whenever you need to sit for long periods of time.

53 *European Spine Journal*, 2007 Feb; 16(2): 283-298. Published online 2006, May 31.
doi: 10.1007/s00586-006-0143-7

BODY IMAGE RITUAL
#73: FEET FIRST

Recover lost awareness of your feet

Your feet are quite literally the foundation of your life. They provide you with support every single day under a great deal of pressure. If you have ever suffered from painful feet, you will know how difficult getting around can be.

Caring for your feet is a crucial part of any self-care routine.[54] Spend a few minutes today washing your feet with warm soapy water. Be sure to dry thoroughly between your toes and then to give both your feet a gentle massage. **Ritualize** by bowing your head to look at your feet and studying them as if it is the first time you have ever seen them. Do they look well cared for? Are your toe nails neat and trim? Is the skin firm and smooth or dry and cracked? If the latter, lavish your feet with moisturizer, especially your heels, as this is often the area that first shows signs of dryness and cracking. Inspect for any signs of corns and callouses and commit to eliminating them with proper foot care and well-fitting shoes in the future.

• • • • • • • • • • • •

54 www.diabetes.org.uk/guide-to-diabetes/complications/feet/taking-care-of-your-feet

BODY IMAGE RITUAL
#74: MAKING STRIDES
Give your legs a lift today

Legs that feel heavy, bloated or swollen, hamper your ease of movement and may also be a warning sign of poor circulation and health. One of the best ways (aside from walking and keeping your weight down) to keep your legs healthy is to put them up about 5 inches (13 cm) above heart level for 10 minutes each day.[55]

Today's ritual encourages you to kick off your heels or shoes. Pick a comfortable position near a wall and lie down on the floor. Lift your legs and shuffle your bottom as close to the wall as you can, stretching your legs up the wall, so you form an "L" shape. Stay there for around 10 minutes. If you can't do this against a wall, sit down and put your feet up in front of you on a chair or lie on your bed and put a pillow under your feet. **Ritualize** by fully experiencing your "legs-up" relaxation time and reminding yourself that you are not being lazy. You are simply caring for your legs and supporting the health of your entire body.

55 www.dailymail.co.uk/health/article-109067/Ten-steps-healthy-legs.html

BODY IMAGE RITUAL
#75: GET TO THE BOTTOM

Support your buttocks as diligently as they support you

A toned posterior will strengthen your back and pelvic floor.[56] Squats and lunges are effective ways to keep your buttocks firm, but buttock clenches can also help.

Today, when you are seated, do ten buttock clenches and releases in a row. This body ritual is quite a small action – all you are doing is shrinking your buttocks inward from the sides, raising yourself a little while remaining seated. Keep your feet on the ground and don't tense your leg muscles. All the focus is on your buttocks. **Ritualize** this exercise by inhaling deeply to a count of five as you clench and then exhaling for five as you release. As you clench and release, feel the strength of your gluteus muscles.

Your buttocks have the crucial and high-pressured job of keeping the trunk of your body erect. They support you every single day, so return the favour and support them by doing all you can to keep them well-toned and strong.

56 www.sciencedaily.com/releases/2014/10/141014152540.htm

BODY IMAGE RITUAL
#76: TAKE YOUR PULSE
Feel your body talking to you

Your pulse is an invaluable measure of your well-being.[57] Today's ritual requires you to take your own pulse, but not to measure it as a doctor would to assess your heart health, but to simply feel it. (Healthy heart normal resting rate is between 60 and 100 beats per minute, but if you are super fit it may be as low as 40 bpm.)

Find somewhere quiet. Set a timer for one minute. **Ritualize** by putting your index and third finger on the inside of your wrist below the base of your thumb, between the bone and tendon to find the radial artery. Notice how many beats you can feel per breath. You don't need to count the beats. You just need to be aware of them. Focus your attention on the thump of your pulse and the flow of your breathing. Most of us don't give our hearts beating away a second thought. Let the experience of sensing how your pulse coordinates with your breath give you an appreciation of the natural rhythms of your body and the energy that flows through your body, quietly supplying your heart with life.

---

57 www.nhs.uk/common-health-questions/accidents-first-aid-and-treatments/
how-do-i-check-my-pulse/

THE RITUAL YEARBOOK

BODY IMAGE RITUAL
#77: DROP YOUR TOWEL
Look at yourself as nature intended

Poor body image has a negative impact on your health and wellbeing.[58]
There is no quick fix if you've spent years hating how you look, but getting
used to seeing yourself naked is a great starting point.

Your ritual today is to take a look at yourself without any clothes on
in a mirror, ideally a full-length one. **Ritualize** by dropping your towel
after you have dried yourself when you step out of the shower or bath.
There is nothing wrong with taking an honest and appreciative look at
your body as nature intended in a full-length mirror. We look at our faces
every day in the mirror, but we are far less likely to look at our bodies
and be as accepting. Study the shape of your body and how it looks.
Remind yourself that nobody is perfect, and it is time to celebrate what
makes you unique. Your body needs you to accept it and not be critical.
The more you familiarize yourself with the way you look naked the
more comfortable you will be loving your body in the way nature always
intended you to.

Note: If your religious or cultural background makes this ritual
impossible, you can do it wearing your underwear or even fully clothed.
The important thing is getting comfortable with all of you, rather than
just the face you see in the mirror.

58 https://academic.oup.com/her/article/22/3/342/595939

BODY IMAGE RITUAL
#78: BE SENSATIONAL
Live more in your senses

Sex is great for your health,[59] so if you are in a relationship the more regular sex you have the better, but if you are not in a relationship you can experience similar health benefits by becoming more sensual. This means enjoying your body as it feels in the present moment without any judgement.

Today's ritual encourages you to reconnect with your sensual self through the simple act of taking a warm bubble bath by candlelight. If a bath isn't possible, spritz yourself with a seductive new perfume or aftershave, or choose silky soft clothes and enjoy how they caress your skin. Become aware of all your physical senses – hearing, sight, touch, smell and taste – and fully experience your bath, your perfume or choice of soft clothing with those five senses. **Ritualize** your sensual act by pausing to acknowledge where you are, what you are doing, what you are feeling in both your body and mind, as well as what all your senses are telling you.

Trust that this sensual approach will bring you a deeper connection to your sexuality.

59 www.telegraph.co.uk/health-fitness/body/surprising-health-benefits-having-sex/

THE RITUAL YEARBOOK

BODY IMAGE RITUAL
#79: YOUR BODY POWER ANTHEM
Let music be your body guide today

Images of bodily perfection via social media, magazines and movies are a major cause of body image anxiety, even though we know these images are heavily airbrushed or the result of clever camera work. There's no point trying to ignore them because they are everywhere. The answer is to step outside of the media hype and change your attitude. A great way to do that is through the power of music.[60]

Today's ritual – the last in your body image series – uses the motivational power of music to help you understand that your body is perfect just the way it is. Simply listen to a personal empowerment anthem, like "This Is Me" from *The Greatest Showman* (if you can watch the video online as you listen, that's even better) or "Beautiful" by Christiana Aguilera. If these songs aren't for you, find a track that makes you feel great to be you. **Ritualize** listening to it by feeling the raw emotional power of the words and the music. Let it empower you to love yourself, just the way you are, today and every day.

60 https://academic.oup.com/musictherapy/article/8/1/78/2756996

ENERGY-BOOSTING BODY RITUAL
#80: ALARM TONES

Make the start of your day fun

Good health and feeling energetic go hand in hand. This next week offers you simple rituals to instantly boost both your health and your energy levels. Let's begin with the side you get out of bed in the morning.

We've all heard that expression, someone "got out of bed on the wrong side", when they are grumpy first thing. The way you start sets the tone for the entire day, so begin with a great big smile on your face. Laughter[61] may not be a cure-all, but it has fantastically positive benefits for boosting energy and overall physical health.

Waking up can be tough but it doesn't have to be if you change your alarm clock ring tone to an energizing tune, preferably one that starts gently and then builds to motivate you to get out of bed smiling. When the alarm goes off, **ritualize** your waking-up moments by losing yourself in your chosen track. Absorb its happiness and positivity. Should you feel like singing or dancing along that's even better. Here are some "wake-up-smiling" song choices:

★ "On Top of the World": Imagine Dragons
★ "Wake Me Up before You Go-go": Wham
★ "Confident": Demi Lovato
★ "Lovely Day": Bill Withers
★ "Viva la Vida": Coldplay

61 www.mayoclinic.org/healthy-lifestyle/stress-management/in-depth/stress-relief/art-20044456

ENERGY-BOOSTING BODY RITUAL #81: CHEW PEPPERMINT

Inhaling peppermint can wake you up

Sucking or chewing peppermint[62] stimulates the same part of your brain that wakes you up in the morning. When you eat aromatic sweets, odour molecules circulate in your mouth and drift up your nose by the back of your throat, multiplying their intensity.

The ideal time to chew a peppermint would be after a meal or when you are feeling a little tired physically and mentally and in need of an instant energy boost. If you don't want the extra sugar intake, you can choose calorie-free gum or mints, or simply smell the mint rather than putting it into your mouth – inhaling peppermint is also effective. As you suck, chew or smell peppermint, **ritualize** by noticing with gratitude how it not only tastes and smells refreshing but, rather like smelling salts, wakes you up too.

---

62 Abbas, M.: 'Instant effects of peppermint essential oil on the physiological parameters and exercise performance', *Avicenna Journal of Phytomedicine*, 2014 Jan-Feb; 4(1): 72-78.

ENERGY-BOOSTING BODY RITUAL
#82: SMILE AND BREATHE

Inhale with a broad smile

All the health and energy-boosting benefits of deep breathing can be enhanced greatly if you inhale with a broad smile on your face.[63]

When you feel in need of an energy boost today, pay attention to your breathing. **Ritualize** by consciously breathing from your stomach rather than your chest. Then, when you are ready, exhale through your mouth and tell yourself you are breathing out stagnation and stress. Ensure that you exhale absolutely all the air. Then, inhale deeply through your nose with a great big smile on your face. Don't worry if your smile isn't genuine, just be aware that the physical action of smiling will send a positive message to your brain and from your brain to your entire body. You are, quite literally, breathing in positivity and better health.

63 Please refer to Foundation Ritual no 4 and 5 for research footnotes.

ENERGY-BOOSTING BODY RITUAL #83: GIVE YOURSELF A NATURAL HIGH

Indoor plants can improve your health

Indoor plants[64] are great for your health and your energy levels because they can help purify and humidify the air you breathe.

For this ritual you need an indoor plant. If you haven't got time to diligently care for a plant, your best bet is to buy or borrow low maintenance plants such as cacti and succulents. Other easy-to-care-for choices include spider plants, dracaenas, ponytail palms and Chinese evergreens, as they won't die on you if you neglect them. (According to NASA scientists, the easy-to-grow English ivy is the best plant for air filtering.) **Ritualize** by taking two minutes of your time today to give your plant your full attention. Notice its colour, shape and texture. Picture in your imagination how that plant will grow or change. Feel deep gratitude for the connection to living nature this plant is bringing you.

---

64 www.bbc.com/earth/story/20160420-how-nature-is-good-for-our-health-and-happiness
Min Sun Lee, *et al.*: 'Interaction with indoor plants may reduce psychological and physiological stress by suppressing autonomic nervous system activity in young adults: a randomized crossover study!', *Journal of Physiological Anthropology*, 2015; 34(1): 21.

ENERGY–BOOSTING BODY RITUAL #84: SALUTE YOUR DAY

Reach for the skies today

Just as there are certain foods that are nutritional superstars, there are also superstar yoga poses that can instantly boost your circulation and your energy.[65] Your ritual today is a yoga pose called the Upward Salute. It's an ideal pick-me-up to do during the day when you feel your energy levels dipping.

Stand in a relaxed position with your feet hip-width apart. Bring your hands into the prayer position in front of your chest and then **ritualize** your actions by focusing on your breath and being fully present and aware of what your body is doing. Inhale and exhale deeply and, as you do so, let stress fade away. When you feel calmer from the inside out, keep your hands in the prayer position and raise them over your head. Press your biceps against your head, tilt your head back slightly and gaze upward toward the ceiling or sky. Keep your back straight and don't allow your belly to push forward. Hold this empowering position for five slow and deep breaths as you salute the day.

65 www.health.harvard.edu/staying-healthy/yoga-benefits-beyond-the-mat

ENERGY-BOOSTING BODY RITUAL #85: SEE THE LIGHT

Your body needs daylight – seek it out

Spending time in natural light[66] can reduce the risk of cancer, boost skin health, elevate mood, and improve both concentration and energy. It also promotes faster healing, better sleep and even aids weight loss.

Your ritual today is to ensure you spend at least 15 minutes outside in daylight, ideally before lunchtime. If it's sunny be sure to wear sunscreen and sunglasses. If it's simply not possible to head outside, open a window instead and sit by it. **Ritualize** your exposure to natural daylight by soaking in and appreciating the energy that natural light is nourishing your body with. Know that it is helping to balance your hormones and body clock and, if it's sunny, feel the vitamin-D rays direct from the sun strengthening your bones. If you have trouble sleeping, make seeking at least 15 minutes of natural light a ritual every morning, as the amount of natural light you are exposed to during the day can tell your internal clock when it is time to sleep.

66 Mohamad Boubekri: 'Impact of windows and daylight exposure on overall health and sleep quality of office workers: A case-control pilot study', *Journal of Clinical Sleep Medicine*, 2014 Jun 15; 10(6): 603–611.

ENERGY–BOOSTING BODY RITUAL
#86: TAKE A STEP BACK

Try walking a few steps barefoot today

The earth we walk on is full of energy and getting in touch with that energy can nourish your body, mind and spirit. Walking barefoot is probably something you only regularly do at home. But there are a number of energy-boosting and health benefits to walking barefoot outside, including better posture and balance, as well as stronger leg and foot muscles and relief from poorly-fitting shoes. There is evidence[67] to suggest that direct physical contact with the earth through "earthing" (the scientific term for walking barefoot) can boost health.

Today's ritual requires you to take your shoes and socks off and walk barefoot, preferably on some grass, soil or sand or any natural surface. Be sure to check there are no stones or sharp objects. Just a few steps in your garden or a local park will do. The ideal time to do this is early morning or evening when the sun rises or sets, but choose the best time for you. **Ritualize** walking barefoot by focusing on how direct contact with nature through your feet feels. If you enjoy the natural reconnection, let this incentivize you to try longer periods of earthing.

67 www.ncbi.nlm.nih.gov/pubmed/22291721

ENERGY-BOOSTING BODY RITUAL
#87: SMILE OUT LOUD
Aim to laugh more today

Laughter[68] doesn't just boost your energy levels and your mood, it is also absolutely fabulous news for your health and physical wellbeing. It seems that laughter can increase antibodies, which boost immunity and lower cortisol, the hormone released when we are under stress.

There isn't a downside to laughing, so your ritual today is to do something that makes you laugh – not smile silently but really laugh out loud. This can be watching your favourite funny movie clip or reading a book of jokes or, if you can't find anything that makes you laugh naturally, simply laugh out loud for five minutes until you are out of breath. It doesn't matter whether you feel like laughing or not, just fake it and exercise those laughing muscles. **Ritualize** by noticing how your body feels when you laugh. As a child laughter came so naturally. But as adults we become so serious. Let your newfound knowledge of all the health benefits of laughter encourage you to seek out more opportunities to be less serious.

68 www.ncbi.nlm.nih.gov/pmc/articles/PMC2814549/

STRESS REDUCTION
BODY RITUAL
#88: TOUCH MATTERS

Hugging is good news, so give it a try today

Stress is a normal and natural part of life. Indeed, it can be good for us as it keeps us alert and focuses the mind, but too much stress is bad news for our health. Stress can cause headaches, poor digestion, depression and insomnia, and can also significantly increase the risk of disease. With up to 80 per cent[69] of trips to doctors linked to stress-related complaints, stress reduction is a vital part of any health-boosting programme and that's why your final week of Body rituals focuses on things you can do to ease stress.

One simple and surprisingly effective way to minimize stress is to hug or touch someone. Even a brief hug[70] has been shown to boost immunity and ease stress. Physical touch has a beneficial impact both on the giver and the receiver, making each hug you give and receive a win-win situation.

Today make a point of hugging someone you feel close to, as the benefits of hugging strangers has yet to be confirmed. This can include your partner, family members, friends or anyone you feel comfortable enough with to hug. **Ritualize** that hug by making it last a little longer than normal and feel deep gratitude for that person being in your life and the health benefits hugging gives you both. If a hug isn't possible, the good news is that touch has similar therapeutic powers. Consider shaking someone's hand when you meet them or even gently touching their arm. Having a massage is also great touch therapy.

69 www.webmd.com/balance/stress-managemtn/effects-of-stress-on-your-body
70 S. Cohen, D. Janicki-Deverts, R. B. Turner, W. J. Doyle: 'Does hugging provide stress-buffering social support? A study of susceptibility to upper respiratory infection and illness', *Psychological Science*, 2014; DOI: 10.1177/0956797614559284

STRESS REDUCTION
BODY RITUAL
#89: IN ONE SIDE
AND OUT THE OTHER

Alternate nostril breathing eases stress

A certain yoga breathing technique has been shown[71] to ease stress and improve overall well-being. You can do it anytime, anywhere and it is called alternate nostril breathing or *Nadi Shodhana*.

Set aside a few minutes today to do some alternate nostril breathing. **Ritualize** by covering your right nostril, inhale slowly through the left nostril, then cover your left nostril and exhale slowly through the right. This is one cycle and you should repeat the cycle at least five times. Focus on keeping your breathing slow, smooth and continuous. Notice how energizing it feels to breathe in this way. The reason is that as your breathing switches back and forth between the right and left nasal passages, this has a stimulating effect on your nervous system as well as physiological functions such as blood pressure, heart rate and respiratory function.

71 Telles, Shirley, *et al.*: 'Blood pressure and heart rate variability during yoga-based alternate nostril breathing practice and breath awareness', *Medical Science Monitor Basic Research*, 2014; 20: 184-193.

STRESS REDUCTION
BODY RITUAL
#90: MAKE SPACE
Set aside some time to streamline

Disorganized living and working environments[72] are a major source of stress. The solution is simple: make space by regularly throwing out, selling online or giving to charity any things you don't use or want any more.

Your ritual for today is to set aside some time, even as little as five minutes, to streamline. **Ritualize** the action of decluttering by reminding yourself just how beneficial it is for your health and happiness. Be sure to get rid of at least one item you don't need or use anymore and to give yourself some empty space. There is overwhelming evidence to suggest that clutter damages your health and interferes with your ability to enjoy life fully. Notice how fresh and light it feels to get rid of something (or several things) you don't need anymore. If you don't want to throw anything out physically today, turn your attention to your digital life. Delete junk emails or tidy up your desktop.

72 Roster, C., *et al.*: 'The dark side of home: Assessing possession 'clutter' on subjective well-being', *Journal of Environmental Psychology*, 4632-41. (2016), doi:10.1016/j. jenvp.2016.03.003

STRESS REDUCTION
BODY RITUAL
#91: BEAT YOUR OWN DRUM
Connect to your natural rhythm

Increasing evidence[73] suggests that the action of beating a drum has many health benefits, from boosting immunity and concentration to easing stress. Indeed, a number of hospitals use drumming to improve the health and mood of their patients.

Try some drumming today. You don't need to read music or buy a drum kit. Obviously if you can get hold of a proper drum kit that would be ideal but, if not, just use a hardback book, plastic box, table or shelf with a couple of pencils for drumsticks or just drum with your hands on your thighs. **Ritualize** by expressing yourself through the action – you can simply improvise or you can beat to the sound of a familiar easy-to-beat song in your head, like "We Will Rock You" by Queen. Focus only on the sound you are making. Ground yourself in the present moment and connect to the natural rhythms of your body and your life.

73 www.ncbi.nlm. nih.gov/pubmed/?term= Drumming+and+blood +pressure

STRESS REDUCTION
BODY RITUAL
#92: SMELL BETTER

Reach for lavender when you feel stressed

Lavender[74] has been shown to help ease insomnia, fatigue, headaches, indigestion and anxiety.

Your ritual today is to seek out lavender or something lavender scented – be that oil, water, soap, perfume or the herb – and then spend some quality time relaxing fully into the lavender fragrance. Drop some lavender oil onto a pillow or cushion, add some lavender oil to your bath, wash your hands in lavender-scented soap or spritz the air with some lavender perfume. **Ritualize** by reminding yourself of the proven therapeutic effects of lavender and allowing yourself to fully experience the scent. Let all thoughts and stresses go, so all you can smell and feel is the refreshing fragrance of lavender inhaled through your nose. Notice and feel gratitude for the gentle and natural power it has to soothe you.

74 www.independent.co.uk/life-style/lavender-scent-benefits-relax-anxiety-kagoshima-university-a8597421.html

STRESS REDUCTION
BODY RITUAL
#93: LET YOUR STOMACH GO

Make time for belly breathing and toning today

As Foundation Ritual 7 makes clear, deep breathing from your belly is one of the simplest ways to boost your health and ease stress.[75] The problem is that belly breathing feels unnatural, as we have got used to breathing shallowly from our chests.

Today's ritual is a yoga breathing technique that can not only encourage deeper belly breathing, but also tone your stomach at the same time. **Ritualize** by closing your eyes and focusing your attention only on your breath. If thoughts come into your mind simply notice them but don't interact with them. When you are relaxed, breathe in through your nose until your lungs are full and your chest and lower stomach rises. Let your abdomen expand fully and then exhale completely through your mouth. Once you have settled into a comfortable cycle of deep breathing for a few minutes use your abdominal muscles to pull in your belly and then force the air out in short sharp exhalations. Do this until all your air is expelled. Repeat ten times before returning to deep breathing.

Note: Do not perform this ritual if you are pregnant and stop if you feel dizzy at any point.

75 www.health.harvard.edu/mind-and-mood/relaxation-techniques-breath-control-helps-quell-errant-stress-response

STRESS REDUCTION
BODY RITUAL
#94: TIDY UP BEFORE BED
Put things back in their place this evening

Tidying up is good for your health[76] because it eases stress. You may think of cleaning and tidying as a strictly daytime activity, but doing a gentle tidy-up before you go to bed is both a beneficial and relaxing thing to do, so this is your ritual for today.

Set aside 15 or so minutes to make sure you have left your living space tidy and it will be a pleasure to wake up to. Put away the dishes, take the trash out, fluff the cushions on your sofa, put the TV remote where it belongs, place your keys, phone and wallet/purse in the same place, so you aren't rushing around in the morning trying to find them, and so on. **Ritualize** your evening tidy-up by focusing on the sacred significance of what you are doing. You are putting things back in their rightful places, saying farewell with gratitude to your day and also setting the scene for tomorrow. You'll sleep better knowing things are a little more organized. When you wake you will feel calm and fully prepared to start a new day.

76 https://health.usnews.com/wellness/mind/articles/2016-11-08/why-decluttering-is-good-for-your-health

STRESS REDUCTION POWER RITUAL
#95: CAST A SPELL

Try an ancient answer to an everyday problem

The last seven days of ritual have specifically focused your intention on ways you can ease stress, because stress is one of the most common causes of poor physical and emotional health. The final ritual in this Body section draws its inspiration from ancient stress reduction practices many of us would consider to be rather alternative. It's absolutely fine if you consider this to be too "out there" for you and this book doesn't want to push anything onto you. All it asks is that you consider giving one of the alternative rituals below a go. None will do you any harm and you may even feel some calming benefits. **Ritualize** what you are doing by reminding yourself of the stress-busting intention behind them.

Crystal work[77]: For centuries crystals have been said to emit healing energy because they are a product of the earth. The thinking is that when crystals are placed on or close to your body, they can help your body connect to the earth's healing energy. One crystal believed to have the power to ease stress is celestite. If you can, buy a small celestite crystal and carry it around with you today. Whenever you feel yourself getting stressed hold the crystal and gaze into its calming blue colours.

Essential oil power[78]: Essential oils from plants and flowers are said to be effective and natural stress busters. It is best to dilute essential oils with a carrier oil before they are used as a healing perfume. Apart from lavender, the best essential oils to ease stress are vanilla or rose. Put a few drops on your handkerchief or scarf and

77 www.livescience.com/40347-crystal-healing.html
78 www.livescience.com/52080-essential-oils-science-health-effects.html

when you feel stressed take a sniff. Feel how the natural scent instantly restores calm.

Cast your spell: For this pagan-inspired ritual you will need to gather some small stones and be near some running water or a stream. Find some quiet time and place the stones in front of you. Choose one stone that calls out to you and meditate on it. Pour any stresses or tensions you have into the stone. Think about the things that make you sad, fearful or angry. Channel all that energy into the stone. When you are finished, pick up the stone and cast it into the water, saying out loud, "Cast into the depths this pain I feel. Water I implore you to heal."

FINDING YOUR STRESS SOLUTION

If you ensure you eat healthily, exercise regularly and get quality sleep and relaxation time, you are taking the very best care of your body. Hopefully, the Body rituals in this book have all motivated you to treat your physical health as something sacred. However, stress isn't just caused by poor physical health. It can be the product of negative thoughts and feelings, and a lack of purpose in life.

The sections in this book that follow on from here all contain potent rituals to help you find meaning and deal with negative thinking, but you are encouraged to work through the Mind section next.

Mind
RITUALS

*Rituals for a more alert
and optimistic YOU*

A healthy mind is just as important
as a healthy body for a happy and
fulfilling life. A foggy brain loses out
on opportunities, limits creativity
and prevents you from noticing and
remembering what matters. It also
stops others noticing you.

096–169

Fortunately, there are many things you can do to improve your mind. In the same way that exercise tones your body, the more you use your brain, the fitter it gets. It was once thought that brain power decreased with age, but we now know that this is not true. Your brain remains highly adaptable and able to acquire new skills and information regardless of your age. The reason most of us feel we can't remember or concentrate as sharply as we used to when we were younger is simply because our brains have got lazy over time. When you were a child your brain was kept constantly busy learning new things every day. But after formal education and possible training for work, the great majority of us just stop using our brain. We let it drift passively on autopilot, typically repeating the same actions and thought patterns that don't get us what we want.

The good news is that brain researchers have now identified the key things you can do to stay mentally fit, and in this section of the book you will find these scientifically-proven activities presented in a series of 74 mind-boosting rituals. These Mind rituals all complement your 21 Foundation ritual programme and should be performed one new ritual a day, over a period of 74 days. Each new ritual builds on the previous ones. Once you have performed a new daily ritual, and understood and hopefully also felt the benefits, you then have a choice: you can continue to repeat it daily or as often as you feel will benefit you the most.

The rituals are organized into mind-nourishing categories: Diet and Lifestyle, Thought Management, Peace of Mind and Brain Training.

HOW MIND RITUALS CAN HELP YOU

If you want to sharpen your mind, this section is definitely for you. It is also recommended if you are prone to negativity, as it contains rituals to help you break soul-destroying thought patterns for good. It will help you understand that negative thoughts have no power over you unless you choose to give them power. Whether the rituals expand your brain power and/or help you become more positive, understanding the reasons why each specific action is so good for your mind and then performing that action with mindful intention and gratitude (so it is **ritualized**) will boost your mind and your chances of happiness.

DIET MIND RITUAL
#96: FEED YOUR MIND GOODNESS

Make your mind happy by consciously choosing a healthy lifestyle

The first 25 Mind rituals follow on naturally from the previous Body rituals section as they focus on brain-boosting diet and lifestyle recommendations. This is because the evidence[1] is overwhelming. Your brain power will significantly benefit if you make sure you eat healthy food, get quality sleep and partake in regular exercise, preferably outdoors. Consciously following simple and healthy lifestyle choices is the best possible news for your mind.

Your ritual today is to take some time out to carefully think about the choices you make every day as far as your diet, exercise and sleep schedule are concerned. Are you eating a balanced diet that is rich in unprocessed and fresh foods? Are you getting between six and nine hours of sleep a night? Are you exercising regularly and spending time in nature? **Ritualize** your lifestyle meditation by writing down exactly what you have eaten over the last 24 hours, how much you have exercised and how much sleep you have had. Then ask yourself how many of the lifestyle choices you made in the last 24 hours were conscious and how many of them were done without thinking. Promise yourself that moving forward you will follow a conscious lifestyle that feeds your mind the goodness it needs to function at its peak.

1 www.livescience.com/2675-good-diet-exercise-brain-healthy.html

DIET MIND RITUAL
#97: CONSIDER YOUR BRAIN
Give your brain something back today

There are certain superfoods that research[2] has shown are particularly beneficial for your brain's performance. One of those foods is the humble walnut, which is rich in brain-boosting nutrients, such as omega 3, vitamin B6 and magnesium.

Today's ritual encourages you to snack on a handful of walnuts. Instead of eating them mindlessly, **ritualize** by taking your time to truly savour their warm nutty taste. Reflect with gratitude on all the incredibly complex tasks your brain does for you effortlessly at lightning speed. It regulates the functions of all the organs of your body as well as your thoughts, memories, movements and sensations, and all it asks from you is the essential nutrients it needs to do its work. Think of the walnuts less as a food but more as a thank-you gift to your brain. Your brain does so much for you, it's time you did something special in return and walnuts truly are special.

Note: If you suffer from a nut allergy, try a handful of blueberries instead as a snack, as they contain similar brain-enhancing nutrients.

2 www.sciencedaily.com/releases/2007/11/071106122843.htm

DIET MIND RITUAL
#98: FOOD FOR THOUGHT

Savour the brain-boosting benefits of brown rice

Your brain works 24/7, even when you are sleeping. It's your body's greediest organ and needs a constant supply of fuel from the food you eat. The optimum brain diet is therefore rich in foods that are broken down by your body at a steady rate, thereby giving your brain a steady supply of nutrients and energy. One of those steady energy-release foods that your brain thrives on is wholegrains[3] – particularly in the form of brown rice.

Your ritual for today is to treat your brain to some brown rice, ideally as a snack during the day when your energy levels dip. You can eat it cold or warm, but be sure to cook it properly. It takes a little longer to cook than white rice but it's well worth the effort. It's bursting with concentration- and brain-boosting vitamins and minerals, in particular B vitamins, magnesium and calcium. **Ritualize** by mindfully savouring the rich, nutty flavour with each bite. Remind yourself why you have chosen to nourish your mind with brown rice today. If you can't tolerate rice, try gluten-free quinoa, which has similar benefits.

3 http://article.sciencepublishinggroup.com/pdf/10.11648.j.ijnfs.20130204.12.pdf

DIET MIND RITUAL
#99: CHOCOLATE BLISS

Magnesium can boost your brain power

No brain-boosting diet is complete without a daily serving of magnesium-rich foods and leafy green vegetables, such as spinach, almonds and avocado. Magnesium deficiency has been linked to cognitive decline, anxiety and poor memory.[4] If your diet is low in magnesium, your ability to focus and recall will suffer. Unfortunately, even if you take care to eat your leafy greens religiously every day, it is still easy to become deficient in magnesium because your body needs a constant supply.

Your ritual today encourages you to turn the spotlight on magnesium in a heavenly way. Buy a bar of quality dark (not milk) chocolate. Dark chocolate is one of the top magnesium-rich foods. Then **ritualize** by carefully breaking off two squares of chocolate. Place one square onto your tongue and chew slowly. Don't put the second square into your mouth until you have finished the first one completely. Focus all your attention on the taste experience. Savour fully. Chew mindfully. Take your time and feel gratitude for the blissful power boost you are gifting your brain.

4 www.sciencedaily. com/releases/2010/01/ 100127121524.htm

DIET MIND RITUAL
#100: MIND SPICE

Turmeric can keep your brain sharp

Most of us know that eating a diet rich in wholegrains and nutritious fresh, unprocessed foods is important for a healthy mind and body. But we may not realize just how useful certain herbs and spices can be for enhancing concentration and mind power. One spice that has been shown[5] to help keep our brain sharp is turmeric.

Your ritual today is to add a sprinkle of this delicious yellow spice to a warm beverage. Turmeric has powerful antioxidant (anti-ageing) properties and contains a chemical called curcumin, which can stimulate stem-cell repair in the brain and protect against memory loss. Add a pinch of turmeric to a glass of warm milk, almond milk or herbal tea and add honey to sweeten. Then **ritualize** by finding somewhere quiet to sit down and, as you drink, offer your gratitude to the universe for your newfound awareness of the benefits of turmeric for your mind. Let this ritual incentivize you to add a sprinkle of turmeric regularly to your cooking to help boost your brain power for years to come.

5 www.ncbi.nlm.nih.gov/pmc/articles/PMC2781139/

DIET MIND RITUAL
#101: GO BANANAS
Give your brain a fruity boost today

Research[6] has shown that students who eat bananas before an exam can concentrate and perform better. Bananas are superb brain food. Your brain needs a constant supply of glucose and bananas are a tasty and healthy way to help replenish depleted glucose reserves and fight brain fatigue.

Your ritual today is to make sure you eat at least one delicious, ripe banana. **Ritualize** your snack by mindfully savouring each bite with the knowledge that not only is a banana delicious to eat, it is also a nutritional powerhouse rich in many of the vitamins, minerals, fibre and amino acids that your brain craves, such as potassium, vitamin B6 and mood-enhancing tryptophan. There is enough evidence to suggest that regularly eating bananas is a great way to improve concentration. So perhaps a banana a day should become another brain-boosting mantra for you from now on.

6 www.livescience.com/45005-banana-nutrition-facts.html
www.mdpi.com/2072-6643/9/1/53

DIET MIND RITUAL
#102: SMELL THE COFFEE
Drink or smell some coffee today

The fact that coffee can make you feel more alert and energetic is something coffee drinkers already know. But what they may not know is that smelling[7] coffee beans can have similar brain-boosting effects to drinking it.

Your ritual today is to drink a cup of your favourite coffee but, before you drink it, to spend a few moments fully appreciating the aroma. If you don't drink coffee, you may want to purchase some quality coffee beans. **Ritualize** your coffee-smelling experience by feeling gratitude that in a world boasting such an expensive and confusing array of mind-boosting supplements and potions, you can boost your brain power naturally and safely simply by smelling some coffee beans.

Note: Coffee can become addictive and drinking excessive amounts is toxic and will keep you awake at night, so it is important to drink it only in moderation. Two cups a day are recommended. If you find yourself wanting to drink more than that, wake up and smell the coffee instead!

7 www.bbc.co.uk/news/health-40567047
www.sciencedirect.com/science/article/abs/pii/S0272494418302615

DIET MIND RITUAL
#103: B IS FOR BRAIN

Ensure your diet is rich in the Bs

There is evidence[8] to suggest that the higher the level of vitamin B in a person's bloodstream, the better their performance in memory, problem-solving and word formation. There is a variety of B vitamins and they all have different brain-enhancing functions, with B6 and B12 perhaps standing out as "supernutrients" for the brain, but they function best collectively. They are brilliant team players. If your diet is deficient in one B vitamin it is usually connected with deficiency in other B vitamins.

Today's ritual shines the spotlight on B vitamins to encourage you to make sure your diet is always rich in them. (You can take a B-vitamin supplement but nutrients are absorbed better from the food you eat rather than pills.) Set aside a few moments to do some investigating online about healthy food sources of the B vitamins. **Ritualize** by writing down B-rich food sources you need to include in your diet regularly and then plan your daily menu around them. Remind yourself of the important role the Bs play in healthy brain function and the life lesson they can teach you about the power of team work.

Note: To get you started, here are some B-rich suggestions: brown rice, lean fish, low fat milk, beans, lentils, almonds, sunflower seeds, broccoli, spinach, bananas and avocados.

---

8 www.ncbi.nlm.nih.gov/pmc/articles/PMC4290102/

DIET MIND RITUAL
#104: GET YOUR DAILY DHA
Your brain needs a constant supply of omega 3

There is a link[9] between eating oily fish or taking fish-oil supplements and improved memory and cognitive function. Fish oil contains DHA, an omega-3 fatty acid that the brain's memory centre absolutely thrives on – indeed, it can't function without it.

Adding fish oil to your diet is a great way to improve your brain health. That's why your ritual today is to ensure you always include omega-3 food sources in your diet. **Ritualize** by reflecting on why many of us tend to be deficient in omega 3 these days and create an action plan of things you can do to help you correct that imbalance. (**Hint:** diets high in processed foods remove vital nutrients, in particular the essential fatty acids.) If you want your brain to function at its peak, omega 3 – ideally consumed in oily fish such as sardines and salmon – is essential. In addition, your body can't store DHA so you may want to consider regular fish-oil supplements to ensure you don't ever become deficient.

Note: If you already take fish-oil supplements or are vegan or vegetarian include more non-fish sources of omega 3 in your diet such as flax, nuts, seeds and soybean.

9 Connor, Steve, *et al.*: 'DHA supplementation enhances high-frequency, stimulation-induced synaptic transmission in mouse hippocampus', *Applied Physiology, Nutrition, and Metabolism*, 20 June, 2012. DOI: http://dx.doi.org/10.1139/h2012-062

DIET MIND RITUAL
#105: LIGHT UP YOUR BRAIN
Think about your vitamin - D levels

One way to light up your brain (and your life) is to think about your vitamin-D levels and whether you are getting enough to keep your bones strong and your brain alert. Vitamin-D deficiency[10] is associated with poor brain function. Your body gets vitamin D from two sources – sunlight and food. If it's summer time, 20 minutes a day in sunlight is sufficient, as your body can make vitamin D each time sunlight hits your skin. Be sure to wear sunscreen if it's very hot. If it's winter you need to ensure your diet contains vitamin-D rich foods.

Your ritual today is to make sure you eat an egg as egg yolk is particularly rich in vitamin D. Eggs are nourishing fuel for your bones and your brain. **Ritualize** by truly savouring your egg as you eat it and letting the golden yellow colour of the yolk remind you to enjoy at least 20 minutes of nourishing sunshine every day. If you can't tolerate eggs, seek out some vitamin-D fortified cereals, salmon or tofu.

10 www.ncbi.nlm.nih.gov/pubmed/19460797

DIET MIND RITUAL
#106: CONSIDER HERBS
Herbs that can boost your brain power

The recommendation today is to do some of your own research into the best herbal supplements for your brain, how they are thought to increase brain performance, what the side effects are and what scientific studies have been done on them. Then consider whether taking a course of herbal supplements is something you want to do and, more importantly, is safe for you to do. **Ritualize** by choosing one herb supplement and writing down the pros and cons of taking it. Then, make a decision. Know that even if you decide not to take a supplement, you are learning about different ways to take care of your brain and forming your own opinion. You will inevitably come across the herb ginseng because it has been extensively researched[11] and has been shown to boost blood flow to the brain, thereby improving memory, concentration and alertness. Ginseng is inexpensive, so why not give it a try today?

Note: If you decide to supplement with ginseng or any other brain-boosting herb such as St John's wort, gingko or evening primrose, you should ideally consult your doctor first to ensure there are no contraindications. If you are pregnant, have high blood pressure or are on medication of any kind, it is especially important to seek medical advice.

11 www.ncbi.nlm.nih.gov/pubmed/18580589
https://bmccomplementalternmed.biomedcentral.com/articles/ 10.1186/s12906-017-1579-5

DIET MIND RITUAL
#107: SAGE ADVICE

Boost your wisdom quotient with sage

Sage has been scientifically[12] proved to improve brain function. Ensure you add some sage to your dressings, soup or juices today.

This ritual is simple and easy to do as sage has a wonderful soft, sweet but savoury flavour and is a great addition to any meal or snack. Fresh, dried whole or powdered, sage is readily available throughout the year. **Ritualize** sage into your diet by reflecting on its name as you cook or taste it. It's called sage for a reason. It contains nutrients that boost circulation to your brain and can improve concentration and focus. It is also rich in mood-enhancing iron, which has been found to ease anxiety. It is particularly delicious when added to tomatoes and lentils. You may also want to make drinking a revitalizing cup of sage tea a regular ritual. Simply steep some leaves in boiling water, add a natural sweetener like honey, put your feet up and relax secure in the knowledge you are increasing your wisdom quotient as you drink.

12 www.whfoods.com/ genpage.php?tname =foodspice&dbid=76

DIET MIND RITUAL
#108: BLESS YOUR DIGESTION
Go live today with probiotic therapy

If your digestion is poor, your mind and your body won't be getting the nutrients they need to function well. Fortunately, poor digestion and the resulting nutritional deficiencies this causes can be easily corrected by eating a balanced diet, exercising more and reducing exposure to toxins. It can also be corrected by a daily serving of probiotic foods rich in bacteria that promote gut health.[13]

Today's ritual encourages you to eat some delicious probiotic food or "live" yogurt, containing *Lactobacillus* and *Bifidobacteria*. (If you can't tolerate dairy, try sauerkraut cabbage, tempeh soybean or miso seasoning.) **Ritualize** by buying some probiotic food and eating it mindfully, relishing the healthy taste. Feel blessed that you are doing something positive to help your gut send your hungry brain the nutrients it needs for greater mental clarity.

13 www.healthline.com/nutrition/probiotics-and-brain-health

LIFESTYLE MIND RITUAL
#109: YOGA FOR THE BRAIN

Perform the Child's pose today

Certain yoga poses[14] are beneficial for your brain. One of these is the *Balasana* or Child's pose, which is your ritual today.

Ritualize by focusing all your attention on performing the pose and opening up space for peace to arise within you. Kneel on the floor and then lower your buttocks until you are sitting on your heels. Separate your knees so they are hip-width apart. Then, exhale and bend your torso forward draping it on top of your thighs. Allow your forehead to rest face down on the floor. You can either tuck your arms behind you with your palms facing up and elbows relaxed or extend them forward with your palms facing down, lengthening from your hips to your armpits and through your fingertips. Either way, keep your buttocks in contact with your heels. Let your upper back expand. Soften and relax your lower back. Let go of all tension in your shoulders, arms and neck. Keep your eyes closed and hold for up to a minute breathing deeply. To release the pose, carefully raise your torso upright to sit back on your heels.

Note: If you can't perform this pose, you can gain similar benefits by sitting at a desk or table and leaning forward to rest your head on it.

14 Yoga and Meditation Boost Brain and Energy Levels, newsmax.com/Health/Health-News/yoga-meditation-boost-brain/2017/09/06/id/812034/

LIFESTYLE MIND RITUAL
#110: HEADSTAND

Train your brain with a yoga pose

Today's ritual requires you to do the *Padahastasana*. It's another yoga pose that is believed to stimulate blood flow to your brain and by so doing boost your brain power.[15]

Stand tall with your feet together. Then bend carefully at the hips as far as you can toward the floor. The ideal is for your hands to touch your feet or the floor beside your feet but only go as far as you are comfortable, even if that is just your shins and thighs. If you can't keep your legs straight, bend them as much as you need to in order to touch the floor. Stay in this position for 20 seconds and then slowly and carefully return to a standing position. **Ritualize** this yoga pose by breathing deeply and focusing mindfully on what you are doing and noticing how refreshing it feels to boost blood flow to your head and brain.

Note: You can also do this yoga pose from a sitting position by bending at the waist and touching the floor, with your head in your lap.

15 www.ncbi.nlm.nih.gov/pmc/articles/PMC3155099/

LIFESTYLE BODY RITUAL
#111: WALK AND TALK

When your phone rings, head outside

The most beneficial kind of physical exercise for your brain is aerobic exercise, or continuous movement that raises your heart rate so you get slightly out of breath. Brisk walking, jogging, swimming and cycling are all forms of aerobic exercise. One study[16] showed that after just 30 minutes of moderate aerobic exercise, brain-processing speed increased significantly.

Go for a brisk walk today whenever your phone rings and you need to have a conversation. Heading outside is best but, if that's not possible, pace around indoors. **Ritualize** what you are doing by noticing the pace you are walking at and how easy it is for you to speak. Be aware of your breathing because for exercise to be aerobic, you should be slightly out of breath but still able to carry on a conversation. Feel gratitude for your ability to efficiently combine two productive things for your brain at once – stimulating conversation and exercise. If it's a day when you aren't scheduled to speak on the phone, call someone you haven't spoken to for a while, or just go for a brisk 30-minute walk anyway. Either way, your brain will be grateful for any movement.

16 https://abcnews.go.com/GMA/exercise-boost-brainpower/story?id=8840026

LIFESTYLE MIND RITUAL
#112: STARTER FOR 10

Brief bursts of exercise can improve focus and problem-solving

Exercise is good news for your brain and there are measurable brain-health benefits after 20 minutes of aerobic exercise. But if you can't commit to a long-term exercise regime because of time or physical capacity, exciting research[17] suggests that even a ten-minute short burst of exercise can boost parts of your brain responsible for decision-making and focus.

Today's mind-boosting ritual encourages you to do a ten-minute burst of exercise. It doesn't matter what that exercise is. It can be brisk walking, running, cycling, dancing, boxing, skipping, stepping or any sport that requires continuous movement. **Ritualize** by focusing on correct technique and how liberating it feels to both move your body and wake up your mind at the same time.

Note: If you can't get up to exercise for ten minutes, there are exercises you can do seated in a chair, such as opening and closing your arms and legs at the same time.

17 www.sciencedaily. com/releases/2017/12/ 171221122543.htm

LIFESTYLE MIND RITUAL
#113: MUSICAL CLEANING

Play some music and clean

Exercising to music can enhance cognitive function. One study[18] showed that listening to music while exercising helped to increase scores on a verbal fluency test among test subjects.

Your ritual today is to exercise while listening to music, preferably something upbeat but anything that motivates you will do. If you don't have time for a specific musical workout, the recommendation is to play some music while you are doing your housework, cleaning and tidying up. Cleaning is exercise when you consider all the bending, stretching and use of muscles involved to clean thoroughly and, if you add music into the mix, this will naturally encourage you to move your body with even more energy. You could also ditch the carwash and clean your car manually while listening to music. **Ritualize** by focusing with awareness on your bodily movements. Remind yourself as you waltz through your exercise and/or cleaning that your actions are music for both body and mind.

18 www.sciencedaily.com/releases/2004/03/ 040324071444.htm

LIFESTYLE MIND RITUAL
#114: BULKING UP YOUR BRAIN
Lift your brain with some weights

While aerobic exercise is believed to be of the greatest benefit to your brain, weight-bearing exercises can also help improve brain function.[19]

Set aside ten minutes today to do some gentle toning. Don't do anything complicated. Start with the basics, such as sit-ups with your knees bent, followed by press-ups from a kneeling position. If you want to tone your arms, grab a couple of cans and do some biceps curls. **Ritualize** by feeling the power of what you are doing. If you are already committed to a muscle-toning routine, either at home or at the gym, approach it today with grateful intention and new understanding that this isn't just good for your body, but for your brain, too. Realizing how beneficial for both brain and brawn gentle toning can be can encourage you to make it a regular part of your brain-boosting exercise.

19 https://well.blogs.nytimes.com/2011/01/19/phys-ed-brains-and-brawn/

LIFESTYLE MIND RITUAL
#115: THE POWER OF FIVE

Do the people you spend most of your time with inspire you?

We have mirror neurons[20] in our brains that encourage us to fit into the environment we are in, whether we are conscious of this or not. In ancient times fitting in was a matter of survival. We needed our tribe to take care of us or we would die. Although our survival is no longer at stake today, we are still wired to adapt to the people around us.

It has often been said that we are the sum of the five people we spend the most time with. Today's ritual encourages you to focus on the five most important people in your life and to think about how spending time with them impacts your mindset. **Ritualize** by writing down their names. Then spend a few minutes focusing all your attention on their names and reflecting on whether you are investing your time in the right company. Do these people lift you up or drag you down? Are you being yourself with them or "fitting in"? If you are completely happy with your five choices, feel deep gratitude for these amazing people being in your life. However, if the latter is true, take steps today to seek out the company of people who allow you to be yourself and inspire you to have a positive outlook on life that motivates and energizes you.

20 www.apa.org/monitor/oct05/mirror.aspx
www.sciencedaily.com/releases/2007/11/071106123725.htm

LIFESTYLE MIND RITUAL #116: COMPLIMENT SOMEONE

Make someone feel special today

When you admire or compliment someone, your brain is activated with the pleasure neurotransmitter dopamine, which generates feelings of alertness in your mind and body. Complimenting other people is a powerful mental stimulant.[21]

Your ritual today is to compliment someone you admire sincerely. This can be your partner if you are in a committed relationship but, if not, just make someone you are attracted to or admire in some way feel a little special. Pay them a sincere compliment or make it known that you admire them. If you can't think of anyone, spend a few moments thinking of someone in the media you find attractive or admire. Visualize meeting them and what you would say to praise them. **Ritualize** your compliment by being fully aware of the intention behind it: you are consciously making someone else feel special. Remember, you don't need to act on your feelings of attraction or admiration, you are just mindfully enjoying their stimulating benefits for your brain. Let complimenting someone light up your mind today.

21 www.sciencedaily.com/releases/2014/02/ 140206155244.htm

LIFESTYLE MIND RITUAL
#117: EXPRESS YOUR LOVE

Feel the benefits of your love today

When the brain of a person who has fallen in love is studied by scientists,[22] they find levels of dopamine and a related hormone, norepinephrine, are released during attraction. These chemicals make the mind feel euphoric and super-creative.

Obviously, you can't fall in love on demand and you aren't going to be asked to do that today. There's also a difference between infatuation and love. The former is temporary, whereas the latter is constant. Although infatuation does wake up your mind immediately, love that endures over time has even more powerful creative and immunity-boosting benefits.

Your ritual today is to spend a few moments thinking about someone or something in your life that you love with all your heart and then to express your love with an affirmation. That someone can be a partner, a friend, a family member or a pet and that something can be your career, your home or even your favourite plant. **Ritualize** your desire to celebrate the mind-boosting benefits of love by saying out loud the following affirmation: *The more I celebrate and express my love, the more love there is in my life to celebrate and express.*

22 http://sitn.hms.harvard.edu/flash/2017/love-actually-science-behind-lust-attraction-companionship/

LIFESTYLE MIND RITUAL
#118: LIGHTEN YOUR MENTAL LOAD

Try a little organization

Getting more organized[23] is a vital ingredient for clear thinking. The more organized you are, the calmer and more in control you will feel and the better you will be able to concentrate, focus and remember. Even genius professors have a certain method to their madness.

A chaotic, disorganized work or study environment stresses your brain. Your ritual today is to spend ten minutes putting your desk or work surface in order. If you don't spend time at a desk, rearrange the desktop of your computer or the screen saver on your phone. If your desk is tidy, congratulate yourself and find something else that urgently needs regulating, such as unsubscribing from junk mail. There will always be something that needs organizing better in your life. Remove what isn't needed and sort what is left into piles, files or categories so you can easily find them or navigate from them to where you need to go. Set up a pending or "to-do" pile of papers or digital files that are urgent and give yourself deadlines, creating reminders for those deadlines. **Ritualize** by noticing as you work how spending a little time getting things better organized, so you can work or study more efficiently, lightens your mental load.

23 https://unclutterer.com/2011/03/29/scientists-find-physical-clutter-negatively-affects-your-ability-to-focus-process-information/

LIFESTYLE MIND RITUAL
#119: KEEP YOUR SOCKS ON
Boost nocturnal problem-solving

When you sleep your brain is busy organizing your memories and helping you gain new perspectives. The morning after a refreshing sleep often brings new insights that seemed impossible the night before. However, getting a good night's sleep isn't always a given, so today's ritual is to put on some comfortable socks before you go to bed tonight,[24] which will immediately improve your chances of getting quality shut-eye.

Socks in bed may not feel sexy, but then neither are cold feet! Warm feet cause dilation of the blood vessels, which signals to your brain that it's time to redistribute heat around your body so you can gently fall asleep. **Ritualize** by putting each sock on mindfully, noticing how wearing them feels cozy in comparison to sleeping barefoot. Remind yourself that sleep is essential for regenerating your mind. There's a reason why the age-old advice to "sleep on it" whenever you have a problem holds true. So, you could even say your night time socks can play an important part in problem-solving, because they help you to sleep better.

24 www.sleep.org/articles/wearing-socks-to-bed/

LIFESTYLE POWER RITUAL #120: THE RULES OF DRINKING

Regularly refresh your mind

Drinking water and brain function[25] are intrinsically connected, as our brains are approximately 85 per cent water. Most of us underestimate just how essential staying well-hydrated is for optimum brain function. Today we have a **power ritual** to enhance the holistic diet and lifestyle advice previously given. It draws its inspiration from Ayurveda, the beautiful ancient Indian mind-body healing system. Make water your first choice of drink today and then **ritualize** drinking it by following these Ayurvedic drinking rules with gratitude and respect for the refreshment and clarity they bring.

★ When you drink water be sure to sit down. You typically sit down to eat for digestive reasons, so pay the same mindful attention to drinking water.
★ Take a sip rather than a gulp. Between each sip be mindful of the refreshment you are giving your mind. Take a small sip, swallow and then breathe. Repeat.
★ Your water should be at room temperature rather than ice cold, as this is easier on your digestion.
★ Only sip a small amount of water when you are eating. If you drink too much when you eat, you interrupt the digestive process. Avoid drinking too much water after a meal for the same reason.

25 www.cambridge.org/core/journals/british-journal-of-nutrition/article/
milddehydrationimpairscognitive-performance-and-mood-of-men/
3388AB36B8DF73E844C9AD19271A75BF

- ★ If your urine is dark yellow and your lips and eyes are dry, you need to drink more water.
- ★ Eight glasses of water a day is recommended but everyone is different. If you sip water throughout the day and immediately pay attention to any thirst cues, you will be drinking the right amount.

PAST TO PRESENT

Ayurveda is an ancient science of life and it is based on the belief that health and wellbeing depend on harmony or balance between the mind, body and soul. The recommendations it gives for boosting brain power are perfectly in line with the latest scientific research. Bringing past to present, Ayurveda suggests our brain functions best when we are well hydrated, get enough sleep, avoid stress, consume natural foods rich in brain-enhancing nutrients and avoid brain-draining salty, fatty, fried and processed foods. We should only drink alcohol in moderation and avoid smoking altogether.

THOUGHT MANAGEMENT MIND RITUAL
#121: MAKE A GOOD BRAIN GREAT
Become good at positive thinking

The next few daily rituals focus on actions that can help you manage your thoughts, so your mind doesn't drag you down. The more upbeat your thinking,[26] the more likely it is that your brain will produce "feel-good" chemicals that can help it function at its peak. If your thoughts are negative, this will produce brain-draining chemicals that cause confusion and tension. Negative thinking can cloud your judgement, ruin your concentration and focus, and limit your creativity and chances of success in life.

From now on use the power of this ritual every time you have a negative thought. When you find yourself thinking negatively, clap your hands loudly and stop what you are doing. Write down that negative thought to dispel its power and challenge it. Don't automatically treat the thought as fact, just because you are thinking it. Ask yourself if you are being realistic or exaggerating, generalizing or worrying too much. **Ritualize** by reminding yourself sharply as you clap that you are not what you *think* but what you *do*. Your thoughts have absolutely no power to define you unless you allow them to. Start talking to yourself in a more realistic, reassuring and positive way. Your negative thoughts aren't used to being challenged, so this ritual is one you may need to practise until it becomes second nature.

26 www.ncbi.nlm.nih.gov/pmc/articles/PMC1838571/?tool=pubmed

THOUGHT MANAGEMENT
MIND RITUAL
#122: JUST SHINE
Turn away from your fear of failure

Positive actions rewire your brain[27] - and that's the basis of this book as rituals are all about the power of positive action - but it's far easier to act positive if your thoughts are on your side and strengthening areas of your brain that stimulate positive feelings. In other words, although you don't need to think positive to perform rituals that can change your life for the better, a happy mindset is a great motivational support for you in your personal development.

   Your ritual today will help create new neural pathways in your brain that encourage you to leave fear of failure behind. The reason most of us don't enrich our minds and learn or try new things - and remember your brain loves the stimulation of learning about new things - is because we are frightened to fail. The truth is you can do almost anything if you stop worrying about what other people think and just have a go. When you hear that familiar voice in your head telling you that you will fail, or you can't do it or you aren't good enough and so on, **ritualize** retraining your brain by standing up and turning around once in an anticlockwise direction. When you have come full circle, say out loud, "I am not afraid to shine" and take a small step forward. Then, take a small step in your daily life to achieve a desired goal or learn something you have been putting off for fear of failure.

27 https://positivepsychologyprogram.com/neuroplasticity/

THOUGHT MANAGEMENT
MIND RITUAL
#123: THINK LIKE A PRO

Focus on the positives and let the negatives go

All the rituals in this book are designed to help reshape your brain and create a positive mindset from the outside in. But you can help things along by also working from the inside out, as research[28] has shown that certain positive-thinking techniques can boost mood and motivation.

Your mind is always communicating with your body through your thoughts and your body is always talking to your mind with your actions. Adding a dose of healthy and happy thoughts into this constant dialogue will encourage a more optimistic and motivational mindset. Today's ritual asks you to focus on a problem you have right now or something in your past you still feel negative about. **Ritualize** by consciously focusing on only the positive aspects and writing down a list of pros. Be aware of the negative aspects but don't invest any emotional energy in them. Don't write a list of cons. Instead, focus all your emotional energy on solutions and try to regard the problem, negative experience or toxic relationship as a learning experience – an opportunity to learn and grow into a much wiser person.

28 Schaffer, J.: 'Neuroplasticity and positive psychology ', *Clinical Practice: A Review for Combined Benefits. Psychology*, 3(12A), 1110-15 (2012)

THOUGHT MANAGEMENT
MIND RITUAL
#124: INTRODUCING YOURSELF

Present yourself in a positive light

The benefits of a positive mindset should never be underestimated for your mental health.[29] If you constantly bombard your brain with negative thoughts, this will have a damaging impact on all areas of your life. Fortunately, you can reprogramme your thoughts with positive-thinking practices. Remember, your thoughts have absolutely no power over you unless you let them. You can choose how you think.

Today's ritual encourages you to think about one person only – yourself. Look in a mirror, smile broadly and introduce yourself. When you introduce someone you typically say their name and then focus on their strong points or their interests, so do the same for yourself today. Choose one or two positive traits or aspects of your life and, after stating your name, tell yourself how interesting you are. Talking to your reflection may feel weird, but it is truly powerful for your mind to hear you presenting yourself in a positive light. **Ritualize** your mirror work by putting all your focus on what makes you interesting. Speak clearly. Your mind is taking note and releasing neurotransmitters to rewire your brain so that seeing yourself positively becomes your default mindset.

29 www.scientificamerican.com/article/your-thoughts-can-release-abilities-beyond-normal-limits/

THOUGHT MANAGEMENT
MIND RITUAL
#125: UPDATE YOURSELF

Compete with the person you were yesterday

One of the biggest roadblocks to thinking positively about yourself is feeling inferior or comparing yourself to others. Social media has been shown to have a damaging impact on our self-esteem[30] because whether we realize it or not, it encourages us to play the comparison game. We focus on what we don't have, rather than feeling grateful for what we do have.

Today ask yourself this question: who have I compared myself to in the last few days? **Ritualize** by writing down who or what has negatively impacted you. Resolve to avoid unhealthy comparison triggers in the future. Limit your time on social media if you can. Remind yourself that outward appearances do not reflect what is going on inside someone and money can't buy happiness. Then, make a sacred commitment to yourself that the only person you are going to compare yourself to from this moment on is the person you were yesterday. Know that it truly doesn't matter what other people are doing because they are not you. You have absolutely no control over what other people do. You do, however, have control over your own utterly unique life. You can choose to become a wiser and better person than you were yesterday.

30 www.forbes.com/ sites/jmaureenhenderson/ 2012/07/11/is-social-media-destroying-your-self-esteem/#2cf7fd174e89

THOUGHT MANAGEMENT
MIND RITUAL
#126: EXPAND YOUR HORIZONS
Boldly go where your mind hasn't gone before

Intelligent and successful people are curious people.[31] Whatever age they are they never lose their desire for fresh perspectives. The problem with negative thinking is that it narrows your mindset. You don't think there are alternatives. Today's ritual encourages you to seek out a motivational quote that will encourage you to think in an optimistic and different way. Find a quote that will help you see the world with a fresh pair of eyes.

Once you have that quote, print it out and post it on your wall or make it your screensaver. If you want a suggestion to start thinking along the right lines, the famous Gandhi quote: "Be the change you wish to see in the world" is a perfect place to start. **Ritualize** by spending a few moments consciously focusing your intention on the words of your quote. Say them out loud and ask the universe to help you live and breathe the motivation. Let your motivational quote push your mind and your life where it has never gone before.

31 https://journals.sagepub.com/ doi/abs/10.1177/ 0956797613499592?papetoc=

THOUGHT MANAGEMENT
MIND RITUAL
#127: SMILE AND WAVE

Combine an attitude of gratitude with smiles today

An attitude of gratitude[32] is a key part of a brain-boosting, positive mindset. What's more, combining gratitude with a physical action dramatically increases your chances of happiness because of the way actions impact your brain.

Today's ritual requires you to practise gratitude with a smile and a wave. Think of things in your life you are grateful for and smile broadly at the same time. You will probably smile naturally when you think of happy things but, if that doesn't happen, fake your smile, because doing so can trick your brain into thinking you are happy. **Ritualize** by reflecting deeply on those happy moments and feeling intense gratitude for them. It could be people or animals or things you've done or seen that made you feel good. Imagine what your life would be like without those people or things and notice how this instantly boosts your mood. If other people are around smile at them and, if you feel comfortable doing so, wave to them and say hello. Smiles are contagious. Chances are the other person will appreciate being noticed and smile back, which will give you even more happiness. Gratitude with a smile and perhaps a wave is a precious way to reshape your mind in a positive way. Let this ritual, and the good feelings it inspires, incentivize you to make being grateful and smiling your natural state of mind and way of life.

. . . .

32 www.abc.net.au/radionational/programs/allinthemind/the-scientific-evidence-for-positive-thinking/6553614

THOUGHT MANAGEMENT MIND RITUAL
#128: MIND YOUR DREAMS

Get into the habit of recalling your dreams

Although we don't yet fully understand the surreal world of our nighttime dreams and even why we dream at all, research[33] suggests that recalling our dreams stimulates our mind and is generally a sign of good mental health.

The recommendation today consolidates Foundation Ritual 20 (*see* page 36). Make it a ritual to have a pen and paper or a recording device by your bed and to write down immediately when you wake up the dreams that flashed through your brain in the night. **Ritualize** your dream recall time by focusing mindfully on the contents of your dreams as you commit them to paper. Ask your unconscious to interpret their meaning for you but, if you can't understand them, simply feel gratitude for the images you received and know that they are a sign of healthy brain function. If you struggle to recall your dreams, your ritual today is to set the intention before you go to sleep to remember your dreams when you wake up. Then, in that twilight world just before you lose consciousness, whisper out loud: "I *will* dream tonight. When I wake, I *will* recall my dreams." Your dreaming mind will take note.

33 Vallat, R., *et al.*: 'Dream recall frequency is associated with medial prefrontal cortex white-matter density', *Frontiers in Psychology*, 9, p.1856 (2018)

THOUGHT MANAGEMENT
MIND RITUAL
#129: LIVING THE DREAM
Make dream recall a way of life

With sleep and dream experts[34] consistently suggesting that dreaming can enhance creativity, intuition and problem-solving, any brain-boosting programme benefits from dream recall.

If you are still struggling to remember your dreams, your ritual today is to make a point of remaining in the same position you were sleeping in, when you wake up. Staying in the same position with your eyes closed helps your brain to hold on to the dream, as any movement will distract it. **Ritualize** by allowing your mind to meander in a meditative state for a while. You'll be amazed how many dream images this can trigger. Then, when images start to form, open your eyes, reach for a notepad and write down everything. Remember, don't put off writing your dream down until later or it will vanish from your memory.

If you can remember your dreams easily, your ritual today is to choose an element from your dream and incorporate it into your daily life. For example, if you saw someone wearing red in your dream, wear something red today to signal to your dreaming mind you are listening, and it will reward you with creative insights gleaned from the dream images.

Note: See also Spirit rituals 233–43

- - - - - - - - - - - -

34 Cai, D. J.: 'REM not incubation improves creativity by priming associative networks', *Proceedings of the National Academy of Sciences* (*PNAS*), June 8 (2009)

Zadra, A., *et al.*: 'Dream recall frequency impact of prospective measure', *Consciousness and Cognition*, vol 21, issue 4, December 2012, pp. 1695–1702

THOUGHT MANAGEMENT
MIND RITUAL
#130: FOCUS AT A DEEPER LEVEL

Create what you think and feel with your mind

Although rituals are all about the power of "I do", rather than dreaming about doing, your imagination can ignite your mind and motivate you to take action. It seems[35] that imagining or visualizing something happening stimulates the same neural networks in your brain as the actual experience. Your body and your brain don't know the difference between reality and visualization.

Your ritual today is to do a simple visualization exercise. You are going to imagine yourself living a happy and fulfilled life. Find somewhere you are unlikely to be disturbed for at least ten minutes. **Ritualize** your visualization by closing your eyes and clearly setting your intention. You are going to envision your ideal life by engaging your thoughts, feelings and all your senses. Don't just see yourself succeeding in your mind's eye, see and feel it happening. Make your visualization as real and as vivid as possible, so you can think, taste, touch, see, hear, smell and feel your dream of success and happiness coming alive at a deep level. Then, when you are ready, open your eyes, stop dreaming – and start doing!

35 https://hbr.org/2014/03/to-reach-your-goals-make-a-mental-movie

THOUGHT MANAGEMENT
MIND RITUAL
#131: ESCAPE THE PRISON OF WORRY
Switch off and leave anxiety behind

Worry is a significant brain drain.[36] It destroys creativity, spontaneity and our ability to focus and be creative. We think we are doing something constructive when we worry, but the resulting anxiety, stress and tension it causes achieve absolutely nothing. If you can do something to make things easier for you, do it. But if there is nothing you can do, worrying is pointless. When have you or anybody ever been helped by your worrying? What has helped you or them is not worrying but positive action.

Your ritual today will help you escape the prison of worry. If there is something you are anxious about, stop thinking about it. Do something repetitive instead, such as tapping your hand or walking up and down. When you keep your conscious brain busy with a repetitive task, this frees up the creative, intuitive part of your brain that can help you come up with solutions. **Ritualize** the repetitive task you choose by focusing mindfully on it. Don't try to force solutions. Let them come to you and, when they do, take action.

36 www.sciencedaily.com/releases/2014/01/ 140130141313.htm

THOUGHT MANAGEMENT
MIND RITUAL
#132: THINK HIGHER

There is more power in a question than in an answer

While affirmations or positive statements have the power to boost concentration and performance, asking yourself questions[37] has more power to ignite your brain. Questions dictate the direction your thoughts flow in. They are a higher form of thought than answers, and stimulate your brain more.

Today's ritual encourages you to ask yourself a seriously important couple of questions: who am I? What do I want for my life? **Ritualize** by first creating a picture in your mind of the answer and then writing it down. Chances are you may not know what the answers are but that does not matter. The mind-boosting power here is in your search for the answers. Brainstorm and put down on paper whatever springs to mind. You may need to repeat this ritual every day until you eventually settle on something that resonates. Think about what you want your legacy to be or how you are serving others. Keep asking yourself these crucial life questions because every time you do so, your brain is creatively searching for inspirational answers.

37 Senay, I., *et al.*: 'Motivating goal-directed behaviour through introspective self-talk: The role of the interrogative form of simple future sense', *Psychological Science*, April 2010; 21 (4), pp. 499–504

THOUGHT MANAGEMENT POWER RITUAL
#133: STOPPING THOUGHTS

Discover healthier thinking patterns

Today's ritual is a power one because it consolidates the thought management techniques you have been learning in previous days. It introduces you to a number of Cognitive Behaviour Therapy (CBT)[38] techniques.

CBT has been shown to be a highly effective way to challenge negative thought patterns and behaviours. Every time you find a negative thought creeping into your mind, **ritualize** by pausing what you are doing and consciously applying the following simple CBT techniques. Focus your mind on the things you can do right now to change your mind for the better. Set a timer on your phone twice a day as a reminder to always challenge your thoughts and reframe them more positively. The more you practise these CBT techniques and integrate them into your schedule, the more you reprogramme your mind for happiness.

★ Whenever you have a negative thought, examine that thought objectively. Look for positives to balance out the negative. For example, if it's raining and you can't go for your daily walk, feel gratitude that the plants in your garden are being watered.
★ Brainstorm whenever negativity strikes. There is never just one answer to a problem. Open yourself up to all possibilities.
★ Challenge your thoughts. Don't believe them because you think them. Most of the time negative thoughts have absolutely no basis in fact.

38 www.bbc.co.uk/news/
health-20625639

- ★ Use visualization in the morning when you wake up and before you go to bed. See yourself having a wonderful day first thing. Then when you retire at night focus on the best bits of your day and, if things didn't go well, visualize them going smoothly. Fill your mind with positive imagery.
- ★ Remind yourself there is no such thing as failure if you learn from the experience. Disappointment, loss and failure are perfectly normal and natural parts of life. They happen to us all.
- ★ Practise an attitude of gratitude. End your day by thinking of at least three things you can be grateful for.
- ★ Learn to distinguish between things you can control, and those you can't. The things that are in your hands can always be improved. Let go in your mind of the things that are out of your control. Always keep your focus on what you can actually do.

PAST TO PRESENT

CBT is a talking therapy that is based on the idea that your thoughts, feelings and actions are interconnected and it looks for practical ways to improve your thoughts, feelings and actions. The idea that your thoughts impact how you feel and behave is not new. It is centuries old and can be seen appearing in many ancient texts, such as the Chinese classic *Tao Te Ching* written by Lao-tzu. The central thesis of the *Tao Te Ching* is based on the simple idea that if you change your thoughts, you can change your behaviour and your life for the better. CBT brings this profound ancient wisdom right into the present day.

PEACE OF MIND RITUAL
#134: LOSE YOUR MIND

Find your calm centre with a "mindless" meditation

The next five days of rituals will turn the spotlight on finding peace of mind. If your mind is calm, you will find it easier to concentrate and think clearly. Research[39] confirms that one of the best ways to reshape your brain and improve your memory and concentration is regular meditation.

Today's ritual is a "mindless" meditation. To do this, sit or lie down comfortably in a place where you won't be disturbed and where there aren't too many noises and distractions. **Ritualize** by setting a timer for 20 minutes and being fully aware of your intention to meditate as a way to grow and access more mind power. Turn the lights down or draw the curtains and close your eyes. Simply experience the silence around you, then move your feeling inward and feel the silence within. Stay in this calm place for as long as you can. Breathe deeply but don't force yourself to breathe in a certain way. Just feel your inner rhythm. Allow your thoughts to run wherever they want to go, like wild horses. Just notice your thoughts without judgement. Give your mind complete freedom to run or roam and play.

Be mindless and let your brain find calm.

39 Holzel, Britta K., Carmody, James, *et al.*: 'Mindfulness practice leads to increases in regional brain gray matter density', *Psychiatry Research: Neuroimaging*, 2011; 191 (1): 36. DOI: http://dx.doi.org/10.1016/j.pscychresns.2010.08.006

PEACE OF MIND RITUAL
#135: SPACE YOURSELF OUT
Do some deep nose inhalation

Scientists[40] have discovered a dramatic difference in brain function when you breathe in through your nose compared to breathing in through your mouth. Inhaling through your nose stimulates your brain and boosts memory.

Most of us breathe shallowly and quickly through our mouths rather than our noses. Your ritual today is to do some serious deep nose inhalation. Sit comfortably with your back straight and your shoulders relaxed. Then close your mouth and take a long, slow, deep breath from your stomach through your nose. When you have completely inhaled, open your mouth and breathe out slowly through your mouth. Keep repeating that cycle for at least five minutes. You will feel a little spaced out because of all the energizing oxygen you are sending to your brain. **Ritualize** by breathing mindfully and with deep awareness that your mind follows your breath. Know that you are filling your mind with the oxygen it needs to generate mental agility.

You are breathing in mental clarity through your nose and exhaling brain fogginess through your mouth.

40 www.telegraph.co.uk/science/2016/12/08/take-deep-breathinhaling-nose-stimulates-brain-boosts-memory/

PEACE OF MIND RITUAL
#136: CLOUD-WATCHING

Indulge in some not-so-idle day-dreaming today

There are cognitive benefits to simply letting your mind wander in any direction it wants to go, according to some brain-scan studies.[41] It seems that when your mind is idle, areas in your brain that can creatively solve problems are triggered.

Your ritual today is to do some cloud-watching. When you were a child you probably lay in the grass at some point and gazed at the clouds changing shape, indulging in some glorious day-dreaming. You don't have to lie down in the grass (unless you want to), you can enjoy the benefits of just standing or looking out of the window letting your mind wander as you watch clouds. However you decide to do it, **ritualize** your cloud-watching by raising your eyes to the skies, being fully present and focusing all your attention on the clouds. The benefits of day-dreaming are at their greatest when you are unaware your mind is wandering. So, focus your attention on observing the shapes of the clouds and their hypnotic slow movements rather than on any issues or problems you have, and give your mind free rein.

41 https://greatist.com/happiness/let-mind-wander-promote-creative-thinking

PEACE OF MIND RITUAL
#137: SHED A TEAR

Cry to detox your body and boost your mind

Holding back the tears may not always be the best thing to do. Psychologists[42] believe that crying isn't just cathartic and healing for our emotions, it can also stimulate brain circulation..

Your ritual for today is to shed a tear. Think of something that makes you sad and **ritualize** by letting the tears flow for a few minutes. Then, after this release, carry on with your day. This may sound like a calculating thing to do, but it is a very powerful ritual, as your intention is to cry because you know the healing, cleansing and brain-boosting power of tears. If you find it hard to cry, watch a scene from a sad but inspiring movie or listen to some melancholy but uplifting music. My recommendations would be to watch the final scenes of the movie *Titantic* or listen to Eric Clapton's song, "Tears in Heaven".

Note: Anyone prone to depression or post-traumatic shock disorder (PTSD), should approach this ritual with caution or avoid it. If you feel that once you start crying you won't be able to stop or that this exercise will make you feel worse in any way, your mind-boosting ritual for today is to go for a mood-enhancing run or a vigorous swim instead.

42 www.psychologytoday.com/us/blog/emotional-freedom/201007/the-health-benefits-tears

PEACE OF MIND POWER RITUAL
#138: TRY *LAGOM*
Not too little, not too much, just enough

Today's ritual is a power one because it complements and enhances the previous peace of mind rituals. One of the biggest threats to peace of mind is stress which, along with high anxiety levels, can cause brain-cell damage,[43] so stress management is of the utmost importance. There is a huge variety of scientifically-proven stress-reduction techniques to encourage inner calm, such as meditation, prayer, relaxation exercises, aromatherapy, massage and drinking herbal teas, but perhaps the most successful technique of them all is the common sense one: moderation in everything.

Today's mind boosting ritual draws inspiration from the Swedish art of *Lagom*.[44] There is no equivalent word in the English language, but translated loosely it means "not too little, not too much, but just enough". **Ritualize** by setting an alarm to go off three times today, three to four hours apart. When the first alarm sounds, find somewhere quiet, close your eyes and practise one minute of conscious awareness of your thoughts and feelings – your inner world. When the second alarm goes off, close your eyes for a minute and focus your meditative awareness on your whole body and the external world outside you, such as the sounds you can hear. Then, when the third alarm goes off, close your eyes again and focus your total attention on your breathing for one minute, breathing in slowly and deeply through your nose and exhaling through your mouth.

43 www.sciencedaily.com/releases/2016/01/160121121818.htm
44 L. Dunne, *Lagom: The Swedish art of balanced living*, Octopus, 2017

Be consciously aware of the reason for these three mini-meditations. They are reminding you of the crucial importance of *Lagom* or balance between your thoughts, your body and your breath or spirit. Balance is an antidote to brain-draining stress and essential for true peace of mind. This ritual and the inner calm and sense of balance it brings can encourage you to apply the "moderation-in-everything" rule to all areas of your life. *Lagom* always puts the focus on slowing down and taking your time and values quality of life rather than material clutter. It's a stress-free, "lighten-the-load" way to live simply and it's also in keeping with the spirit of this book as it promotes positive actions, not empty words. Here are some other *Lagom* guidelines:

★ Slow down; be in the moment; enjoy the simple pleasures in life.
★ Spend more of your time in nature.
★ Clear out your wardrobe and only keep what is practical and easy to wear.
★ Take regular breaks during the day.
★ Enjoy quality time alone.
★ Seek clarity and fairness in all situations.
★ Cultivate the art of listening – really listen to and reflect on what you can learn from others.

PAST TO PRESENT

Lagom derives from the Swedish phrase "laget om", which means "pass around the team". Translated literally it means "the middle or the appropriate amount for everyone" and probably dates back to Viking days when mead would be passed around, so everyone could have a sip. Fast forward to the present day and little has changed as *Lagom* means there is something of value for everyone as long as they all take the moderate or right amount. The virtue is always in moderation. Apply this measured approach to your life and your thinking, and notice the clarity, peace and inner calm it brings.

BRAIN-TRAINING MIND RITUAL
#139: UNFAMILIAR FOLDING
Do something the same differently today

Research[45] shows that you can improve your brain power regardless of how old you are. The remaining 30 days of rituals in this section will offer you a variety of successful brain-training techniques.

Among the most successful cognitive training programmes are ones that offer your brain novelty. Today's ritual requires you to make a familiar action unfamiliar. When you do something new or unfamiliar your brain grows new neural pathways. Fold your arms. Notice which arm, right or left, automatically goes on top and how comfortable this position feels. Now slowly and carefully try folding your arms the other way round, with your other arm on top. Stay in that position. **Ritualize** this arm-folding experience by being fully aware of how it feels to adopt this unfamiliar position. Notice how it challenges you. Later in the day try the same ritual with something else you always do exactly the same way, such as crossing your legs. Cross the other leg over instead of the one you normally do. Notice how doing something unfamiliar with your body energizes your thinking.

· · · · · · · · · · · ·

45 Motes, Michael A., *et al.*: 'Higher-order cognitive training effects on processing speed-related neural activity: a randomized trial ', *Neurobiology of Aging*, 2018; 62: 72, DOI: 10.1016/j.neurobiolaging.2017.10.003

BRAIN–TRAINING MIND RITUAL
#140: BRUSH AWAY
Wake up your brain with your other hand

Occasionally using your non-dominant hand for an activity normally done with your dominant hand can strengthen neural connections in your brain.[46]

Your brain-training ritual today is to brush your teeth with your non-dominant hand and that includes opening the tube and applying toothpaste to your toothbrush. If you prefer you can substitute a different daily activity, such as brushing your hair, buttoning up your shirt, holding your fork when you eat or even doodling. The important thing is to choose an activity that you always do with your dominant hand on autopilot every day. **Ritualize** by noticing how using your non-dominant hand feels challenging to you, both physically and mentally. Using your non-dominant hand in this way will stimulate the opposite side of your brain rather than the side you normally use.

46 www.researchgate.net/publication/315417110_Changes_in_motor_cortex_excitability_for_the_trained_and_non-trained_hand_after_long-term_unilateral_motor_training

BRAIN-TRAINING MIND RITUAL
#141: AGAINST THE FLOW

Ease your brain in the right direction

Exercises that challenge your brain by going against what feels natural or comfortable are beneficial because they can increase neural connections in your brain's cortex and in the process stimulate your entire brain.[47]

Today you are going to perform a ritual that sounds simple but, when you try it, you will be surprised how tricky it is. Sit down and start slowly making clockwise circles with your right ankle and foot. Then, while you are circling your right foot, attempt to draw a huge figure of six in the air with your right hand. It will be easy for you to **ritualize** this exercise because to do it properly you have no choice but to concentrate fully in the present moment. It's impossible to think of anything else. You have to focus your mind only on the actions of your foot and hand. Notice when your foot wants to return to what it knows and circle in an anti-clockwise direction (trust me, it will!) and simply correct it. Keep trying until you find this ritual easy and can mentally stop your mind and your foot going with the flow.

47 www.ncbi.nlm.nih.gov/pubmed/27212059

BRAIN-TRAINING MIND RITUAL
#142: MIND GYM

Learn and feed your brain as you walk

Exercise is linked[48] to improved brain function. Keeping fit improves blood flow to your brain cells, increasing the supply of oxygen, glucose and other nutrients it needs to function at its best.

Your ritual today requires you to select an audio book or a podcast about a subject you know very little about and then to go for a walk outside for 20 to 30 minutes with your headphones on and the audio book playing. Walk briskly and **ritualize** by listening mindfully to what you hear in the audio. Your body will soon settle into autopilot with the walking, but your mind will be consciously absorbing new information. Remind yourself that by listening and learning as you exercise you are associating absorbing new information with physical activity. You are expanding your brain and training your body at the same time.

Note: It's best to do this ritual away from traffic, but if this is not possible, ensure your active listening does not distract you from keeping safe.

48 http://time.com/4752846/exercise-brain-health/

BRAIN-TRAINING MIND RITUAL #143: SURPRISE YOURSELF

Do something unexpected today

Routines are often a good thing. For example, your body thrives on routines, like waking up and going to sleep at the same time each day. But your brain is different. Your brain thrives on variety.[49]

If all your daily routines are predictable, your brain will carry them out with the minimum of energy, on autopilot. Routine offers your brain no opportunity to form neuro-pathways with new experiences. Your ritual today is to break a familiar routine. It doesn't matter what that routine is, just do something different in its place. It can be going to work via a different route; shopping at a different supermarket; sitting at a different place at the dinner table for a change of perspective; or even using a cup and saucer instead of a mug to see if it changes the way your drink tastes. The possibilities to surprise your novelty-hungry mind today are endless, so be imaginative. **Ritualize** your break from routine by mindfully monitoring how doing something out of the blue puts your brain on high alert.

---

49 www.scientificamerican.com/article/new-experiences-help-speed-up-brain-development-in-mice/

BRAIN-TRAINING MIND RITUAL #144: MAKE BELIEVE

Lose yourself in a story today

Neuroscientists[50] have discovered that reading fiction can enhance connectivity in your brain.

When was the last time you read a good novel? If you are like many people, you probably only devote time to reading fiction when you are on holiday. The recommendation today is to go to a bookstore, a library, or an online store and obtain a work of fiction. It doesn't matter what the novel is about, just choose something that you find intriguing. Then, this evening, set aside 30 minutes and start reading it. **Ritualize** by switching off your phone and finding somewhere you won't be disturbed and can lose yourself in the land of make-believe. If at any point you feel that you are wasting time on things that aren't real or relevant to daily life, gently focus your mind on the evidence that proves conclusively that reading fiction can significantly improve your brain function and boost your creativity.

Reflect on how much you probably enjoyed being read to before you went to sleep when you were a child. Even though you are older now, your brain hasn't lost its appetite for a really absorbing good-night story.

50 www.liebertpub.com/doi/full/10.1089/brain.2013.0166

BRAIN–TRAINING MIND RITUAL
#145: *RONDO ALLA TURCA*

Jumpstart your brain with a little Mozart

Educators the world over have linked listening to music and music-making to improved cognitive ability ever since a 1980s study that showed regularly listening to Mozart could significantly boost a child's brain power. Other studies[51] followed and they confirm that music can stimulate areas of the brain used for problem-solving.

Today's ritual encourages you to set aside four minutes to listen to Mozart's *Rondo Alla Turca* for piano and, if you have more time, you can also try listening to Mozart's *K448 Sonata*, or any other pieces for free online. Before you listen, set your intention. The music will wake up both sides of your brain – your left brain will try to process tune and rhythm, while your right brain simultaneously conjures up images and feelings inspired by the music. **Ritualize** by turning up the volume and absorbing yourself in the world of sound. Let the notes flow through you. If you are listening intensely there are so many riches for your ears and mind that there won't be room for any distracting thoughts. You will be experiencing the music fully and the mind-boosting genius of Mozart, too.

51 www.sciencedirect.com/science/article/pii/S1053810015001130

BRAIN–TRAINING MIND RITUAL
#146: SAY IT ANOTHER WAY

Add a new word to your vocabulary

Adding new words to your vocabulary can not only improve your memory, speech and cognitive function, but, according to language experts, it can also increase your chances of success in life.[52]

Find a dictionary and search in it until you land on a word you don't know the meaning of. Learn how to spell and say that word. If you want a ritual-themed suggestion try "hodiernal" (*ho-di-ER-nal*), which means "relating to the present day" and originates from Latin. **Ritualize** by saying the new word out loud three times and paying attention to how it feels as you say it. What images does this new word conjure up in your mind to make it easier to remember? Do you feel that the sound of the word matches its meaning? What are its historical origins? Then, make a point of finding a relevant way to use the new word today, either in conversation or in your writing.

Looking ahead, you may wish to make learning a new word, and incorporating it into your everyday speech and writing, a daily ritual.

52 www.ascd.org/publications/books/113040/chapters/What-Does-the-Research-Say-About-Vocabulary¢.aspx

BRAIN-TRAINING MIND RITUAL #147: BACK TO SCHOOL

Make a resolution to learn a new skill

Every time you learn how to do something new your mind grows stronger.[53] Most of us wait until the New Year to start something new, but why wait when you can do it today?

Instead of watching television or scrolling through your social media feed in your down time, make a resolution to learn something novel instead. **Ritualize** by understanding that learning a new skill expands your brain, even if it's something simple like folding a napkin properly. Remember, your brain is led by your actions. It doesn't matter what you decide to learn or how long it takes you to learn how to do it, just make sure you choose something you haven't done before. It could be knitting or skating or building a shed – the possibilities are endless. Once you have decided, sign up for a class or teach yourself, but take action. Start learning how to do something new today.

53 www.npr.org/ sections/health-shots/ 2014/05/05/309006780/learning-a-new-skill-works-best-to-keep-your-brain-sharp

BRAIN-TRAINING MIND RITUAL
#148: REPEAT AFTER ME

Wake up your memory muscle through simple repetition

Memory is like a muscle and the more you use it[54] the stronger and fitter it gets, regardless of your age.

Your ritual for today uses the simple memory technique of repetition. Read the following two statements from mind-map expert Tony Buzan. Next, find a sheet of paper and a pen and copy them out. Then, using fresh paper, try to write them out from memory. Keep repeating until you are word perfect.

Like our physical bodies, our memory becomes out of shape. As children, we are constantly learning new experiences, but by the time we reach our 20s, we start to lead a more sedentary life, both mentally and physically. Our lives become routine, and we stop challenging our brains, and our memory starts to suffer.

Your brain is like a sleeping giant. Through using our memory to its fullest, we can unlock the vast reservoir of human potential that isn't currently being used.

It will be easy to **ritualize** this task, as you need to focus completely to do it successfully.

54 Smith, G. E., *et al.*: 'A cognitive training program based on principles of brain plasticity: results from the Improvement in Memory with Plasticity-based Adaptive Cognitive Training (IMPACT) study', *Journal of the American Geriatric Society*, 57(4), pp.594-603 (April 2009)
http://www.ncbi.nlm.nih.gov/pubmed/19220558

BRAIN-TRAINING MIND RITUAL #149: LET YOUR FINGERS DO THE TALKING

Doodle to boost your creativity

There is evidence[55] to suggest that learning how to draw or paint stimulates both the creative and logical parts of your brain. The beneficial effect of making art may also be connected to the experience of creative flow, which happens whenever you are so fully immersed in an enjoyable activity that you lose track of time. Flow has similar benefits for your brain as meditation or mindfulness.

Your ritual today starts with you gathering up a piece of blank paper, a pencil and/or some colouring pencils. Write the title "My Brain" at the head of your paper and set a timer for three minutes. Then, set your intention to be fully present and doodle or draw whatever comes into your mind. Let the title inspire you but not direct you. You can literally depict anything. It doesn't have to be a masterpiece as nobody is going to see this except you. **Ritualize** by giving your mind free rein and letting your fingers do the talking. Lose yourself in the freedom and enjoyment of this ritual. Notice how drawing or doodling calms you and inspires creativity.

55 https://psmag.com/social-justice/making-creative-art-boosts-seniors-psychological-resilience-85117

BRAIN-TRAINING MIND RITUAL
#150: FROM BETA TO ALPHA
Give brainwave entrainment a try

Our ancestors knew intuitively that the brain's wave patterns could be manipulated into a meditative state using rhythm and syncopation. Brainwave entrainment attempts to harmonize brainwave frequencies with the rhythm of external stimuli. Research[56] suggests that brainwave entrainment may improve cognitive function and change the brain's normal beta frequencies (between 13 and 30 Hz) to the lower alpha, theta or even delta frequencies, which happen in meditation.

Today's ritual is especially helpful if you find it hard to settle into a meditative state. Search online for some brainwave entrainment meditation music – but do remember this isn't actually music but a brainwave harmonizing sound. If you can listen to the sound with your headphones on that would be ideal. When you are ready, close your eyes and simply listen. **Ritualize** by losing yourself in the sounds and by reminding yourself that ancient cultures all over the world had methods, such as chanting or beating drums, to induce mind-harmonizing, meditative states. If you already subscribe to brainwave entrainment, experiment with a different entrainment method, such as binaural beats or sacred acoustics.[57]

56 www.researchgate.net/publication/289030858_Alpha_brainwave_entrainment_as_a_cognitive_performance_activator
57 www.sacredacoustics.com

BRAIN-TRAINING MIND RITUAL #151: SOLVE PUZZLES

Enhance your brain with logic problems

The more regularly you challenge[58] your brain with puzzles and problem solving, the better it gets at thinking critically and processing information. There are stacks of free puzzles and problem-solving exercises you can seek out online, but to get you started today's ritual offers you a couple of brain teasers. **Ritualize** by relishing this opportunity to challenge your brain. Notice the urge you have to immediately discover the answers in the footnotes. Don't act on it. Give your brain a chance to work out both solutions for at least five minutes. All the information you need to answer the puzzles correctly can be found in the question. You don't need any specialist knowledge, just logical thinking. It doesn't matter if you can't solve them. Simply musing on brain teasers like these will ignite your thinking and hopefully encourage you to seek out others to solve every day.

★ In Egypt, why can't you take a photo of a man with tattoos?[59]
★ What is the slowest and fastest thing in the world, and the longest and shortest, as well as the most neglected and the most regretted, without which nothing can ever be achieved?[60]

---

58 www.bmj.com/content/363/bmj.k4925
59 Photos are taken with cameras, not tattoos.
60 Time.

BRAIN-TRAINING MIND RITUAL
#152: CHECK MATE

Playing chess can make you smarter

Chess is a fantastic way to give your brain a vigorous work out. It can improve your problem-solving skills, reasoning power, concentration and logic.[61]

If you don't know how to play chess, you may want to learn the basic rules of the game. If you do know how to play, but haven't for a while, you are encouraged to return to the game. It's ideal to play against another person, but there are plenty of chess apps or free online chess websites where you can pit your wits against the ultimate logic of a computer. A game of chess can take hours, so your ritual today is to make the first move in a game of chess. Then, tomorrow make your next move and continue one move a day until you either win or lose.

It is easy to **ritualize** playing chess because the only way to play successfully is to focus all your concentration on the game and your next move. If you are distracted you will soon be facing check mate from your opponent. If you are already a committed chess player, congratulate yourself. Chess is much more than a game – it's fantastic news for your brain.

61 Burgoyne, Alexander P., *et al.*: 'The relationship between cognitive ability and chess skill: A comprehensive meta-analysis', *Intelligence*, 2016; DOI: 10.1016/j.intell.2016.08.002

BRAIN-TRAINING MIND RITUAL
#153: PICK UP A PEN AGAIN

Writing boosts brain function more than typing

Intriguing research[62] suggests writing by hand can make you smarter. If you are like most people these days, you probably type everything. But the proven mind-boosting benefits of doing even a little handwriting might just encourage you to pick up a pen again.

Your ritual today is to write something by hand. The ideal place to start would be with a diary entry at the end of the day about what happened today or anything you like, as that's the beauty of personal diaries – nobody ever sees them but you. If keeping a diary isn't for you, write your to-do list by hand. Doesn't matter what you write, just be sure to do some writing by hand today. You may even want to go online and find some exercises to help you improve your handwriting or a poem you love and copy it out. **Ritualize** by focusing mindfully on the words you write and the feel of your pen on the paper. Remind yourself that writing by hand isn't a waste of time – it's actively boosting your brain power.

---

62 www.rd.com/advice/parenting/why-handwriting-makes-you-smarter/

BRAIN-TRAINING MIND RITUAL
#154: SPEAK ELVISH

Learning a new language can improve your brain

Speaking in another language[63] improves the brain's speech centres. Obviously, enrolling in a language class would be ideal but, if that's not for you, there are D-I-Y language-learning apps and courses online. Choose a language that you enjoy the sound of and make learning new words a daily ritual. You don't need to become fluent and may forever stay at beginner's level, but that doesn't matter. Simply learning to say a few words each day in another language, even if it's a fantasy language like Elvish, gives your brain a boost.

Indeed, the foreign words you are going to learn for your ritual today are Elvish (the fictional language of elves). This is to remind you that language learning should be fun and you don't necessarily have to have a serious reason to learn a new language. It's just great stimulation for your brain. **Ritualize** by saying out loud the following in Elvish.

★ *Mellon* (Friend)
★ *Emma lath* (My love)
★ *Dareth shiral* (Safe journey)

Saying the words out loud will emphasize the magical impact foreign words can have on your mind. You may even want to memorize these words and their meanings, so you have your own secret language no one can understand except you ... and perhaps a nearby elf.

63 www.ncbi.nlm.nih.gov/pmc/articles/PMC3259110/?tool=pubmed

BRAIN-TRAINING MIND RITUAL
#155: TURN IT DOWN
A focused mind is a powerful mind

Lack of sleep, stress and an unhealthy diet can all contribute to poor concentration, but distractions[64] are also a major reason. To focus your mind, you need to be able to tune out outside distractions, both the obvious ones and not-so obvious ones.

Today's ritual is designed to help improve your ability to focus using your sense of hearing as your teacher. At some point today turn on the TV or an online video and lower the volume until you can barely hear anything. Then, turn up the volume slowly until you can hear what is being said. Write down the volume indicator. Do some deep breathing and stretching for a minute and then repeat the exercise and try to hit a volume point earlier each time. It will be effortless to **ritualize** this exercise because the only way you can hit a lower volume point is by focusing completely on the sound you are trying to hear and ignoring all the other distracting sounds and thoughts competing for your attention. As you perform this ritual you will naturally find yourself touching your ears. Let this action remind you that a focused mind is a powerful mind.

64 https://news.stanford.edu/news/2009/august24/multitask-research-study-082409.html

BRAIN-TRAINING MIND RITUAL #156: YOUR 60 SECONDS

Become an instant expert

The size and structure of your brain expands both when you learn *how to do* something new – because your brain is led by actions – and also when you learn *about* something new.[65]

Today's ritual encourages you to expand your brain with mental exploration. Choose a subject you don't know enough about yet or a well-known book you haven't read and look it up online. If you need a suggestion for a subject try "brain training techniques" and for a book, Stephen Hawkins' *A Brief History of Time*. Read up online for ten minutes about your chosen subject or book. Then **ritualize** by setting a timer for one minute, and hitting record on your phone. Talk about your subject or book for one minute. If you find yourself hesitating or saying "um" too much or repeating what you have said, stop the timer and try again until you can speak fluently for one minute. Then listen back to yourself. Focus mindfully on what you are absorbing and retelling. Remind yourself that gathering information is enhancing your knowledge, and recapturing and summarizing that information in 60 seconds is improving your communication skills.

65 *American Journal of Geriatric Psychiatry*, 2009 Feb;17(2), pp. 116-26.

BRAIN-TRAINING MIND RITUAL
#157: PLAY WORD GAMES

Crosswords can make you smarter

Crosswords and word games[66] can sharpen cognitive function, so your ritual today is to buy a newspaper that has a daily crossword puzzle section or to find a crossword online and print it out. If you prefer word searches to crosswords they are just as beneficial. Then, head somewhere you can relax (a coffee shop is ideal as you combine the brain-boosting benefits of coffee with doing crosswords) and gift yourself at least ten minutes to complete the crossword or word search.

Ritualize by mindfully focusing on completing the crossword and not letting other thoughts distract you. Be clear in your intention. Doing this crossword is not just about passing the time or playing a game. You are training your brain with a mentally invigorating challenge that encourages you to think critically and dip into your memory stores. There's also a tremendous feeling of satisfaction (you may hopefully get hooked on) when you successfully complete a crossword. Try to resist Googling for the answers unless you really get stuck.

• • • • • • • • • • • •

66 http://freedailycrosswords.com/puzzles-boost-childs-brain-power/

BRAIN–TRAINING MIND RITUAL #158: PLAY NUMBER GAMES

Turn off the TV and play some number games instead

Watching TV in moderation is positive. You can learn a great deal from the news and documentaries, and there is nothing like watching a great drama or movie to inspire brain-boosting empathy and creativity. Too much TV, however, is bad news.[67] It can slow down your brainwaves and cause a decline in brain function. Experts recommend no more than two hours of screen time a day.

Your ritual today is to do some Sudoku in the time that you typically devote to watching TV or videos online. In much the same way as crosswords can challenge and improve your brain, Sudoku is a fun way to improve your problem-solving skills. Sudoku is a Japanese logic number game, where you have to fill in blank boxes based on easy-to-understand rules. If you search online you will find many free Sudoku challenges with the rules clearly laid out. You can also buy Sudoku challenge books and apps. **Ritualize** by focusing mindfully on the number games and feel gratitude for the free brain training these puzzles offer you.

67 www.livescience.com/52959-television-cognitive-function.html

BRAIN-TRAINING MIND RITUAL #159: JUST 50 WORDS

Write a very short story

As we saw in Ritual 153, writing[68] by hand can improve memory, communication skills and enhance creativity.

Your ritual today is to write a very short fantasy story. Don't be tempted to type, you need to write this by hand. Your story must have a beginning, a middle and an end, but the catch is you have to write your story in under 50 words. **Ritualize** this task by setting your intention – tell your mind that you are going to compose a story.

Visualize your story in your mind's eye first. Take as long as you need to do this. Then, write down the most concise summary of your story that you can. Don't set any limits on your creativity. If you get stuck for ideas think of fantasy stories you admire and summarize them in 50 words. For example, Harry Potter all started for the author J K Rowling when she was day-dreaming on a train journey and had one simple idea: a human boy going to wizard school on a train in his school holidays. Doesn't matter what your very short story is about. Just write it down in a concise 50 words.

68 www.wsj.com/articles/SB10001424052748704631504575531932754922518

BRAIN-TRAINING MIND RITUAL
#160: LOOK TO YOUR PAST
Research your family tree

Intriguingly, there is research[69] indicating that knowing your family history or the history of your genetic origins may boost your intellectual performance. The researchers aren't exactly sure why this is the case, but they hypothesize that people thinking about their ancestors increases their sense of control over everyday activities.

Today your ritual is to reconnect with your ancestral past. If you know very little about your ancestors or your genealogy, perhaps this is the time to do some investigation or ask your grandparents or family members to share their memories. If you were adopted or didn't know your parents, focus on the culture you were born into and how it has shaped you into the person you are today.

Ritualize by getting a notebook and spending some time writing down information and time lines. Feel gratitude for what the lives and experiences of your ancestors can teach you, and appreciate the perspective that knowing your past and where you came from can give you. Looking ahead, you may wish to set out regular periods of time each day or week to find out more about your family tree. See how far back in time you can go.

69 https://onlinelibrary.wiley.com/doi/full/10.1002/ejsp.778

BRAIN-TRAINING MIND RITUAL
#161: READING ALOUD

Hear yourself to remember better

The dual action of speaking and hearing yourself speak at the same time when you read something out loud helps your brain process and store information better. This process is called the "production effect".[70] In short, reading out loud improves your memory.

Choose a poem and read it aloud for today's ritual. Ideally pick a poem that you might like to commit to memory because the words are so immortal and inspiring. I suggest: Rudyard Kipling's evergreen poem "If" or Coleridge's "Kubla Khan", or a famous passage from Shakespeare, such as "the quality of mercy" speech from *The Merchant of Venice*. You can just focus on the first ten lines or so if the poem is long. Simply choose a passage that inspires you or sounds great out loud. **Ritualize** by reading the words slowly and clearly and adding some emotional intensity. Read it out several times and then see how much you can recite from memory.

Note: Looking ahead, you can use this ritual whenever you need to commit a phone number to memory or a to-do list or a car licence plate. By saying the words or numbers out loud to yourself, you are more likely to remember them.

. . . .
70 www.medicalnewstoday.com/articles/320377.php

BRAIN–TRAINING MIND RITUAL #162: TURNING TIMES TABLES AROUND

Challenge your mind by speaking and writing different sums at the same time

The more you challenge your mind, the sharper it gets. Research[71] suggests brain-training games really can improve your memory, concentration and cognitive function, regardless of your age.

Your brain-training ritual today can help improve your logic, mental maths and problem-solving skills. Try reciting the five times table out loud while writing down the two times table. Don't be surprised if this dual exercise takes you quite a while to do, especially if maths has never been your strong point. This ritual isn't meant to be easy and indeed the more your brain feels under pressure the better. You are flexing your mental muscle. If you find this easy, challenge yourself by reciting the six times table out loud while writing down the seven times table, and so on. It will feel natural to **ritualize** this task because you will need all your mental focus and concentration to successfully do both verbal and mental calculations at the same time.

71 Landau, Susan M., *et al.*: 'Association of lifetime cognitive engagement and low β-amyloid deposition ', *Archives of Neurology*, Published online January 23, 2012. http://dx.doi.org/10.1001/archneurol.2011.2748

BRAIN-TRAINING MIND RITUAL #163: QUESTION TIME

The inquisitive brain is a stimulated brain

The more curious you are, the more questions you ask of yourself, others and life itself, the more you will learn from the answers you think, hear or read. Research[72] consistently shows that inquisitive minds are stimulated minds.

Today your ritual is to make a point of asking other people as many questions as you can. Other people have different opinions, experiences and insights to share, and their words and ideas can provoke new thoughts and ideas within you. You don't have to agree with the answers other people give you. Simply learn a new perspective and add it to your store of knowledge.

Ritualize your question time by mindfully paying attention to the answers you receive. Allow others to have their say and reflect deeply on their point of view. Don't interrupt. See where they are coming from; treat their words with sacred respect. If you prefer not to ask someone questions in person, the online world is a great place for information gatherers - just be sure to check the accuracy and credibility of your sources, as sadly we live in a world where misinformation is rife. Quora is an amazing Q&A app for people with inquisitive minds.

72 www.scientificamerican.com/article/curiosity-prepares-the-brain-for-better-learning/

BRAIN-TRAINING MIND RITUAL
#164: THE EYE OF THE STORM

No idea is too ridiculous when you brainstorm

Brainstorming[73] or mind mapping, can help solve problems and generate new ideas, and brainstorming alone is more beneficial than doing so in a group. Simply pour out ideas without worrying about organization, logic or whether the ideas make any sense or how they fit together.

Today your ritual is to unlock your creative power with some brainstorming. You need a pen and a piece of A4-size paper. **Ritualize** by writing down an idea or a problem you want to solve and then write anything related to that idea or problem that comes into your mind. Think and write fast. If you can't think of an idea or problem, try answering this: *Based on my daily actions, where can I expect to be in five years?*

Then, when you have exhausted random thoughts, use prompter words, like who, what, why and when or the word opposite to trigger more ideas and associations. When your page is full of writing, take a break and come back and review what you have brainstormed. Can you identify the eye of the storm or a central theme? Allow your mind to freely wander where ever it wants to go during this task. Trust that this different way of thinking will give your brain a creative boost.

73 http://mechanicaldesign.asmedigitalcollection.asme.org/article.aspx?articleid=1449997

BRAIN-TRAINING MIND RITUAL
#165: BEAT THE CLOCK

Timed games and activities force your mind to focus

Your brain loves to be stimulated by puzzles and it especially enjoys the challenge of working against the clock.[74] This is because when activities are timed you are forced to focus intensely and think quickly.

Set aside ten minutes today to do some mind or memory-boosting drills using a timer. There are many free brain-training resources online you can seek out to do this ritual and they are well worth the effort because online brain-training games typically tend to be timed.

To get you thinking along the right lines, try this simple mind drill to get you started. Set a timer for two minutes and see if you can successfully recite the alphabet forward and then backward and then forward and backward again.

It will feel natural to **ritualize** this beat-the-clock brain teaser because the only way to complete it successfully is to focus and be in the present moment 100 per cent.

74 Jaeggi, S., *et al.*: 'Improving fluid intelligence with training on working memory', *Proceedings of the National Academy of Sciences (PNAS)*, 105(19): 6829-6833. April 28, 2008. DOI: http://dx.doi.org/10.1073/pnas.0801268105

BRAIN-TRAINING MIND RITUAL
#166: UPSIDE DOWN TIME
Stretch your brain with "neurobics"

Experiments show that when we do things differently to the way we always do them, or use our senses in novel ways, we stimulate nerve cells and contribute to the growth and agility of our brains.

Your ritual today is to try two "neurobic" exercises. These exercises[75] are simple, practical ways to shake up your mental routines and give your brain a workout. The first exercise will stimulate your brain by turning an everyday action on its head. Wear your watch upside down or, if you don't wear a watch, turn the screen saver photos on your phone upside down. This small change will force your brain to make sense of time or an image upside down every time you look at it.

The second exercise is to listen to a piece of classical music while smelling lavender scent or any aroma that you find relaxing. This forces you to combine two senses in an unexpected way. An alternative would be to put on a blindfold while you get dressed, so you are forced to rely on other senses to get the task done. It will feel entirely natural to **ritualize** neurobic exercises because when you do them, they feel unnatural and you will therefore have complete awareness of your reason or intention for doing them.

75 www.keepyourbrainalive.com/the-authors/

BRAIN-TRAINING MIND RITUAL
#167: MEMORY GAMES
Start flexing your memory muscle

Regularly flexing your "memory muscle" with memory games and "hooks" to jog recall will strengthen and improve your memory, however old you are.[76]

Your ritual today is to remember the titles of the 21 Foundation rituals in their correct order. Experiment with simple memory techniques if that helps. You can use repetition. For example, write out the titles and repeat them out loud as you write them. Then keep writing and reciting them until you are fluent. (This technique is especially helpful when you want to remember someone's name – say the name out loud and keep repeating it in your head.) Or you can associate familiar words or images with each title. For example, for the Impress Yourself ritual (*see* page 26) think of that famous Madonna song, "Express Yourself" to jog your memory. You can also set the titles to a familiar piece of music or create a story that helps you remember them.

Ritualize by focusing 100 per cent on this task and not giving up until your memory has emerged victorious.

76 Johnson, Jeffrey D., *et al.*: 'Recollection, familiarity, and cortical reinstatement: A multivoxel pattern analysis', *Neuron*, Vol. 63, Issue 5, September 8, 2009. DOI: http://dx.doi.org/10.1016/j.neuron.2009.08.011

BRAIN-TRAINING MIND RITUAL
#168: A WHOLE NEW WORLD

Take your thoughts to where they have not gone before

Your brain loves novelty. Having said that, repetition and routine are also key because if we were constantly seeking out new things, we would never move beyond novice or learner stage. The secret to wisdom is to find a balance between curiosity and perseverance. In other words, seek variety when you can and do things in a new way to learn to use your imagination creativity[77] when you can't.

Today's ritual will encourage your brain to reach in new imaginative directions without you needing to do anything new and stimulating, like learning a new language or changing your daily routine in an unexpected way. Set aside some time to imagine what it would be like to be something that you can't ever experience in this life (*see* list below). **Ritualize** by seeing yourself in an alternative existence and reality. Visualize and feel what that reality would be like. Write down a few key words or phrases that encapsulate that reality for you in reply to the following questions.

★ What is it like to be a tree?
★ What is it like to be a butterfly?
★ What is it like to be the wind?
★ What is it like to be fire?
★ What is it like to be time?
★ What is it like to be eternity?

77 www.livescience.com/49244-imagination-reality-brain-flow-direction.html

BRAIN-TRAINING POWER RITUAL
#169: FREE YOUR MIND

Change your mind and your life in alternative ways

If New Age or alternative rituals are out of your comfort zone, then this might be a good reason to give them a try today, as a constant theme in this Mind ritual section is the brain's love of novelty. Each time you think about, learn or try to do something new, your mind expands. So, consider trying out one of the perfectly safe New Age techniques for your **power ritual** today. **Ritualize** your actions by reminding yourself of their brain-boosting intentions.

Crystal mind power: There's no hard-core science yet but crystals have been believed to contain healing[78] energy for centuries because they are a product of the earth. If you place a crystal on or close to your body, this may help your body link to the earth's natural healing powers. One crystal believed to aid concentration better is fluorite. Carry some fluorite around with you or put it on your desk. When you need to study, concentrate and focus clearly, place and hold the crystal lightly on your forehead. Other crystals for improving concentration are tiger's eye and clear quartz.

Essential oils: It is best to dilute essential oils with a carrier oil before they are used as a healing perfume. The best essential oils for concentration and memory according to health experts[79] are: rosemary, lavender, sage, basil, cypress and lemon. You can simply sniff the stimulating scent directly from the bottle, inhale from a drop of oil on a tissue, or diffuse the essential oil in your room, office or car.

78 www.livescience.com/ 40347-crystal-healing.html
79 www.takingcharge.csh.umn. edu/explore-healing-practices/ aromatherapy/what-does-research-say-about-essential-oils

Emotional freedom technique (EFT) is a mind/body/emotion programming technique that can help you stay calm and focused. When you feel stressed you use your fingertips to gently tap different parts of your body three to seven times, while repeating a sentence like this: "Even though I feel anxious and distracted, I choose calm and focus." The tapping points are the top of your head, your eyebrows, the side of your eyes, under your eyes, under your nose, your chin, your collarbone, under your arm and then return to the top of your head. Notice the intensity of your stress as you tap, and stop this ritual when you feel calmer.

TAKING GOOD CARE OF YOUR MIND AND YOURSELF

The best way to take care of your mind is to use it. Curiosity is superfood for your brain. Never, ever think you are too old to learn something new. Hopefully, the Mind rituals in this book have encouraged you to learn something new every day. Of course, your mind also needs your body to be healthy to function at its peak so, if you haven't already, you may want to refer to the Body section of this book now. Before moving onto the Spirit and Heart sections, it makes sense to stay with the material world a while longer and work through the Success rituals section next.

$\mathscr{S}$uccess
RITUALS

*Rituals to help YOU work
smart and live well*

What does success mean to you?
For many people the definition
of success is money, career and
popularity. But if that is the case,
why do we read media stories about
famous, rich and successful people
who are deeply unhappy? These
people seem to have it all, but
"having it all" is not enough for them.
The reason for their dissatisfaction
is that their lives lack meaning. They
have been chasing success through
external sources.

170–197

External things can't give your life meaning unless you find peace from within first. Feeling content with who you are and not with what you have is the true definition of success. Fulfilment and happiness are inside-out jobs and the upcoming Spirit and Heart sections of this book will reinforce that point powerfully. However, we live in a material world and we need to find positive and life-affirming ways to navigate through it. That's why before you enter the mystical world of Spirit and Heart you are encouraged to keep your feet on the ground and work through this section. The focus here is on money and material success. It's a four-week programme divided into four sections: Feel Rich, Finance, Networks and Attracting Abundance.

You need 28 days for the "worldly-wise" rituals here to have a noticeable impact on your life. Remember, it takes at least three weeks for newly introduced rituals to reshape your brain and for you to feel the benefits. As long as you keep things in perspective, there is absolutely nothing wrong with using rituals to help attract greater wealth and material success into your life. Apart from making your life more comfortable and pleasurable, it is easier to help others if you have the means to do so – you can't offer someone a drink from an empty cup. This section will help you fill your own cup. It will remind you that you deserve material success and the very best for yourself.

Just be sure, as you work through the next 28 days of rituals, that you remind yourself daily that nobody on their death bed ever says, "I wish I had spent more time at the office". The dying only speak about the priceless things money can never buy: love, truth, peace, knowledge and time.

FEEL RICH SUCCESS RITUAL #170: DITCH THE POVERTY MINDSET

Pay for things with gratitude

Many of us think of money as something that is scarce. We feel we can never have enough of it. We dread bills and bank statements. This attitude is called a poverty mindset[1] and it can be very hard to shift, especially if you were brought up to think of money in this way or you believe that spiritual people should not value the material. The problem is if you have a poverty mindset, the chances are life will reflect that lack of abundance back to you. That's why the next nine days of rituals will all encourage you to think richer.

The best way to shift your poverty mindset to a more abundant one is with positive action. Today's ritual asks you to say "thank you" out loud every time you pay someone in cash or via card, however large or small the amount. They may look surprised as they should be thanking you for the money you are giving them, but know in your mind why you are doing this. **Ritualize** by focusing your intention not on the money leaving you when you sign or hand it over, but on the gratitude you have for the ability to pay for the product, work, time or service you need.

1 www.epi.org/blog/is-poverty-a-mindset/

FEEL RICH SUCCESS RITUAL
#171: GADGET GRATITUDE
Say thank you to technology

Just as money itself is not evil – indeed, you can do an incredible amount of good with it if you spend it wisely – so technology is not a completely negative force either. Technology transforms lives. If you want success today you have to be switched on digitally. Many people start getting technophobic as they get older, when they should be doing the opposite for their wellbeing, because research[2] shows keeping up with technology keeps you mentally young.

   Yes, addiction to phones can be damaging but, used in moderation, the digital world truly is one of infinite possibility. Imagine how a medieval person would react if they were given a phone. They would be filled with shock and awe. So, your ritual today is a little gadget worship. Pay mindful attention to the hugely important role the digital revolution plays in your daily life. Whenever you search online for information, spend a few moments appreciating the real magic of what has just happened. The same applies before you call or text anyone. Marvel at your ability to instantly connect to someone who is miles away. At the end of your day, do an online search about a subject that interests you, preferably on a mind-expanding information app like Quora. Then, when you switch off your computer or put your phone to charge, **ritualize** by bowing your head in gratitude for all the connections, joy and wonder that technology can give you.

2 www.pewinternet.org/2014/04/03/older-adults-and-technology-use/

THE RITUAL YEARBOOK

FEEL RICH SUCCESS RITUAL
#172: TOP READING

Learn about money and make friends with success

Your success-building ritual today is to start to read at least one of the following best-selling books. They are all easy to read and contain fantastically helpful information that can help you achieve career, financial and life success.

Ritualize as you read by being fully present and absorbing the information. Read slowly and carefully and understand the importance[3] of what you are reading. Too many spiritual people neglect their finances and this can cause considerable stress. Taking care of yourself financially is just as important as taking care of yourself physically, mentally, emotionally and spiritually. Learn about business and make friends with money and success as you read these books. If you have read all these books before, choose one to re-read. Great books always yield more on second reading.

★ *The 7 Habits of Highly Successful People* by Stephen R. Covey
★ *Think and Grow Rich* by Napoleon Hill
★ *Good to Great* by Jim Collins
★ *Emotional Intelligence* by Daniel Goleman
★ *The E Myth* by Michael Gerber
★ *How to Win Friends and Influence People* by Dale Carnegie
★ *The Intelligent Investor* by Benjamin Graham
★ *The Outsiders* by William Thorndike
★ *Business Adventures* by John Brooks

3 Investor, Warren Buffet said the secret of his success was reading at least 500 pages of a good book a day because "that's how knowledge works. It builds up, like compound interest."

FEEL RICH SUCCESS RITUAL
#173: THINK OF CAPABLE OTHERS
Pretend for a day

Research[4] suggests that thinking about the stereotype of someone who excels in their chosen field can improve your performance. For example, if you want to learn something academic, identifying with or mimicking the behaviour or stereotype of a professor can result in higher performance at a general knowledge test. Or if you want to improve your performance in physical exercise, priming yourself with the athlete stereotype shows higher persistence in a physical exercise.

Your ritual today is to think of someone you admire, who has achieved success. It doesn't matter who that person is or whether or not they are famous. Then, just for today, adopt one of their mannerisms or way of speaking, doing things or dressing. Copy their behaviour. **Ritualize** by understanding that when you mimic them you are consciously using them as a role model to improve your own performance. At the end of your day, reflect on what you have learned from copying someone successful for a day and integrate whatever boosted your confidence into your own unique personality.

4 www.researchgate.net/publication/247839239_Think_of_Capable_Others_and_You_Can_Make_It_Self-Efficacy_Mediates_the_Effect_of_Stereotype_Activation_on_Behavior

FEEL RICH SUCCESS RITUAL #174: WORK SMART

Improve your productivity and efficiency

You've probably been told how important it is to work hard. While this is true, perhaps more important than working hard is working smart.[5] In other words when it comes to work you should always focus on quality rather than quantity.

Your ritual today is to make a conscious effort to work smart. Some of the recommendations below may seem counterintuitive, but that is the whole point. You are consciously changing your behaviour. **Ritualize** by reading them out loud before you begin your day and letting them remind you to be as productive, creative and efficient as possible today.

★ Get up earlier.
★ Plan your day the night before or first thing in the morning.
★ Approach tasks like a lazy person – they find the simplest and easiest ways to do something.
★ Do less and delegate work when you can.
★ Prioritize work that is important.
★ Stop procrastinating and tackle important work first thing.
★ Leave what is not important for later or another day.
★ Review your work and get feedback.
★ Feel passionate about and proud of your work.
★ Take regular breaks.
★ Leave work on time – your work-life balance is important.

5 www.bakadesuyo.com/2018/02/work-smarter-not-harder-2/

FEEL RICH SUCCESS RITUAL #175: WRITE YOURSELF A CHEQUE

Dream big

The days of writing cheques to pay bills or purchase goods are receding, but writing one to yourself can be a powerful symbol to attract prosperity from the universe. The Hollywood star Jim Carrey[6] famously wrote a cheque to himself for $10 million when he was an unknown actor.

Your ritual today is to take a blank cheque (if you don't have a cheque book, find an image online and print it out), then write today's date and make it out to your full name. You can either enter a specific amount or leave it blank for the universe to decide. On the signature line write "the law of prosperity" and on the stub or the back write "PAID" in large letters. **Ritualize** by focusing your attention with gratitude on all the things you have in your life, rather than what you lack. Feel abundant and deserving of prosperity.

6 www.mindpowernews.com/JimCarrey.htm

THE RITUAL YEARBOOK

FEEL RICH SUCCESS RITUAL #176: WRITE DOWN YOUR GOALS

Use your journal to map out your future

Write down your long-term goals today in your journal. Numerous experts[7] recommend journalling as a tool to increase your chances of future success in life. **Ritualize** by visualizing an abundant future as you write. See it happening in your mind's eye, as you write down where you want to be. Then, at the end of your day, record whatever you did today to help make those goals a reality. If you don't think you did anything, write down what you can do tomorrow to help you on your way. It doesn't have to be anything big. Remember, the journey of a thousand miles begins with one step.

By writing down your goals clearly and thinking about what you are going to do to achieve them, you are creating your road map for success. Let today's ritual incentivize you to keep recording your progress toward your goals every day.

Note: See also Foundation Ritual 7.

---

7 https://psychcentral.com/lib/the-health-benefits-of-journaling/

FEEL RICH SUCCESS RITUAL
#177: FORGET ABOUT ONE DAY

Consciously create your own life with smart goals

A structured goal-setting plan[8] is an absolutely crucial factor for success because it helps you break away from passively allowing others to direct you and, instead, you can proactively and consciously create your life.

Yesterday you were encouraged to think about and write down your goals. Today you are going to focus on what exactly you need to do to achieve those goals. Most people fail to achieve them because they have no plan or are too vague, so be specific. Saying you will do something or go somewhere "one day" is as good as saying you are never going to do it. Do your research and clearly identify the steps and time frame needed to complete them now. **Ritualize** by noticing how excited you feel as you write down your action plan to achieve your dreams. If you don't feel excited, this is a clear sign that you need to rethink your goals.

Note: Your goal-setting ritual yesterday and your action plan to achieve those goals today have set the ball in motion and reminded you that you are in charge of the direction of your life. Looking ahead, check in with your action plan as often as you can, as even the best plans need constant revision, evaluation and adjustment.

8 http://users.nber.org/~sewp/Davis_SurveyAnalysis20060201.pdf

THE RITUAL YEARBOOK

FEEL RICH SUCCESS RITUAL
#178: ACTION PICTURE
Create a vision board

Vision boards can increase your focus and improve your chances of achieving your dreams. They help create a strong emotional connection between you and your life goals. They also help you to clarify your goals and believe they can be possible. There is transformative power in clearly seeing a visual reminder of your dreams laid out in front of you every day. If you aren't convinced, give today's ritual a try to see if it helps. You have nothing to lose and everything to gain.

You will need a large piece of blank paper and some glue. Search online for pictures that you feel best depict your life goals, then print them out. If you prefer to do this online, create a document and gather your images there or on Pinterest. Then arrange the images in a way that looks and feels pleasing to you. Make your vision board beautiful. **Ritualize** by visualizing yourself achieving these goals as you create your vision board. Then, at the top of your poster or file, add the following words in bold: *Without action my vision will remain a dream.*

Display your vision board on a wall that you see every day or on your desktop or screen saver. Whenever you see it, repeat the words you added and make reciting them a daily ritual. You can add or update the images whenever you feel you need to. Trust in your dreams but remember the greatest value a vision board offers is that it motivates you to *take action.*

FINANCE SUCCESS RITUAL
#179: KEEP TRACK
Record your spending

The next five rituals will all focus on things you can do to improve your income. As the previous rituals have shown, money is not evil or to be feared. It is something that can enhance and empower your life. The first step to improving your financial situation is to be aware of what that situation is. You need to know exactly what is coming into your account and what is going out. Then you can look at your spending and start cutting back on things that don't matter much to you and direct it toward things that do.

Your ritual today asks you to keep a daily record of your spending.[9] Write down every single thing you buy today, even inexpensive items like a newspaper. **Ritualize** by pondering and understanding the importance of monitoring your finances. Unless you are aware of what you are spending your money on, you can't make educated decisions about where savings can be made. You may well find that your actual expenditure is very different from what you think it is. Let today's ritual encourage you to keep better financial records every day.

Note: If you are too overwhelmed by your finances to see clearly, consider booking an appointment with a financial advisor or expert.

9 www.forbes.com/sites/learnvest/2014/05/13/9-financial-habits-that-can-make-you-wealthy/#5f1efe457183

THE RITUAL YEARBOOK

FINANCE SUCCESS RITUAL
#180: KEEPING ON TRACK

Know the time, place and reason

Continue with your spending record for today's ritual, but this time include the time, location and reason for spending. **Ritualize** by focusing not so much on the amount you spend or what you purchase but the reason why you are buying it. What are the emotions[10] behind your purchase? Hopefully, this will help you start questioning how valid or essential your purchases are. Did you really want what you bought or were you trying to satisfy another feeling? Don't pressure yourself to know all the answers immediately. The important thing is that you are starting to ask questions, which are often the catalysts for transformation in all areas of life, including finances.

Note: If you have understood the benefits of keeping a spending log, moving forward you may want to download a free app like Learnvest that can help you.

10 www.investopedia.com/articles/pf/08/emotional-spending.asp

FINANCE SUCCESS RITUAL
#181: SPENDING RULES

Self-imposed rules improve finances

Keeping track of your spending can certainly help you identify areas of unnecessary spending, but today's ritual encourages you to think in the opposite way.

Behaviour experts[11] believe that self-imposed spending rules can really help improve our finances, so you are going to create rules for yourself that put a cap on your spending for specific things. For example, decide that you will only spend X amount in restaurants or coffee shops per week. The same applies if you are in debt – sit down and work out a repayment plan to help you pay it off. **Ritualize** by understanding that creating your own spending rules and sticking to them gives you real control over managing your own finances.

11 https://learnvest.com/article/ready-for-a-no-spend-month-heres-how-to-start

THE RITUAL YEARBOOK

FINANCE SUCCESS RITUAL
#182: INCREASE YOUR INCOME

Look for additional income streams

If you want more money you can either spend less or earn more. Today's ritual encourages you to think of ways that you can earn more.[12] Set aside at least half an hour to sit quietly and put all your mindful attention on other possible income streams.

Ritualize by reminding yourself that actively seeking new ways to boost your income, whether that income materializes or not, is an act of loving self-care. It is showing the universe that you are approaching your life proactively with an attitude of abundance. If you already have a job, consider applying for a part-time position to supplement your income or look online for earning opportunities there. If nothing seems suitable, consider visiting a careers advisor, starting your own small business or even running a podcast, YouTube channel or blog to generate potential income. It is easy to get despondent but one thing is for sure: if you don't take action nothing in your life will ever change. Be sure to devote time today to actively start looking for ways to increase your income.

12 www.forbes.com/sites/learnvest/2014/05/13/9-financial-habits-that-can-make-you-wealthy/#5f1efe457183

FINANCE SUCCESS RITUAL
#183: SAVE FIRST

Live like a secretly rich person

Contrary to what you may have been led to believe, many of the world's richest people don't live lavish and flamboyant lifestyles. They are extremely careful with their money and instead of spend, spend, spend, they invest and save, save, save. They prioritize their savings over and above everything else.

Your ritual today is to live like a secretly rich person.[13] Take some time to think about what you can realistically save each month. Work out what that amount of money is and write it down. **Ritualize** as you write by saying out loud this abundance boosting mantra: Save first; pay bills, then spend.

Make a sacred promise to yourself that from now on you will make saving rather than spending your financial motivation and priority.

13 William Danko, *The Millionaire Next Door*, Rosatta, 2010

NETWORKS SUCCESS RITUAL
#184: REFLECT BACK
Mimic the body language of someone you are talking to

Networking is a key ingredient for success in work and life, so that's why the next five rituals are designed to improve your people skills. People tend to offer opportunities to people they feel comfortable with, so knowing how to make other people feel comfortable when you interact with them is a crucial life skill. Research[14] shows that one of the best ways to win friends and influence people is to mimic them physically. For example, if you are sitting with someone and they cross their legs, cross your legs the same way.

You often see this kind of body language mimicking in romantic couples where it happens naturally. Your ritual today is to consciously mimic the body language of someone you are having a conversation with. Obviously do this in a subtle rather than an obvious way! **Ritualize** by noticing how adopting the same body language as the person you are with increases your empathy and sense of connection with them. It may also impact your thinking and help you consider their point of view.

14 www.researchgate.net/publication/5400170_Mimicking_Attractive_Opposite-Sex_
Others_The_Role_of_Romantic_Relationship_Status

215

NETWORKS SUCCESS RITUAL
#185: A IS FOR EFFORT

Praise effort rather than ability

Research[15] shows that when children are praised for their efforts rather than their ability or intelligence, they significantly improve their scores moving forward, whereas those who were told they were clever or smart or a natural did worse than they did at the beginning.

Your ritual today is to make a conscious effort to praise someone out loud (and that person can be yourself) for the effort they have put into a task rather than the outcome or their ability to perform the task. Put the focus all on their time and effort and the importance of learning from trial and error. **Ritualize** by speaking calmly and positively. Understand that praising someone's work ethic and valuing their efforts ahead of what is achieved is highly motivating.

15 http://mereworth.kent.sch.uk/wp-content/uploads/2015/04/growth_mindsets_dweck-praise-effort.pdf

THE RITUAL YEARBOOK

NETWORKS SUCCESS RITUAL #186: PRESS PAUSE

Reflect on the quality of what you put out there

We live in an era of high-speed communication. We send messages on the go. The crowded inbox is a feature of modern life. All this constant communication has its benefits, as good communication is a key to success. But there are also serious downsides.[16] A lot of messages come across as vague, rambling, indifferent or cold when that wasn't our intention when sending them.

Every time you are about to send a text, a message or an email today, pause for a few moments. Sit quietly and shift your attention away from the message by looking outside the window or up at the sky. **Ritualize** by imagining the impact of that message on the person who is going to receive it. Imagine if this was a century ago and you had to send that message in letter form. Then re-read that message after you have taken some time out. Have you expressed yourself well? Is your message helpful or necessary? Would it be better to pick up the phone and talk to the person instead? Nothing beats person-to-person interaction. Most of our work revolves around messaging today, so make sure monitoring the quality of what you put out there in writing becomes a daily ritual.

16 https://onlinelibrary.wiley.com/doi/abs/10.1002/jclp.21916

NETWORKS SUCCESS RITUAL
#187: OPEN UP

Let others help and support you in your career

Successful people allow themselves to be helped, advised and mentored by others in both their lives and their careers. Of course, you must always carry yourself forward – and do what feels right to you – but sometimes the advice or support of others can make all the difference.

Asking for help is not a sign of weakness but a sign of open mindedness, trust and optimism in your fellow human beings. If someone offers to help, advise or mentor you today, accept it with gratitude and **ritualize** by making a conscious effort to listen carefully. You don't have to agree, just see what you can learn and thank the person for their interest in you.

If nobody offers you help or advice today, you can always ask someone for help, support or advice. If they turn you down there is nothing lost, but you have opened yourself up to accepting help from others and the universe will take note. You can also get great advice free of charge from free online talks, such as TED talks,[17] given by experts, business leaders and life coaches, which I highly recommend as a listening ritual.

17 www.ted.com/talks

NETWORKS SUCCESS RITUAL
#188: MENTOR SOMEONE
Look out for others

There's often a belief when it comes to work or money matters that you should only look out for yourself, but this could not be further from the truth. Helping others succeed can be the best way to succeed yourself[18] because the more you help others, the more likely it is that they will help you. Of course, hoping that your good deeds will come back to you isn't the reason you should help. The best reason is the joy it brings you knowing you have made a positive difference to someone else's life.

Your ritual today is to think of someone in your life. It could be a family member, friend or colleague or someone you meet by chance who can benefit from your help or from mentoring them in some way. Perhaps you could offer to connect them to someone you know. Perhaps you can teach them some of your skills. Perhaps you can help them in a practical way or support what they are doing in some way. Perhaps you can inspire them or offer them constructive feedback free of charge. Or perhaps you could share your knowledge about the power of rituals to transform your life. **Ritualize** your altruism by writing down at the end of the day exactly how you have helped someone else succeed. Notice how helping others makes you feel connected to something greater than yourself. If you enjoy the feeling, consider committing some of your time each week to mentoring someone.

18 www.forbes.com/sites/amyanderson/2016/01/06/the-fastest-way-to-achieve-success-is-to-first-help-others-succeed/

ABUNDANCE SUCCESS RITUAL
#189: PLANT SUCCESS
Grow a money tree

The final set of rituals in this section offer you a variety of different rituals to help attract abundance and also boost your motivation to succeed. Let's begin with some ancient wisdom.

In Feng Shui[19] – the ancient Chinese art of placement – certain plants are believed to attract the energy of prosperity into your life and are therefore, not surprisingly, called money plants. Although jade tree plants are commonly used, there is a debate about which is the true money plant. However, you can use any green and vibrant plant for this purpose – picking a healthy, flourishing plant is the important thing, rather than what type it is.

Your ritual today is to decorate your home or office with a money plant of your choice. Just ensure the plant is mostly green and is growing in a pot. Green is the colour of prosperity in Feng Shui. **Ritualize** by thinking of an idea, project or a pot of money that you want to grow as you buy the plant, and position it where you can see it every day, preferably in a place associated with work. Do not put it in your bathroom or bedroom. Commit to taking care of that plant every day. Keep it healthy. Watch it grow.

19 www.thespruce.com/get-to-know-the-feng-shui-money-plant-1275013

ABUNDANCE SUCCESS RITUAL
#190: EVERYTHING IS YELLOW

Attract success with colour

According to research[20] and colour therapists, yellow is the colour for promoting confidence and attracting prosperity and success into your life. Yellow is often associated with falling leaves in autumn and therefore symbols of fulfilling the purpose of life. In other words, yellow is about finishing the race successfully.

Your ritual today is to focus your attention on the colour yellow. Seek out foods that are yellow in colour. Wear a yellow item of clothing. If yellow really isn't your colour, purchase a citrine quartz crystal or a yellow item of jewellery. Before you wear or carry something yellow with you or whenever you notice the colour yellow today, be sure to pause and visualize the energy of yellow within and all around you. **Ritualize** by saying out loud, "I attract prosperity to me."

Notice yellow wherever you go.

20 www.ncbi.nlm.nih.gov/pmc/articles/PMC4383146/

ABUNDANCE SUCCESS RITUAL #191: LIGHT A PROSPERITY CANDLE

Open your heart to wealth

Every year we light candles on our birthdays and some of us even make a wish when we blow them out.

Today's ritual encourages you to light a candle for prosperity.[21] A white candle is fine, but if you can find a green or yellow candle, even better, as green and yellow are the colours of abundance. **Ritualize** by sitting quietly for a few moments before you light the candle. Then, focus your intention on what you have, as all too often we focus on what we lack rather than the blessings we already have and the universe reflects this feeling of lack back to us. Next, light your candle and bow your head silently in prayer or contemplation. Keep feelings of abundance in your heart. If negative thoughts appear, just notice them and let them go. Tell yourself out loud that you are worthy of prosperity. When you feel your inner wealth and a warm glow inside your heart, give thanks to the universe for the external prosperity it will bring to you. Blow out your candle.

21 www.thoughtco.com/ light-a-candle-with-intention -3857353

ABUNDANCE SUCCESS RITUAL
#192: COFFEE BREAK

Savour a perfect cup of coffee

In recent years the world has fallen in love with coffee. Along the way this beverage has lost many of its negative health associations, with recent studies[22] suggesting that people who drink coffee in moderation (say, two cups a day) can not only concentrate and remember better, but live longer. Coffee is only a problem if you drink it in excess. When drunk in moderation coffee, it now seems, is the drink for successful people.

Your ritual today involves your coffee break. If you don't like coffee or can't tolerate caffeine, a fantastic concentration-boosting substitute is orange-blossom tea or green tea, so use that drink instead. **Ritualize** your coffee break by savouring the taste, pausing between each sip and reflecting on the rich, intoxicating power of this utterly pleasurable drink. Some people meditate for hours searching for inner peace and a heightened sense of alertness, but perhaps you can find it instantly. Serenity, tranquillity and zest for life are all right there in your cup or mug.

---

22 http://time.com/5326420/coffee-longevity-study/

ABUNDANCE SUCCESS RITUAL
#193: CROSS YOUR ARMS

Project an aura of strength

Today's ritual may feel counter-intuitive if you have been told that crossing your arms looks defensive. This is certainly true if your aim is to deepen your emotional or intellectual connection with someone. But if your aim is to project persistence and boost your chances of success, research[23] shows that crossing your arms sends a powerful message, both to yourself and to others, that you mean business. Arm-crossing boosts persistence and projects an aura of strength.

At some point today when you feel your motivation or resolve ebbing, stand up with your back straight or sit tall in your seat, pull your shoulders back, lift your chin up and cross your arms defiantly. **Ritualize** by understanding that you have now deliberately arranged your body in an "I-can-do-this" position. You have taken action with this ritual. Not only will others notice your resolve expressed through this stance, but you will feel it, too.

23 https://onlinelibrary.wiley.com/doi/abs/10.1002/ejsp.444 Source: "The effect of arm crossing on persistence and performance" from *European Journal of Social Psychology*

ABUNDANCE SUCCESS RITUAL #194: INCONVENIENCE YOURSELF

It's time for change

The problem with staying in your comfort zone is that nothing exciting happens there. It's too predictable. Success lies in reinventing yourself, making changes, inconveniencing yourself and taking risks. Of course, you should not change for change's sake, as reinvention should always build on your skills and previous accomplishments but, as you get older, your goals and plans need to be reinvented regularly. Successful people constantly reinvent themselves. They learn new things. They leave things, choices, places, people and personality traits behind them on their journey through life. They embrace change because they know that change is essential for personal growth.

Today's ritual reinforces this point. Search online or download the original six-minute version of Queen's "Bohemian Rhapsody".[24] This smash-hit iconic song struggled to see the light of day because record producers at the time felt it broke too many rules, didn't make sense, couldn't be labelled, didn't conform and was way too long. Now listen to the recording. **Ritualize** your listening by tuning into the courage, eccentricity and revolutionary genius of this rule-breaking song. Let that rebel feeling inspire you to embrace reinvention and innovation within your own life.

24 www.songfacts.com/facts/queen/bohemian-rhapsody

ABUNDANCE SUCCESS RITUAL
#195: STAY MOTIVATED
Keep going and don't stop

Staying motivated is the key ingredient for success. If you are motivated you are far more likely to overcome challenges, learn from setbacks and take the necessary action to achieve your goals. There are a number of motivational strategies you could look into but perhaps the most important is that your life goals mean something to you. Meaningful goals are inspiring goals. They give you the willpower you need.

Research[25] shows that willpower is something that can be drained if you aren't in touch with your goals and taking care of yourself, and that is why your daily rituals are so important for achieving success. Rituals keep you focused on self-care and give you the motivation to keep going in the right direction when you want to stop or hit challenges. Your ritual today reinforces the motivational power of rituals. Learn by heart the following quote from Confucius:

It does not matter how slowly I go, as long as I do not stop.

Ritualize by saying the words out loud. Remind yourself of the fable of the Tortoise and the Hare as you learn and recite this quote. The hare was a natural runner but the tortoise's slow and steady approach won the race. From now on, whenever you hit a setback or challenge, or your motivation to perform your daily rituals is low, recite Confucius, visualize yourself as the tortoise and keep going forward.

25 Muraven, M. and Baumeister, R.: 'Self-regulation and depletion of limited resources: Does self-control resemble a muscle?', *Psychological Bulletin*, 126(2), 247-259 (2000)

ABUNDANCE SUCCESS RITUAL #196: DOUBLE YOUR FAILURE RATE

Fail, fail and fail again

The road to success is paved with failure[26] and today's ritual encourages you to take more calculated risks. When you look back on your life, you will not regret what you did, you will regret what you did not do. It really is better to try and fail than not to try at all. Fear of failure keeps you living in your head with only your thoughts for company. Rituals bring you out of your head and encourage you to take the action you need to move forward.

Your ritual today is to get yourself a small notebook. On the first page, write the title Lesson 1. Now, spend five minutes thinking about something in your life that you totally failed at. Then, write down ten lessons you learned from that experience. **Ritualize** by feeling gratitude for the gift of failure and the important discoveries you have made about yourself and life from the process. In the coming days, weeks, months and years, fill that notebook until you reach Lesson 100. Then get another notebook and start again. Never stop learning because when you learn, you grow and live your life with purpose.

26 www.forbes.com/sites/johnkluge/2014/02/26/why-the-road-to-success-is-paved-with-failure/#51fc0a911222

ABUNDANCE SUCCESS RITUAL #197: LIGHTEN YOUR LOAD

Free – the opposite of heavy

The final ritual in this section is unique and stands alone in that it should only be performed once a year. It is designed to prepare you for the Spirit and Heart ritual sections which follow on next.

All you need to do is read out loud the following true story.[27] It will remind you that material success should never become so important that you neglect what truly matters. **Ritualize** by reading slowly and solemnly as if you were reading a sermon, so the words and the eternal message within them truly sink in. Career, money and material success can bring great happiness, but never let them overshadow the voice of your spirit and your heart.

In 2001 Businessman Karl Rabeder, 47, gave up his entire fortune. The reason he gave for this dramatic gesture was that his fortune didn't make him happy. The Austrian sold his $2.5 million villa, which had a lake, a sauna and spectacular views of the Alps, and his stone farmhouse in Provence. He also sold his luxury car and six gliders, as well as the interior furnishings and accessories business that had made his $4.8 million fortune. All the proceeds went to charities he had set up.

Rabeder had the idea to downsize everything in his life while on a luxury holiday in Hawaii. He noticed that everyone he had taken along on his holiday was being friendly because he was paying them to be and the other people vacationing in luxury alongside him were full of self-importance because they had money. Nothing felt real. All his life he had believed that wealth and luxury would automatically mean happiness. But when he finally became a millionaire and achieved all he wanted to, materially he still wasn't happy. Since selling all his material possessions, Rabeder says he feels, "free, the opposite of heavy".

27 www.telegraph.co.uk/news/worldnews/europe/austria/7190750/Millionaire-gives-away-fortune-that-made-him-miserable.html

THE RITUAL YEARBOOK

$\mathcal{S}pirit$ RITUALS

Rituals for a self-actualized, enlightened YOU

Spirituality is the search for deeper meaning in life. It directs attention away from the distractions of the material world to the insights of the inner world. Spiritual practices focus on increasing love, compassion, gratitude, forgiveness and empathy to discover meaning and purpose.

198–271

Studies[1] have consistently shown that popular spiritual practices, such as meditation, mindfulness and prayer, can increase feelings of emotional, mental and physical calm and wellbeing. People[2] with a strong spiritual life tend to live longer, happier lives.

You can be spiritual without being religious. The 74 Spirit rituals are designed for anyone and you are advised to perform one new ritual a day over a period of 74 days. Each Spirit ritual builds on the one before it. There are no categories in this section as there were in the previous sections, just continuous flow from one ritual to the next because in spirit there are no categories – everyone, every moment and everything is interconnected.

HOW SPIRIT RITUALS CAN HELP YOU

Spiritual awakening is discovering and celebrating your originality, walking your own path. It is about distancing yourself from attachment to material things. Spirit is invisible. It is light. It is free. It is an empty space of pure potential for you to grow. It is not defined by your words but by your actions. Rituals are therefore perfectly attuned to spiritual awakening and growth. They are meaningful actions that bring your body, heart and mind into a deeper connection with your true self, your spirit.

Each ritual connects you to your higher self, the wise part of you. If you want to discover deeper meaning to your life this section of the book is definitely for you. It will help you make a sacred commitment to your spirit every single day. This section is also recommended if you want to become more self-aware. It contains rituals to help you find out who you truly are and what you were born to do. Whether the rituals feed your spirit and/or help you become more enlightened about yourself and your purpose in life, understanding the reasons why each specific action is so good for your spirit and then performing that action with mindful intention and gratitude (so it is **ritualized**) will significantly increase your chances of living a fulfilled life.

1 www.sciencedaily.com/releases/2012/07/120711104811.htm
2 www.webmd.com/balance/features/spirituality-may-help-people-live-longer

THE RITUAL YEARBOOK

SPIRIT RITUAL
#198: SACRED SPACE

Make space in your life for an altar

Rituals bring sacredness into your life by honouring your spiritual connection to something greater than yourself.[1] Today's ritual encourages you to find a space in your home for an altar. It doesn't have to be a big space and can just be a small corner or a top drawer. **Ritualize** by putting images of people and things you love there. Place your spiritual reading there (including, I hope this book) and if you use crystals, candles and essential oils place those there, too. Anything that connects you to spirit should go there. From now on, when you need to meditate, connect to your spirit, listen to sacred music or perform a ritual, do it beside your altar. In this way you create your own sacred personal space.

Note: You may wonder why making a sacred space hasn't appeared earlier in this book. It was to avoid the association between altars and religion. Hopefully by now you understand that rituals have nothing to do with religion and everything to do with treating yourself and every day of your life with sacred reverence.

1 https://journals.sagepub.com/doi/abs/10.1177/0956797613478949

SPIRIT RITUAL
#199: BOW YOUR HEAD
Say a little prayer today

As we saw in Foundation Ritual 21, prayer is a life-changing spiritual practice. It is a conversation with Spirit or the higher power within and all around you. It is a dialogue about what truly matters in your life. It gives you a chance to be honest with yourself, express gratitude and ask for insight and/or strength to deal with life's challenges. The healing and comforting benefits of prayer have been extensively researched.[2]

Today's ritual encourages you to bow your head whenever you pray because the action of bowing your head is a sign of humility and trust in the universe. You may already do this naturally when you pray but you are encouraged to focus your attention on the bowing action today. When you have bowed your head, **ritualize** by closing your eyes and saying out loud: "Grant me the strength to accept the things I cannot change, the courage to change the things I can and the wisdom to know the difference." If you want to say "Amen" at the end or "Blessed Be", feel free to do so. Personalize your prayer. Bowing your head as you pray signals to the universe that you are a person of humility, dignity and quiet strength. .

2 www.ncbi.nlm.nih.gov/pmc/articles/PMC2802370/

SPIRIT RITUAL
#200: COMMIT TO SILENCE

Dedicate one hour of your day to being alone and still

There is tremendous creative and spiritual power in solitude.[3] Feeling content when alone is the first requirement for spiritual growth, as during periods of solitude you become aware that your spirit is separate from your body and your worth is not determined by what is outside you but what is within you. Your ritual today is to aim for ten minutes in the evening, when you just sit quietly and do not speak or interact with anyone or anything. You are silent. There will be resistance at first, but just acknowledge that inner tension and patiently wait for peace, calm and silence. Trust yourself, your spirit will surface.

Ritualize your silent time by noticing that your thoughts do not define you. Consciously experience stillness and say out loud to yourself, "I am still. I am not my thoughts. I am always enough."

---

3 Anthony Storr, *Solitude*, Flamingo, 1997

SPIRIT RITUAL
#201: RETURN TO YOURSELF
Enter into the quietness of your spirit

Yesterday you were encouraged to separate yourself from identification with externals by becoming comfortable with solitude. Today's ritual encourages you to separate yourself from identification with your own thoughts. Contrary to what you might think, meditation isn't doing nothing. Research[4] confirms that it is doing something healing for yourself.

Find a place where you are unlikely to be disturbed. Set a timer for 15 minutes. **Ritualize** by sitting upright and setting your intention to become fully aware of your inner or true self. Then close your eyes and focus on whatever is occurring within you – your thoughts, your feelings and internal bodily sensations. Notice how it is possible for you – your true essence – to be separate from these and just observe them. Gently relax your body and notice your breathing. Don't alter it. When the timer goes off, slowly open your eyes and reflect on your meditation and meeting your true essence – your spirit free from your ego and fear.

4 www.ncbi.nlm.nih.gov/pubmed/24395196

SPIRIT RITUAL
#202: SMELL THE FLOWERS
Get your nature fix today

Spending time in direct communication with nature is great for your health[5] and it's also bliss for your spirit. When you are close to nature you sense the harmony and interconnection that sustains all life. You feel the energy or spirit that forms the basis of everything, including you.

Your ritual today is to smell a flower or a plant you find in the garden or a park, or have in your home. Don't sniff it hastily. Let the smell linger for at least a minute. **Ritualize** by noticing the childlike surprise the scent of a flower or a plant always inspires. Imprint the scent on your mind, then recall it throughout the day. Spirit expresses itself through what is natural within you and around you. Let the scent you recall help connect you to your true self and to what is honest and natural in your life.

5 Florence Williams, *The Nature Fix: Why nature makes us healthier, happier and more creative*, Norton, 2018

SPIRIT RITUAL
#203: COMMIT TO NON-JUDGEMENT
Get rid of labels

Reconnecting with what is natural reminds you of your true essence. Nature does not judge or label. Every day we tend to put people and things into categories labelled good or bad, or right or wrong. All this labelling does is create noise in your mind that distracts you from your true essence.[6]

Your ritual today is to say to yourself when you get up in the morning: "Today I will judge nothing that I encounter." **Ritualize** by saying it out loud with a bowed head. Then, during the day, whenever you catch yourself judging and labelling others, remind yourself of the sacred commitment you made to the universe in the morning and practise non-judgement. If you become aware of self-criticism, sit quietly and name without judgement what you are feeling.

Don't worry if you find this hard to do at first as you are overcoming a life-time of conditioning, just keep practising non-judgement until it becomes second nature.

6 "Today I shall judge nothing that occurs" is a prayer from *A Course in Miracles*, Foundation for Inner Peace, 2008

SPIRIT RITUAL
#204: REMOVE THE BARRIER

Judgement is blind

Judgement distorts our vision of ourselves, others and events.[7] It is a hard habit to shake because we think it helps protect our identity. But judgement does not protect us, it prevents us from genuinely connecting to others and our true essence or spirit.

Your ritual today is to visualize yourself removing the barrier of judgement from your thoughts. **Ritualize** by sitting down and gently covering your eyes with your hands. Leave a tiny gap between two of your fingers to peep through. Imagine your hands are a blindfold with two very tiny holes to look through. Stay like this for a while. Then, as you remove your hands from your eyes, imagine you are taking a blindfold off and seeing the world with beautiful clarity and without judgement for the first time. You understand just how much the blindfold of judgement has narrowed your view of yourself, others and the world. Observe, but don't judge, what thoughts and feelings this eye-opening ritual inspires in you.

7 www.berkeleywellbeing.com/non-judgement.html

SPIRIT RITUAL
#205: JUST BLINK
See others with fresh eyes

Continuing yesterday's theme of non-judgement, today's ritual encourages you to embrace your shared humanity with others. We are all on our own unique journey but we are also all members of the human race. We share so much in common but, too often, we focus on our differences rather than our similarities.[8]

   Ritualize by consciously blinking a few times before you have a conversation with someone today, whether that conversation be in person, online or on the phone. Let the blinking be your reminder to let go of any pre-judgement of that person. Instead, send that person silent understanding and your acknowledgement that they are a human being just like you, with their own dreams and hopes, struggles and insights. Empathize with that person's similarities to you rather than dwell on their differences.

8 https://blogs.psychcentral.com/mindfulness/

SPIRIT RITUAL
#206: REDIRECT YOUR INTERNAL SATNAV

Shift your internal focus away from self-judgement

Not only do we judge others, we also constantly judge ourselves. If you think and feel negative things about yourself, this will create inner noise and conflict, and make it impossible for spirit to break through.[9]

Every time you feel yourself getting self-critical today, slow down. **Ritualize** by directing your inner focus to your breath. Breathe in deeply through your nose, hold your breath for a count of three and then exhale slowly through your mouth. As you breathe, ask yourself what exactly you are feeling and thinking about yourself. Then, with your next deep exhalation release any negative thoughts and feelings about yourself that you have identified. Tell yourself you are going to breathe in compassion and peace.

Continue directing your attention to the positivity you are breathing in until you notice the negativity you are breathing out loses its hold over you. You are not fighting or denying negativity here, you are simply redirecting your internal satnav to a more spiritually empowering destination.

9 www.consciouslifestylemag.com/self-acceptance-self-judgment/

SPIRIT RITUAL
#207: FEED YOUR SELF-ACCEPTANCE
Nourish yourself from within

The last few days of rituals have focused on non-judgement for a reason. If you are constantly criticizing yourself, this is a sign that you don't feel comfortable being you. The foundation stone for spiritual growth is self-acceptance. Without self-love it's impossible to find inner peace. Your ritual today is a meditation[10] designed to feed your self-acceptance. You will also need some grapes or raisins.

Set your timer for five minutes and put the grapes or raisins in front of you. **Ritualize** by sitting down, breathing with long slow deep breaths and clearly setting your intention to feed your self-acceptance. Close your eyes and allow negative judgements about yourself to surface in your mind. See if you can find a theme, for example, "I'm not good enough" or "nobody likes me" or "I am a disappointment". Notice how your body reacts. What physical sensations do you feel and where do you feel them when you consciously focus on these negative feelings? Chances are you will notice tension in your stomach or your head. Visualize golden light entering the tense area, bringing peace and healing. Then, when the timer goes off, open your eyes and eat your grapes or raisins. Relish the feeling of strength and warmth your body draws from the nutritious snack, as well as spiritual nourishment from within.

10 www.ncbi.nlm.nih.gov/pmc/articles/PMC3679190/

SPIRIT RITUAL
#208: BECOME NOBODY
Appreciate being yourself

Today's ritual encourages you to think of yourself as nobody. This doesn't mean you are insignificant, quite the opposite. It means you aspire to be nothing but your authentic spiritual self.[11]

Ritualize by saying out loud three times, "Tension is who I think I should be. Peace is who I am." Allow your mind to absorb these words as you hear yourself say them. If you feel tension, it is probably because you are trying to be someone else or thinking of yourself in terms of your relationships, your work or material things. Remind yourself that you are not meant to be someone or something else – you are meant to be authentically *yourself*.

Accepting and being content with yourself in the present moment is spiritual enlightenment and the only true path to happiness and fulfilment.

. . . .

11 "You spend the first half of your life becoming somebody. Now you can work on becoming nobody, which really is somebody. For when you become nobody there is no tension, no pretence, no one trying to be anyone or anything. The natural state of your mind shines through unobstructed." Ram Dass

SPIRIT RITUAL
#209: GIVE WHAT YOU SEEK
Bless all those you encounter today

Spirituality is contentment with who you are. It is understanding that true happiness comes from within and not from other people and things. It is giving to others for the sheer joy of it because you know that you are already affluent and you lack nothing,[12] regardless of how much money you have.

Your ritual today is to silently bless everyone you encounter. **Ritualize** by gifting each person something tangible, be that a compliment, a helpful suggestion, a helping hand, a listening ear, a small favour or simply a smile. If you can't do anything to help someone, close your eyes and send them a silent prayer. Know that your good deeds and prayers are not only for others, but also for yourself. You grow spiritually whenever you give.

12 Deepak Chopra, *The 7 Spiritual Laws of Success*, Bantam, 1996, Spiritual Law no. 2

SPIRIT RITUAL
#210: ALLOW OTHERS TO HELP YOU

Open yourself to receiving

Today's ritual balances yesterday's in that a common misconception about being a spiritual person is that it means sacrifice, always placing the needs of others above your own. But your needs matter, too. There must always be a balance between giving and receiving. So, make a point today of consciously noticing, accepting and expressing gratitude for what others offer you, even if the gift they give you is simply their time and attention. Listen to what they say, accept any compliments and offers of help and **ritualize** your willingness to receive from others by saying "thank you".

Know that in accepting gifts from others you are also helping them experience the joy of giving. In spiritual terms, giving and receiving are interchangeable. If you find it hard to accept help, compliments or gifts from others, start opening yourself up to receiving. Try asking them for help. Say "thank you" out loud to the universe for the gifts it sends you every day, such as sunshine or the birds singing. The more you open yourself up to receiving and cultivate an attitude of gratitude,[13] the more likely you are to attract good things into your life.

13 Robert Emmons, *Thanks: How practising gratitude can make you happier*, Mariner, 2008

SPIRIT RITUAL
#211: FORGIVE SOMEONE

You grow whenever you forgive

Forgiveness[14] leads to inner peace. There is no doubt forgiveness is one of the most healing and powerful spiritual principles to live by, but it is also the hardest. It takes strength to forgive.

Today, your ritual is to empower yourself to practise forgiveness, for yourself and/or someone else. **Ritualize** by taking some quiet time alone and identifying someone or something in your life that urgently needs forgiveness. It could be someone who has treated you unfairly or it could be a mistake you made that you still beat yourself up about. Then, close your eyes and silently send thoughts of forgiveness to that person or yourself. Radiate healing to the source of your pain and feel the weight lift from your shoulders and your heart. Remind yourself that forgiveness is not turning a blind eye or avoiding confrontation, as it is important to speak your truth. Forgiveness is about letting go of the anger weighing you down, so your energy can be directed away from them toward your own spiritual growth.

14 www.hopkinsmedicine.org/health/healthy_aging/healthy_connections/forgiveness-your-health-depends-on-it

SPIRIT RITUAL
#212: A SACRED CONTRACT

Commit to a decision and act on it

One of the roadblocks to forgiveness is feeling that our mistakes and failures define us and limit future opportunities. From a spiritual perspective there is no such thing as failure, if you learn from your mistakes. Similarly, there is nothing wrong with experimenting, but there is with letting your life stagnate with indecision. A lot of us fear making decisions about our lives. We worry about making the wrong choices. But not making a choice is actually a decision – one that stops you dead in your tracks. In other words, doing something – even if you mess up – is better than doing nothing.

In spiritual terms intention is detached and trusts that everything happens for a reason. Your ritual today is to choose something that you want to do or have been meaning to do for a while and to **ritualize** it by writing it down as a clear statement of intention. Remember (*see* Evening Foundation Ritual 17, page 33), all the evidence[15] suggests that writing down your goals increases your chances of achieving them. So start small by choosing something that you know is achievable. Then, sign your name at the bottom with the date, as if you were signing a sacred contract, and pin the paper on your fridge or bedroom wall so you see it every day. Now, take action today in the direction of your written goal. You have set your intention and signed up to it. You are committed to taking the first steps towards achieving your goals.

· · · · · · · · · · · · · ·

15 www.forbes.com/sites/ellevate/2014/04/08/why-you-should-be-writing-down-your-goals/#767ad2b83397

SPIRIT RITUAL
#213: TAKE A BOW
Let go of the need to position yourself above others

Yesterday you signed a sacred contract. Today you are going to take a sacred bow. Several religions have rituals expressing humility, such as by bowing,[16] but many of us misunderstand what being humble means. Humility is not being subservient, denying your own needs, feeling inferior or letting others take advantage of you. It simply means letting go of the desire to place yourself above others, and being aware that you are a drop in the ocean of life, no more, no less. The mark of a spiritual person is that they treat everyone as an equal, the same as themselves.

Today's ritual encourages you to practise humility and let go of any need to prove that you are better or "bigger" than anyone else. Creative energy is wasted trying to impress others with your importance. It is far more productive to divert that energy to your own creative growth. At some point today **ritualize** your intention to practise humility by standing upright with your hands placed on your upper chest. Take a deep breath in to centre yourself and bow down slowly from the waist, exhaling as you do. You don't have to bend far, just enough to signal to the universe that you will not place yourself above others. If bowing while standing makes you feel dizzy, sit down and bow your head gently as a sign of reverence and humility.

16 Andi Young, *The Sacred Art of Bowing*, Skylight Paths, 2003

THE RITUAL YEARBOOK

SPIRIT POWER RITUAL
#214: THE SPIRIT OF YOGA

Enjoy the yoga and spirituality connection

The previous Spirit rituals have offered different ways to help you reconnect with your spiritual self. Today's ritual is a power one because it turns the focus on the spiritual potency and potential of Yoga. Research[17] shows that the true beauty of yoga is its ability to help us develop inner peace. Yoga isn't just about posing, breathing deeply and stretching, it's an inward journey to meet our true spiritual self.

Yoga can encourage you to let go of worry and anxiety and become appreciative of the present moment. In this alert state you understand that you are more than your body and you sense your true spiritual being. In short, understanding that yoga is an experience that unites body, mind and spirit brings the greatest rewards. Through each yoga pose you are encouraged to listen to the signals your mind and spirit are sending you through your body.

Your ritual today is a simple yoga balance pose called Tree pose.

Stand and shift your weight to your right foot, lifting your left foot off the floor. Keep your right leg straight, but don't lock the knee. Bend your left knee and place the sole of your left foot high onto your inner right thigh. Focus your gaze so you don't lose your balance. Take deep breaths, lower your left foot and repeat on the other side. **Ritualize** by performing the pose with deep awareness of both your body and your internal state. Feel your standing foot rooted to the ground like a tree and hold your balance with patience, allowing feelings of calm, peace and strength to flow through you. (*Note:* It's impossible to successfully perform this pose without calming yourself.) If you enjoyed this centring and calming ritual, why not sign up for a regular yoga class or study yoga further? If you are unable to practise

17 www.health.harvard.edu/ staying-healthy/yoga-benefits- beyond-the-mat

yoga due to injury or illness, your ritual today is to research the spiritual benefits and philosophy of yoga.

SPIRITUAL AWAKENING

For centuries yoga has been a catalyst for spiritual awakening, and it remains so today. Yoga is not a religion, it is a spiritual path. Millions of people around the world practise it for the physical benefits of its stretching exercises, but also because it enhances spiritual growth. Translated from the ancient Sanskrit, *yoga* means "to unify". A practitioner of yoga, known as a yogi, consciously strives to avoid internal tension and conflict, and to open themselves to higher consciousness by practising poses and breathing exercises designed to unify body, mind and spirit and bring a feeling of wholeness, peace and joy.

SPIRIT RITUAL
#215: SIMPLE IS BETTER

Live the simple life

Sometimes your living and working environments can make it hard for you to reconnect to your spirit. Clutter, and the chaos and confusion it brings, isn't just bad news[18] for your body and mind, it weighs heavily on your spirit, too. Simplifying your life and letting go of unnecessary complications is an important step toward inner peace.

Your environment impacts your inner well-being, so your ritual at the beginning of the day today is to quietly think of ways to simplify or streamline your life. **Ritualize** by finding a picture of a white dove in a book or online. Touch that picture and feel a sense of lightness of being and peace. Then, ask yourself if there is any unnecessary material clutter you can get rid of today. Also think about your schedule and cut down on what isn't strictly necessary – for example, avoid reading junk mail, make your email responses shorter or say "no" to the demands of others if you need your energy for yourself. Moving forward, make simplifying all areas of your life a spiritual priority.

18 www.psychologytoday.com/us/blog/fulfillment-any-age/201705/5-reasons-clear-the-clutter-out-your-life

SPIRIT RITUAL
#216: REDEFINE OPTIMISM
Don't dream about rainbows, chase them

Taking action to simplify your life will naturally encourage you to avoid negativity and cynicism and focus on what really matters to you. In other words, it will encourage you to have a more optimistic outlook. But optimism as an approach to life can't change your life unless you combine it with positive *doing*. This is why rituals work – they are positive actions.[19] Optimism is not positive thinking, nor the glass-half-full approach to life. Optimism is positive doing. When you redefine your understanding of optimism in this way you realize that your actions are the architect of your life. Things may not always turn out as you want them to but you can always adapt your actions to make the best of things.

Your ritual today is to notice and pause for a few moments whenever you switch a light on. **Ritualize** by reminding yourself of the thousand attempts Thomas Edison took to invent the lightbulb. If he had given up at attempt 129, or attempt 999, we would not have a world of light. He simply regarded each attempt as an experiment that taught him what didn't work and an important step toward his final goal of finding what would work. From now on, regard each challenge or setback in your life, not as a failure, but as a step towards greater illumination.

19 www.scientificamerican.com/article/why-rituals-work/

SPIRIT RITUAL
#217: LOVE THE PRESENT
Live in the "right now"

You're practising non-judgement and you are finding ways to simplify your life and cultivate a more positive approach. The next step on your ritual path of spiritual awakening is to fall in love with the present. This moment right now is truly all you have or can ever be sure that you have. So much of the time we focus on the past or worry about the future and all the time we lose the gift of the present. The contented life is not lost in what *has* happened or what *might* happen. The contented life is engrossed in appreciating fully the power of *now*.[20]

Your ritual today will help you commit to living in the now, not just today but every day. Simply choose to say "yes" to the present moment. **Ritualize** this by observing your breath and connecting with the aliveness that exists within you and which is separate from your thoughts. Then say "yes to now" out loud whenever you find yourself regretting what could have been or wondering what might happen. Feel gratitude for all you currently have in your life *at this moment*. It is all that there is.

20 Eckhart Tolle, *The Power of Now*, Yellow Kite Publishing, 2001

SPIRIT RITUAL
#218: HAVE A LITTLE PATIENCE
Lose sight of time

It's impossible to be content in the present moment if you don't know how to practise the spiritual art of patience. Anything worth doing needs to be done in its own time. It shouldn't be rushed and the same principle applies to your life. Patience is a virtue but it is increasingly a lost art in this age of instant gratification, text messages, Googling and smartphones. Learning to be patient[21] can significantly increase your chances of finding happiness and inner peace.

This ritual will help you notice how accurate your inner sense or awareness of the passage of time is. Set a timer but turn away from it so you can't see it, and sit quietly. **Ritualize** by emptying your mind of thoughts and focusing on your breathing and your awareness of time. When you feel that one minute has passed, stop the timer. Then, check how much time really passed.

Did you lose sight of time? Did you over estimate or underestimate the time? Reflect on what you have learned from this exercise.

21 https://greatergood.berkeley.edu/article/item/four_reasons_to_cultivate_patience

SPIRIT RITUAL
#219: GO ON A SELF-DATE
Treat your spirit today

Airplane safety instructions[22] urge you to put on your own oxygen mask *before* helping children put their masks on. The reason is simple: you can't help others effectively if you are in a weakened physical state. The same applies to your spiritual life. You need to nourish and value your own spirit first.

Your ritual today returns to the crucial theme of self-love for spiritual growth. You are going to go on a self-date where you spend time alone doing something that nourishes you, whether that be reading, taking a relaxing scented bath, going to the cinema or anything else you enjoy. It doesn't matter what it is, just *do* something that uplifts you today. **Ritualize** by reminding yourself on your self-date that your spirit needs to be nourished and the best person to do that is you, because you know what makes you feel good far better than anyone else.

22 https://cockpitvoice.wordpress.com/2015/07/02/oxygen-mask-adult-first-and-then-children-why/

SPIRIT RITUAL
#220: BE IMPECCABLE WITH YOUR WORDS

Speak with integrity

If you love and respect yourself, your words will reflect that you are a person of integrity. The essence of a spiritual life is being impeccable with your words.[23] It is speaking with integrity, avoiding negative talk about yourself and others and, most important of all, following through on your promises.

Today make a promise to yourself that from now on you will only say what you truly mean. **Ritualize** by tapping your heart with your hand and reminding yourself that speaking with integrity takes you to love and truth whenever you find yourself tempted to tell a white lie, criticize or gossip. Before you speak today ask yourself the following three questions: Are my words truthful? Are they necessary? Are they kind? Remember the sacred commitment you made to yourself and honour it. If you need to say something that you feel is necessary but may be hurtful, say it in a kind way or don't say anything at all.

23 Don Miguel Ruiz, *The Four Agreements*, Amber Allen, 1997

SPIRIT RITUAL
#221: CHOOSE WISELY
Visualize the consequences of your choices

It's not just your words that you have choice over. Every day is filled with powerful decisions. If you believe in the spiritual law of karma, every action generates an energy that returns to you in kind. If you choose actions that help or bring joy, that healing energy will return to you either through success in your life or peace of mind. Most of us live our lives on autopilot and make choices without much thought or feeling, but research[24] shows if we tune into our emotions, we make far better decisions.

Your ritual today is to become conscious of your choices and the active part you play in creating your karma. If you don't believe in karma, then think of everything you say and do in terms of whether it is progressive for you and others. **Ritualize** by asking yourself what the consequences of each choice you make are and whether they will bring you and others happiness. Visualize the consequences of your choices and notice how this makes you *feel*. If you don't like these feelings, do something different – make a different choice.

· · · · · · · · · · · · · · ·

24 www.medicaldaily.com/science-decision-making-5-surprising-ways-we-make-life-choices-337546

SPIRIT RITUAL
#222: DON'T TAKE THINGS PERSONALLY

Free yourself from the opinions of others

Yesterday you examined your own actions. Today you are going to examine the actions of others. One theme that spiritual teaching returns to time and again is that whatever other people do or say, it's not personal. We are brainwashed from birth to think the opinions of others matter, but nothing other people say or do is because of you. It is always because of themselves.[25]

Your ritual today is to reprogramme your natural reaction when other people upset you in some way. Instead of allowing them to dictate how you feel, stop and take a few deep calm breaths. **Ritualize** by telling yourself you are not going to give your power away to anyone. If the criticism is constructive, learn from it. But if not, simply delete it from your mind and accept that not everyone has to like you. Get busy choosing more productive things to think about and do, and seek out people who "get" you.

25 Don Miguel Ruiz, *The Four Agreements*, Amber Allen, 1997; Deepak Chopra, *The Seven Spiritual Laws of Success*, Bantam, 1996

SPIRIT RITUAL
#223: THE SKY AT NIGHT
Lift your spirit with stargazing

Sometimes it can be hard to get a sense of perspective, especially if other people are criticizing you or being negative. One way to get that sense of perspective about what really matters is to lift your head up and look at the beauty and wonder of the night sky. Stargazing reminds us we are part of something so much bigger and greater than ourselves. It can be a deeply spiritual exercise. Research[26] shows it helps us slow down and can also boost creativity and altruism.

Your ritual today is to do a stargazing meditation. Simply go outside when it's dark and find a comfortable, safe place to lie down on a blanket. Then, relax and look deeply at the stars above you. **Ritualize** by allowing your breathing to connect you to the earth and your gaze to connect you to the vast beauty of the night sky. Allow your awareness to alternate between your grounding breath on earth and your spirit floating among the stars. Let the infinite depth of the night sky fill your spirit.

26 www.dailymail.co.uk/news/article-3090259/Gazing-stars-make-kinder.html

SPIRIT RITUAL
#224: SPIRIT BATH

Enjoy a ritual cleansing today

One tried and tested way to soothe yourself when life drags you down is to take a warm bath, which is known to soothe away physical and mental tensions.[27] It's less well known that warm baths can also be cleansing and healing for your spirit. Your skin is the largest organ for absorption and elimination. When you are immersed in water you are receptive to discharging negativity and receiving spiritual healing.

Find time to treat your spirit to a power bath today. Ensure the water is as hot as is comfortable. **Ritualize** by understanding that this is not a normal bath but a spiritual experience. You are not using your normal soaps and bubble bath, instead, add a few handfuls of unprocessed salt to cleanse away toxins and a few drops of lavender oil to help you relax. As you soak for around five minutes, let go of negativity and ask for spiritual healing.

27 www.newsweek.com/exercise-bath-calories-health-572054

SPIRIT RITUAL
#225: EMBRACE UNCERTAINTY

Click your fingers whenever you feel uncertain

Many of us struggle with uncertainty. We want answers, resolution and closure for everything and feel anxious when we don't get them. What we fail to realize is that there can be tremendous value in ambiguity.[28] The previous rituals have suggested ways to help you find inner calm during times of crisis. But being spiritual doesn't mean never feeling anxious or uncertain again – quite the opposite.

Your ritual today encourages you to let go of your resistance to uncertainty and see it as an opportunity for spiritual growth in disguise. **Ritualize** by clicking your fingers every time you experience uncertainty. In much the same way a tennis player bounces a ball before facing the uncertainty of a serve, clicking your fingers will bring you calm and focus. It will also be your ritual reminder that the greatest lessons in life happen during times of uncertainty, set-backs and challenge. It's the journey rather than arriving that makes your life rewarding. Accept all your disappointments, problems and unanswered questions as the spiritual lessons they are. Embrace the opportunity uncertainty brings into your life every single day.

28 www.scientificamerican.com/article/the-power-of-embracing-uncertainty/

SPIRIT RITUAL
#226: WHAT DO YOU LOVE TO DO?

Follow your bliss

There's one very simple way to grow spiritually and connect with your true essence and that is to do what you love. Research[29] confirms that being fully engaged in what you are doing brings more satisfaction than money. The problem is that most of us don't know what we love to do.

Your ritual today encourages you to discover what it is you love to do - what makes you feel alive. **Ritualize** by lighting a candle. Fire is a universal symbol of passion and new beginnings. If you don't want to use a candle, search for a picture of a lighted candle on your phone. Set your intention, which is to express your bliss, and then write down on a piece of paper your answers to the following questions.

★ **What did you love to do when you were a child?**
★ **If money was no problem, what would you do with your life?**

When you have finished, blow out the candle. Read your answers and absorb them without judgement.

29 https://thoughtcatalog.com/brianna-wiest/2014/02/10-scientific-reasons-why-its-better-to-study-something-you-love/

SPIRIT RITUAL
#227: WHAT IS MY PASSION?
What engrosses you fully?

Today you are going to continue focusing on your heart's desire. **Ritualize** by following the same ritual guidelines as yesterday, but this time ponder your answers to the following questions.

★ **What makes you feel truly alive?**
★ **What absorbs you so fully you lose track of time?**

SPIRIT RITUAL
#228: WHAT IS MY PURPOSE?
Ask yourself how you can serve or help others

The last two days of ritual have encouraged you to think about what you love to do. Your ritual today is to make a list of all the things you are good at. But be sure to only list out the things that you love to do as well as being good at. If you love to do something but haven't had the time to study to get good at it, feel free to list that here too. **Ritualize** following the same guidelines as the two previous days.

When you have written everything down, study the list of things that you love to do and are good at (or could be good at if you put the time in) and *then* identify on that list those things that can also be used to help others or serve the planet.

Within those things lies your true spiritual meaning and purpose.

SPIRIT RITUAL
#229: CAREFUL IS THE WAY
Always do your best

All too often we underestimate the value of the small and steady steps we need to take each day to succeed and live with meaning and purpose.[30] Change doesn't typically happen overnight. Your ritual today encourages you to give yourself a few quiet moments at the end of the day to ask yourself if you gave everything you did today your very best.

Ritualize by visualizing yourself as a free solo mountain climber. Every single movement of your hands and feet is of crucial importance. If you don't concentrate fully you will fall. Giving your best isn't an option, it's a matter of life and death. What if you carried that careful and focused concentration into your daily life? Talk to your higher or spiritual self or the part of you that knows all that you are capable of. Are you committed to doing your best? Are you taking the steady, small and careful steps you need to fulfil your true potential? Your higher self knows the answer. Let it inspire you to give your best tomorrow and make every day one when you climb a little closer to the top.

30 Robert Maurer, *The Spirit of Kaizen: Creating lasting excellence one small step at a time*, McGraw-Hill, 2012

SPIRIT POWER RITUAL
#230: FOLLOW YOUR *IKIGAI*
Find fulfilment the Japanese way

Today's ritual is a power one because it consolidates the previous few days of rituals that have focused on finding your purpose. In Japanese culture there is a concept that the secret to fulfilment lies in finding the reason for or meaning of your life, called *ikigai*.[31] Instead of you slowing down to smell the roses, it encourages you to actively get out there and find your life's meaning, to help others as well as for your own fulfilment. Meaning is discovered through what we give to the world. It's all about being proactive and taking positive action. In this way it is perfectly suited to a life of ritual.

Today's ritual draws inspiration from *ikigai*. It encourages you (as Ritual 227, page 261, also did) to actively seek your meaning first thing in the morning by asking yourself some defining questions.

★ What do I love?
★ What am I good at?
★ What does the world need?

Ritualize your *ikigai* mindset by starting small and setting yourself small rituals during the day. For example, in answer to the first question, ensure that during your day you seek out three small joys that make you feel alive. Write them down and give thanks for them. In answer to the second question, write down three things you are good at and look for ways to utilize your skills during the day. In answer to the third question, you can discover what the world needs by actively connecting to it and being in the here and now. Make a point of noticing what is going on in your environment and appreciating its

31 Ken Mogi, *The Little Book of Ikigai: The secret Japanese way to live a happy and long life*, Quercus, 2017

sensory beauty mindfully. Hear what other people are saying. Be curious. Be proactive. Constantly look for ways you can help others and make the world a better place.

_Through small but positive changes empowered by ritualization, you can reshape your brain, boost your mood, shift your mindset and train yourself to live a life of actively seeking your purpose or *ikigai*.

SPIRITUAL AWAKENING

Research[32] shows the average lifespan of a Japanese person exceeds that of people in other countries. Their diet of fruit and vegetables and fresh rather than processed food is a big reason for their high life expectancy, but perhaps their search for *ikigai* is part of the story, too. *Ikigai* sounds mysterious and complicated, but it truly isn't. It simply describes the need within all of us to always seek purpose in life. It is a metaphor for spiritual awakening. If you feel despondent or repeatedly wonder what the meaning of your life is, your spirit is urging you to find your purpose, your *ikigai*.

32 www.independent.co.uk/life-style/health-and-families/health-news/high-life-expectancy-in-japan-partly-down-to-diet-carbohydrates-vegetables-fruit-fish-meat-a6956011.html

SPIRIT RITUAL
#231: WASH THE DISHES

Practise self-discipline

Successful people live lives filled with meaning and purpose and they are also highly disciplined. Self-discipline is a defining feature of a spiritual lifestyle, too.

Rituals[33] encourage self-discipline and this is why they are so successful in changing all aspects of life for the better. Your ritual today is a reminder of the vital significance of self-discipline. If you want something, you have to put in the time and effort to obtain it or make it happen. There are no short cuts. **Ritualize** by making a point of mindfully washing your mug, glass and dishes each time you eat or drink from them. If you have a dishwasher, stack it neatly. Don't let things pile up in the sink – and clean the sink while you are at it. This may seem like a small step but notice how it motivates. Let it encourage you to take other small steps to train your self-discipline, so that doing what needs to be done to get you to where you want to be – even if it's unpleasant or hard work – becomes a way of life.

---

33 www.scientificamerican.com/article/need-more-self-control-try-a-simple-ritual/

SPIRIT RITUAL
#232: TAKE FIVE

Everything has a message if you take the time to look

We often rush through life barely noticing what is happening around us. Yesterday's mindfulness ritual encouraged you to slow down and become more observant. From a mystical perspective[34] everything and everyone you encounter has a spiritual message, if you take the time to look for it.

Today's ritual encourages you to become more aware of the spiritual influence in your life in the form of coincidences, hunches or unusual or beautiful phenomena. **Ritualize** by making a point of writing down or recording at least five things that you notice or encounter, which could have hidden messages for you. It doesn't matter how far-fetched. For example, a car number plate you see has the same numbers in it as your house number, and so on. The important thing is you are training yourself to look beneath the surface of ordinary things for deeper meanings or, in the words of the British visionary Romantic poet Blake, "seeing the world in a grain of sand".

34 James Redfield, *The Celestine Prophecy*, Bantam, 1994

SPIRIT RITUAL
#233: TAKE TIME
Make the ordinary feel extraordinary

Today's ritual further encourages you to slow down and notice[35] the whole picture of an experience. Choose an ordinary activity you do every day. It could be travelling to work, cooking, answering emails or folding laundry. It doesn't matter what activity you choose, **ritualize** it by pausing for a moment before you begin. Close your eyes and consciously connect with your five senses – your hearing, sight, smell, touch and taste. Become aware of what you are perceiving with all your physical senses. Then move your awareness to your inner world or sixth sense, the gentle promptings that are independent of your physical senses.

Open your eyes and carry this heightened spiritual awareness with you as you complete your chosen task. Notice how connecting with your inner world brings a sense of the sacred into the everyday.

35 https://upliftconnect.com/sacred-rituals/

SPIRIT RITUAL
#234: SKYGAZING

On a clear day you can see forever

How often do you take the time to stop and notice the wonders above you? Skygazing[36] is a Tibetan Buddhist spiritual practice. It's a beautiful way to strengthen your connection with spirit.

Today's ritual will remind you of your spontaneous and natural state. **Ritualize** by finding a good view of a clear sky. Stand or sit quietly for a few moments and take some deep breaths. Then straighten your back so your posture is good and look upward as if you were a king or queen surveying their kingdom. Simply gaze, without straining, at the clear sky. If the sun is shining do not look directly at the sun. Feel your spirit merging with the sky. After a while you will notice your thoughts simply evaporate like clouds becoming rain. You are now open, expansive and experiencing your natural spiritual state. Relish this spontaneous experience as long as you can before you return to the world of distractions.

---

36 http://yourskillfulmeans.com/knowledgebase/sky-gazing/

SPIRIT RITUAL
#235: EXPLORE YOUR DREAMS

Your dreams can be your spiritual guides

Continuing the spiritual theme of seeing the extraordinary in what we often take for granted, today's ritual encourages you to explore the world of your dreams. When you fall asleep and dream, you link to your inner wisdom.[37] In your dreams your spirit transcends physical or material limitations and enters a timeless world of limitless potential. Recalling and working with your dreams is a powerful tool for personal and spiritual development. You can learn so much about yourself and what really matters in life from analysing your dreams.

Most of us dismiss our dreams as nonsense and barely give them a second thought. Your ritual today is to commit to one week of recalling and analyzing your dreams. **Ritualize** this commitment by placing your dreams notebook beside your bed with a pen before you go to sleep tonight and then follow the guidelines for the next seven days of rituals. Before you fall asleep each night, say out loud that you will dream and you will recall them when you wake up – there is a dream-recall tip included for each day to help you. Remember that your dreams have to be written down immediately when you wake up, otherwise you will easily forget them. You can also refer back to Evening Foundation Ritual 20 and to Thought Management Mind Ritual 128 (*see* pages 38 and 154).

Make writing down your dreams a morning ritual. You don't need a dream dictionary to interpret the symbols. The best person to interpret your dreams is you. Every image or sensation in your dream is a symbol for your thoughts, your feelings, your relationships, your interests, your life. Become an expert on your dreams and trust your spirit to interpret their hidden messages.

37 www.ncbi.nlm.nih.gov/
pubmed/19159131

SPIRIT RITUAL
#236: DREAM RECALL DAY 1

★ Date

Recall Tip: If you can't remember anything, simply write "no dream to record". Keep doing this every morning and you will soon start to recall your dreams, as the more you think about dreaming the more likely you are to do so.[38]

★ **Describe your dream or dreams in one or two sentences.**
Tip: Take notes even if they don't make sense.

★ **Identify your feelings in your dreams.**
Tip: Feelings in dreams are your teacher, helping you gain deeper understanding of your daily life.

★ **Identify images in your dreams that have similarities to your daily life.**
Tip: Remember dreams are not predictive but symbolic expressions of your inner world. If your dreams are alarming, analysing them can be cathartic and healing. Your dreams also give you an opportunity to role-play scenarios or be someone else in a safe way.

★ **Ask yourself questions about your dreams.**
Tip: There is always something insightful and deeply meaningful for you to learn about yourself from your dreams, even mundane ones, like driving in a car. Where were you heading? Who was with you in the car? Were you in the driving seat? Did you feel in control? Was the car your own? Remember, everything in your dream is about you. You don't always need answers to the questions you ask, sometimes the power is in the asking.

38 www.sciencedirect.com/science/article/pii/S1053810012001973
39 www.sciencedaily.com/releases/2018/04/180427100258.htm

SPIRIT RITUAL
#237: DREAM RECALL DAY 2

★ Date

Recall Tip: Let your mind meander a bit when you wake up. Keeping your eyes closed and staying in the same position you woke up in can also boost dream recall.

★ Describe your dream or dreams in one or two sentences.
★ Identify your feelings in your dreams.
★ Identify images in your dreams that have similarities to your daily life.
★ Ask yourself questions about your dreams.

SPIRIT RITUAL
#238: DREAM RECALL DAY 3

★ Date

Recall Tip: Making sure your diet is rich in vitamin B6 can boost dream recall.[39] Food sources include: sunflower seeds, tuna, turkey and dried fruit.

★ Describe your dream or dreams in one or two sentences.
★ Identify your feelings in your dreams.
★ Identify images in your dreams that have similarities to your daily life.
★ Ask yourself questions about your dreams.

SPIRIT RITUAL
#239: DREAM RECALL DAY 4

★ Date

Recall Tip: Do some research about the health benefits of dreaming, as research shows the more you think about your dreams, the more likely you are to recall them.

★ Describe your dream or dreams in one or two sentences.
★ Identify your feelings in your dreams.
★ Identify images in your dreams that have similarities to your daily life.
★ Ask yourself questions about your dreams.

SPIRIT RITUAL
#240: DREAM RECALL DAY 5

★ Date

Recall Tip: Placing an azurite crystal under your pillow while you sleep is thought to facilitate dreaming and aid recall.

★ Describe your dream or dreams in one or two sentences.
★ Identify your feelings in your dreams.
★ Identify images in your dreams that have similarities to your daily life.
★ Ask yourself questions about your dreams.

SPIRIT RITUAL
#241: DREAM RECALL DAY 6

★ Date

Recall Tip: A few drops of lavender and sage oil on your pillow may help dream recall.

★ Describe your dream or dreams in one or two sentences.
★ Identify your feelings in your dreams.
★ Identify images in your dreams that have similarities to your daily life.
★ Ask yourself questions about your dreams.

SPIRIT RITUAL
#242: DREAM RECALL DAY 7

★ Date:

Recall Tip: if you are still struggling to recall your dreams, the simple act of focusing your mind on dreams and whether you will recall them is ritual enough. Keep repeating this ritual every day moving forward and your dreams will come back to you.

★ Describe your dream or dreams in one or two sentences.
★ Identify your feelings in your dreams.
★ Identify images in your dreams that have similarities to your daily life.
★ Ask yourself questions about your dreams.

SPIRIT RITUAL
#243: NEVER STOP DREAMING
Dream with your eyes open

Analyzing your dreams at night will help you become more self-aware, and the more self-aware you are, the more you develop spiritually. Re-read your dream log later in the day to bring your dream perception into your waking life. To repeat, the more attention you give your dreams in your waking life the more likely you are to recall them.

I hope your dream recall week has encouraged you to pay greater attention to your dreams, but it isn't just the dreams you have at night that can empower you, daydreams are just as nourishing for your spirit. Even when they don't come true it is important to keep on dreaming.[40] Don't ever let the frantic pace of daily life kill your dreams.

Today's ritual is very simple. You are going to treat yourself to some day-dreaming. **Ritualize** this by finding a picture of a stunningly beautiful waterfall. Then, set a timer for five minutes and sit down comfortably. Close your eyes and imagine yourself stepping through that waterfall into the world of your dreams. Spend some time there. When the timer goes off take some of the magic potential you saw there with you back into your waking life.

40 Paulo Coelho, *The Alchemist*, HarperCollins, 1995

SPIRIT RITUAL
#244: LIGHT UP THE WORLD

Reach out to someone you don't know with compassion

Time now to switch your attention from yourself to other people. With the steady rise of materialism and narcissism, the world urgently needs the spiritual principles of empathy and compassion right now. Sometimes the situation seems hopeless but there is something that can be done and it starts with you.

Your ritual today is to reach out to someone with compassion. Research[41] shows that compassion can make both you and them feel happier. The next time you are in a crowd or with a group of strangers, focus your attention on one person. Then silently repeat each of the following sentences in your mind.

★ Just like me this person is seeking happiness and trying to avoid pain.
★ Just like me this person has known sadness and loneliness, and is seeing fulfilment.
★ Just like me this person is learning about the meaning of life.

Ritualize this exercise by turning your empathy into compassionate action. Smile warmly at that person or send them your loving thoughts for no reason but to celebrate your shared humanity. Let this ritual inspire you perhaps to buy the next homeless person you see in the street a hot drink and a sandwich or to donate some money to a good cause. For every small *act* of compassion, the world becomes a lighter and a happier place.

41 www.pnas.org/
content/103/42/15623.full

SPIRIT RITUAL
#245: VOLUNTEER WORK

Give some of your spare time to a good cause

There are spiritual benefits[42] to volunteering to help others. Donating your time, energy or money without receiving anything in return is incredibly rewarding. It can give your life a sense of meaning and purpose it might otherwise lack if everything is just centred around your own needs.

Your ritual today is to consider doing volunteer work. The word "consider" is used here because even if you decide you simply don't have the time and energy right now, the fact you are thinking about it will lift your spirit. You can always keep it as an option for the future. **Ritualize** by actively looking for volunteer work in your area for a cause you believe in or to help people less fortunate than yourself. Search online and see what is out there. If anything appeals, take action and put yourself forward. You won't regret it.

42 www.health.harvard.edu/blog/volunteering-may-be-good-for-body-and-mind-201306266428

SPIRIT RITUAL
#246: BE KIND
Make kindness your state of being

Kindness, like compassion, is a basic principle of spirituality and a path to greater peace in the world. It differs from compassion in that the focus is less on feeling and understanding someone else's condition and more on being actively considerate or generous. Research[43] shows that kindness benefits you, the person you help and there is also a magical third-party effect in that when others witness it, they are more likely to be kind themselves. In this way every act of kindness has a ripple effect.

Today's ritual encourages you to make kindness your state of being. **Ritualize** by going out of your way to be kind to someone you know or a stranger. Give up your seat to someone elderly or pregnant, hold the door open for the person behind you, drop a few coins into a charity collection, offer to make someone a cup of tea or coffee, and so on. Perform your good deed secure in the knowledge that kindness changes you and everyone for the better.

43 www.sciencedaily.com/releases/2016/10/ 161005102254.htm

SPIRIT RITUAL
#247: THE GRATITUDE PRINCIPLE

Say "thank you" to someone in writing

Along with kindness, gratitude is another basic principle of spirituality. It is noticing and saying "thank you" for all the good people and things in your life. When you neglect to appreciate what you have, you limit your chances of joy and fulfilment.[44]

Your ritual today is to imagine your life without the people and things you love. Notice how this suddenly makes you appreciate and feel gratitude for what you take for granted. **Ritualize** by beginning and ending your day by saying "thank you" out loud to the universe for all the things you already have to be grateful for in your life.

44 www.forbes.com/sites/amymorin/2014/11/23/7-scientifically-proven-benefits-of-gratitude-that-will-motivate-you-to-give-thanks-year-round/#4a66e7b0183c

SPIRIT RITUAL
#248: MORNING ESCAPE
Meet your sacred potential first thing

The previous Spirit rituals you've performed have encouraged you to look beyond the obvious and seek deeper meaning in your life from the inside out in a variety of ways. It's time now to pause and reinforce all these rituals. Perhaps the best way to do that is with the spiritual practice of meditation, first thing in the morning.

Over the course of our lives most of us will greet tens of thousands of mornings. If at this stage in your ritual year your mornings are still chaotic or you find it hard to get out of bed, no more excuses. It's time to make a change with a morning meditation[45] to encourage inner calm.

Today's ritual will help you set up your day as the once-in-a-lifetime opportunity it is to express yourself and experience this beautiful world. **Ritualize** your gratitude by getting up 15 minutes earlier and dedicating that time to a simple morning meditation. Find a sitting or lying position that works for you, close your eyes and focus on your breath. Let your thoughts float by. Empty your mind. Simply be. Then return to your life 15 minutes later, ready to take action to jumpstart your day.

45 www.psychologytoday.com/gb/blog/feeling-it/201309/20-scientific-reasons-start-meditating-today

SPIRIT RITUAL
#249: TEA BLISS

Refresh your spirit with herbal tea

Your ritual today, which you may wish to perform after a morning or evening meditation, is to switch your regular cup of tea, coffee or hot chocolate for a cup of herbal tea.

Set aside ten minutes to make your herbal tea and put your feet up. **Ritualize** your tea-drinking by not rushing the experience. There is a spiritual art to preparing the perfect cup of herbal tea that dates back to the ancient Japanese tea ceremony. As you prepare it and watch the leaves seep in hot water, notice the steam and how the tea smells. Take your time preparing it beautifully. When you drink it, savour it fully and feel it gently warming your mind, body, heart and spirit. Here are some proven[46] spirit-warming herbal tea recommendations: ginger, chamomile, peppermint, rosemary, thyme and rose.

46 www.sciencedaily.com/releases/2011/03/ 110301122055.htm

SPIRIT RITUAL
#250: STUDY GREAT ART
Visit an art gallery or view art online

Meditation and mindfulness are tried-and-tested ways to help you connect to spirit, but there are other less obvious ways. One of those ways is to study great works of art. Research[47] has shown that when you look at beautiful or great artwork, your brain reacts in much the same way as when you fall in love or when you have a transcendent experience.

Art is your spirit calling out to you, so your ritual today is to visit an art gallery or view a great work of art online or in a book. **Ritualize** your art appreciation by choosing a work that uplifts or interests you and lose yourself in contemplating it for a few minutes. You may even want to get a poster version and put it on your wall so you get a daily dose of spiritual inspiration. If you aren't sure where to start, here are some works of art that are enduringly famous for reasons you may want to discover yourself.

★ *Mona Lisa* by Leonardo da Vinci
★ *The Creation of Adam* by Michelangelo
★ *The Birth of Venus* by Botticelli
★ *Girl with a Pearl Earring* by Vermeer
★ *The Thinker* by Rodin
★ *Starry Night* by Van Gogh
★ *Waterlilies* by Monet
★ *The Persistence of Memory* by Dali

47 www.vislab.ucl.ac.uk/pdf/Daedalus.pdf

SPIRIT RITUAL
#251: SACRED SOUND
Find music that speaks to your spirit

In much the same way that great art can speak to your spirit, so can great music or music you love. Research[48] has shown the healing potential of music. Your ritual today is to find music that nourishes your spirit.

Classical music with a steady and calm pulse tends to be the best place to find spiritually nourishing music, but feel free to choose any piece of music that has the ability to both calm and uplift you at the same time. **Ritualize** by feeling gratitude for the deep sense of joy the music gives you as you listen. Pay close attention to the sound and also the pulse and pauses in between, because there is great peace to be found in silence. To get you thinking and choosing along the right lines here are some suggestions.

★ Beethoven's *Moonlight Sonata, first movement*
★ Allegri's *Miserere Mei Deus*
★ Chopin's *Nocturne, Opus 27, no. 2*
★ For more recent music try Enya's "Orinoco Flow" or Yiruma's "Kiss the Rain"

48 https://hms.harvard.edu/sites/default/files/assets/Sites/Longwood_Seminars/
Longwood%20Seminar%20Music%20Reading%20Pack.pdf

SPIRIT RITUAL
#252: BECOME A MASTERPIECE

Make your life a work of art

The previous two rituals encouraged you to grow spiritually through an appreciation of art and music. Great art arises from a place of inspiration, creativity and passion - that is what makes it great and why it touches our spirits - so your ritual today is to think about your own life as a potential work of art.[49]

Take a few moments to yourself today to think of your life as a work of art. **Ritualize** by visualizing what that work of art would look like. Paint or mould it in vivid detail in your mind's eye. Make it your masterpiece. Then, carry that spirit of creativity and inspiration into your daily life. Pay attention to details. Look for beauty, originality and truth. Express your bigger picture.

49 Marjory Jacobson, *Art for Work*, HBR Press, 1993

SPIRIT RITUAL
#253: GO *AL FRESCO*
Experience the great outdoors

Nature is a rich source of inspiration for artists for a reason. The more time you spend outdoors, the better for your holistic wellbeing because human beings were not meant to live indoors.[50] We are a part of nature.

   Make a conscious effort today to do an activity outside that you would normally do inside. For example, if you exercise inside, do it outside. If weather permits dine *al fresco* and, if you get a chance, visit the seaside or go for a walk in the woods. **Ritualize** by breathing in the fresh air deeply, listening closely to the sounds of nature, feeling the elements on your skin and appreciating your deep connection to the earth underneath your feet and all around you.

50 http://norwegianjournaloffriluftsliv.com/doc/122010.pdf
51 www.natureandforesttherapy.org/about/science

SPIRIT POWER RITUAL
#254: FOREST BATHING
Find natural joy in the woods

Continuing the theme of communing with nature, today's **power ritual** may need more time to complete than usual because it encourages you to embrace forest bathing. This means immersing yourself in a forest setting for the therapeutic benefits this can offer and taking time away from the bustle of the modern world to re-energize. Studies[51] show that forest bathing eases stress, and boosts concentration and creativity. It is also soothing for your spirit and deep within us all is a need to feel that natural connection.

Seek out a forest or wooded area and spend as much time there as you can spare. **Ritualize** your experience by leaning against a tree and drinking in with all your senses the sights, smells and sounds around you. Touch the tree to experience its texture. See, hear and feel nature around you. Then, leave the tree behind and walk mindfully, breathing in the forest air and touching leaves, plants and trees as you go. Find a spot where you can quietly sit and observe your surroundings. Intersperse walking and sitting mindfully until it is time to return to your daily life. Mark that transition by drinking a cup of soothing herbal tea or eating an apple or other piece of fruit.

If it's too cold or rainy to visit a forest or you simply haven't got time, your ritual today is to schedule a visit to the forest or woods in your diary for at least 30 minutes. If you still feel you don't have the time, you may want to reassess your priorities. You could also try micro doses of nature therapy instead of full-blown forest bathing. Head outside, even if it's just for five minutes, to connect to the natural world – the grass, the trees, the mud, the wind, the sun, the light and the sky. Take in nature whenever you can or sit beside a window for nature appreciation, immersion and reconnection.

SPIRITUAL AWAKENING

Forest bathing originated in the 1980s in Japan, where it is called *Shinrin Yoku* by the forestry commission, who recognized the need to reconnect with the natural world as advances in technology were distancing people from their natural state. Many Japanese employers schedule regular forest bathing sessions for their employees. Although there are lots of guidelines to help you make the experience as fully immersive as possible, forest bathing really is just another way to reconnect with your natural state or true essence, which is where all spiritual awakening and transformation occurs.

SPIRIT RITUAL
#255: LEARN FROM ANIMALS

Choose your animal guide

Studies have shown that pets truly have healing powers for their owners. It's not just that stroking pets reduces stress and blood pressure, there is an added spiritual dimension. Pets give their owners unconditional love and this is incredibly comforting. They can also teach us a lot about happiness.

Spending time with animals is good news for your ego and your spirit, so your ritual today is to appreciate the pets in your life. If you don't own a pet or don't want one, the next time you pass someone walking their dog, ask if you can pet them. Or visit an animal shelter to pet an animal in need of a home or adopt an animal online so you can contribute to their wellbeing. **Ritualize** your animal appreciation by reflecting on all that animals give to humans from their love to their lives. Animals give us everything they have. The least we can all do is appreciate them back.

SPIRIT RITUAL
#256: GROW UP AGAIN
Reconnect with your inner child

Spending time with animals can help you connect to your inner child – the child that you once were. It's the part of you[52] that is spontaneous, natural, sensitive, creative, joyful, passionate, playful, curious, trusting, loving and truthful. Many of us lose touch with our inner child as we grow up, but spiritual growth involves learning to reconnect with that forgotten part of ourselves.

Your ritual today will help you meet your inner child. All you need to do is find a photo of yourself laughing or smiling when you were a child. **Ritualize** by studying that photo and using it as a prompt to reconnect with the living energy of your inner child. If you don't have a photo, be sure to smile broadly when you meet anyone or before you begin any task. Remind yourself that smiling is your physical prompt to consciously see and share the wonder and joy in everyone and everything in your life, just as your inner child longs for you to do.

52 Theresa Cheung, *Angel Babies*, Harper Collins, 2009

SPIRIT RITUAL #257: RECOMMENDED BOOKS FOR YOUR SPIRIT

Immerse yourself in spiritual reading

Remember how exciting reading was when you were a child? Reading took you on adventures. It also helped you learn. It's well known that reading is great for your mental and emotional health, so why not increase the healing benefits of reading by choosing books that feed your spirit, too. Today's ritual encourages you to start reading some timeless spiritual classics.

Ritualize your sacred reading time with the knowledge that the words you are absorbing truly can change your life for the better. You can, of course, start with ancient spiritual texts, but here are some easy-to-read modern spiritual classics to get you started. Try to read a few chapters a day or to complete one book every month.

★ *The Power of Now* by Eckhart Tolle
★ *The Seven Spiritual Laws of Success* by Deepak Chopra
★ *The Four Agreements* by Don Miguel Ruiz
★ *The Celestine Prophecy* by James Redfield
★ *The Alchemist* by Paulo Coelho
★ *Man's Search for Meaning* by Viktor Frankl
★ *The Untethered Soul* by Michael Singer
★ *Return to Love* by Marianne Williamson
★ *The Road Less Travelled* by M. Scott Peck

SPIRIT RITUAL
#258: LIVE HEALTHIER
Nurture your mind, body, spirit connection

The spiritual reading recommended yesterday will, of course, focus on your spiritual development. But even though you are a spiritual being, don't let this make you forget that you are also human. Through your body your spirit can experience all the wonders of life on earth, so it is important to treat your body with the reverence it deserves.

Poor physical health is going to drain[53] your spirit, so your ritual today encourages you to make a sacred commitment to take special care of your body. **Ritualize** by writing out the following on a piece of coloured card so it stands out: I will treat my body as the sacred home, or temple, of my spirit.

Put that card where you can see it every day. Use it as a visual reminder to help you become fully conscious of all the decisions you make regarding your physical wellbeing. Be aware of how these choices impact you spiritually. Eat mindfully and seek out fresh, nutritious foods. Don't indulge in negative habits, like smoking or eating too much. Ensure you get enough exercise, fresh air and quality sleep. Treat your body like the sacred home, or temple, it is for your spirit.

53 www.webmd.com/depression/news/20070906/depression-a-big-factor-in-poor-health#1

SPIRIT RITUAL
#259: IGNITE YOUR INTUITION

Trust your instincts over all else

Today's ritual focuses on one of the most powerful ways spirit or your inner wisdom speaks to you and that is through the voice of your intuition.

Intuition is your ability to understand or know something without conscious reasoning. It speaks to you in sudden hunches or realizations or through dreams and emotions that seem to come out of nowhere. It is the part of you that already and always knows what is the right thing to do.[54] Sadly, in the rational world we live in today, many of us neglect our intuition and if we do notice it, we don't trust its wisdom. As your intuition is the voice of your spirit, all the rituals in this section will help ignite your intuition, but today's ritual specifically asks you to tune into and trust your gut instinct or hunches. These typically express themselves through your body - butterflies in your stomach, raised heart rate or unexplained aches and pains. **Ritualize** by consciously focusing your attention on your stomach and heart rate and other physical responses whenever you interact with someone or make a decision. Listen to what your intuition - your inner guide to what action you should take - is saying and start trusting it.

At first you may feel uncertain, but if you keep tuning into your intuition before making decisions, in time you will learn to recognize and respond to that sense of quiet knowing.

54 Theresa Cheung, *21 Rituals to Ignite Your Intuition*, Watkins, 2019

SPIRIT RITUAL
#260: SACRED CALLING CARDS

Respect those who have gone before you

It's impossible to talk about spirituality without considering the possibility of an afterlife. Whether you believe in life after death[55] or not, spirit is an incredibly powerful word. It is the part of you that gives your life meaning and purpose and, if you believe in an afterlife, it is the eternal part of you that lives on after you die.

Your ritual today encourages you to reflect on what the word spirit, and/or soul,[56] means to you by asking you to send loving thoughts to someone in your life who has died. **Ritualize** by taking a few quiet moments to yourself and finding a picture of that person to focus your intention on. If you don't know anyone personally, choose someone you respect. Bring that person to life in your mind's eye, think about their spirit or legacy and how they touched or changed your life and what lessons they taught. Then, throughout the day, look for meaningful signs in your daily life that remind you of them, such as a familiar song or the appearance of a white feather, a bird that hops unexpectedly into your path or a butterfly that passes by. Honour the memory of those who have gone before you.

55 Theresa Cheung, *Answers from Heaven*, Schuster, 2017
56 The two words are interchangeable but "soul" refers to your spirit in its human form, whereas "spirit" refers to the part of you that is believed to be eternal in that it has existed before you were born, is your soul during your life on earth and continues to exist after your death.
57 www.theguardian.com/science/2009/feb/15/psychology-usa
www.urmc.rochester.edu/encyclopedia/content.aspx?ContentID=4552&ContentTypeID=1
www.apa.org/monitor/jun02/writing.aspx
psychcentral.com/lib/the-health-benefits-of-journaling/

SPIRIT RITUAL
#261: CONSIDER SPIRITUAL QUESTIONS
The spiritual practice of journalling

Thinking about the possibility of life after death and the meaning of life, along with self-reflection, are sure-fire signs of spiritual awakening. It's also the ideal time to start the spiritual practice of journalling.

Research[57] has shown that journalling has benefits for emotional and mental health but, above all, it is a spiritual practice. When you write with your authentic self, you discover honest truths about yourself and the meaning of your life that you would not otherwise uncover. You don't have to be a great writer or have perfect spelling and grammar. What matters is the intention to learn more about yourself, as that is the whole point of journalling. The more self-aware you are, the more authentic and spiritual you are.

Journalling isn't for everyone, but it has so many benefits for your spiritual growth that your ritual today is to commit to one week of spiritual journalling. Lots of us keep records of our lives on social media, but this week of journalling is strictly for pen and paper as nothing beats this for authenticity, intimacy and privacy. **Ritualize** your commitment to spiritual journalling today by getting a blank notebook. Then, write out the following and sign your name on the first page.

★ **On this day of my ritual year I commit to a week of spiritual-growth journalling, beginning today.**
★ **During that week I will spend a few minutes each day answering the spiritual question or questions of the day as honestly as I can. I will write my answers in this notebook.**

★ Sign your name here ....

SPIRIT RITUAL
#262: SPIRITUAL QUESTION TIME DAY 1

Pick up your pen and pour out your thoughts and feelings

Making journalling a ritual requires you to set aside some time each day, preferably the same time, but there are no rules. It's not always easy to get started with journalling, so for the next seven days you will be given a spiritual question to answer as a catalyst for self-reflection. **Ritualize** by spending a few minutes meditating on the questions before you write. If you want to refer back to previous spirit rituals, feel free to do so as there will be ample inspiration there. Then pick up your pen and pour out your authentic feelings and thoughts onto the page. As you write, be aware that you are actively trying to understand who you are and what you value at the deepest most profoundly spiritual level.

Today's questions:

★ Do I take things personally?
★ Am I guided by my own moral compass?

SPIRIT RITUAL
#263: SPIRITUAL QUESTION TIME DAY 2

Today's questions:

★ Do I listen?
★ Do I gossip?

SPIRIT RITUAL
#264: SPIRITUAL QUESTION TIME DAY 3

Today's questions:

★ Is there a spiritual lesson in a challenging situation I am facing or have faced?
★ If I didn't know how old I was, how old would I be? Why did I choose that age?

SPIRIT RITUAL
#265: SPIRITUAL QUESTION TIME DAY 4

Today's questions:

★ Am I a good friend to myself?
★ Do I have compassion for others?

SPIRIT RITUAL
#266: SPIRITUAL QUESTION TIME DAY 5

Today's questions:

★ What am I most afraid of and why?
★ What really matters to me?

SPIRIT RITUAL
#267: SPIRITUAL QUESTION TIME DAY 6

Today's questions:

★ What does it mean to live in the present moment?
★ What are my values?

SPIRIT RITUAL
#268: SPIRITUAL QUESTION TIME DAY 7

Today's questions:

★ Have I improved as a result of my experiences?
★ What if today was my last day? Am I who I want to be?

SPIRIT RITUAL
#269: LEARN FROM YOURSELF

Spirituality is a journey of self-discovery

Your ritual today is to go back and read your journal entries for the last week. **Ritualize** by reflecting deeply on your own insights and what they teach you about yourself. Appreciate the increased self-awareness your spiritual journalling has brought you. Let it incentivize you to keep journalling every day.

Spirituality is a fascinating journey of self-discovery. The more you write from your authentic self, the more you will understand that you are not who you think you are, what you have been taught to be, what you want to be or what you feel or even believe you are. Why? Because all these identities are temporary. They are not real or authentic. They are not *you*.

For the spiritually awakened soul this realization liberates you from the belief that "I am this" or "I am that" to the realization of "I am".

Your authentic self is the only truth.

You are enough.

SPIRIT RITUAL
#270: LEARN FROM THOSE WHO ARE PRESENT

Notice people who live in the now

Most of us know someone who has mastered the spiritual art of living in the now.[58] They aren't filled with anxiety, worry and regret. They aren't afraid to take risks and learn from their mistakes but, most important of all, they seem to be totally engaged with the present moment or what they are currently doing.

Your ritual today is to identify people in your life who are engaged in the "now" of their lives. **Ritualize** this by sending those people your gratitude for the light and inspiration they bring to the world and seeing what you can learn from them.

Hint: Children can be great spiritual teachers, as can elderly people or grandparents. If you don't know anyone, then study the teachings of famous spiritual teachers like the Dalai Lama, Osho or Eckhart Tolle.

58 Eckhart Tolle, *The Power of Now*, Bantam, 1996

SPIRIT POWER RITUAL
#271: SEE WITH YOUR THIRD EYE

Suspend disbelief and see your way ahead

One of the most enchanting qualities of spiritual people is their youthful ability to suspend disbelief. Today's **power ritual** encourages you to suspend disbelief and set aside a few quiet moments to place your attention on your third eye, which is the area in the centre of your forehead between your eyebrows. Your third eye is believed to be the door to your spirit or your inner wisdom and intuition. It is also known as the pineal gland; research[59] suggests an association between the pineal gland and transcendent experiences.

Gently massage this area with your hand for a few moments to relieve any tension and then close your eyes. You will feel a post-massage dull sensation. **Ritualize** by visualizing the third eye on your forehead opening. Think of yourself as a spark of the universe, a star in the sky, a drop in the ocean. Keep your awareness on being part of something far greater than yourself until you experience a feeling of peace and infinite potential that surpasses understanding. Savour this spiritual experience for as long as you can and then slowly open your eyes. Visualize your third eye closing with the quiet and confident awareness that whenever you wish to open it again, you can.

Your third eye is one of seven chakras or centres in your body through which spiritual energy is thought to flow, according to ancient Indian and Tantric tradition. If any of these energy centres are blocked, this can lead to poor health and tension. While the third eye is linked to your intuition and ability to see the bigger picture, there is also a chakra point on the top of your head that governs your ability to experience bliss. In addition, there are five other main chakras: the throat chakra, which links to communication; the heart chakra to

59 www.researchgate.net/publication/278301447_The_pineal_gland_and_the_possible_neurobiology_of_psi

emotions; the solar plexus or upper stomach to self-confidence; the sacral or lower abdomen to the ability to give and take; and the root chakra, at the base of the spine, to survival and being grounded through material things like money and food. Use your knowledge of these chakra centres in your body to listen to the spiritual messages they send you whenever you experience physical sensations associated with them.

Working with your third eye will naturally increase your intuitive or psychic powers so you may also want to research ancient divination tools, such as Tarot, astrology and numerology, as they can all be used to help you develop greater foresight. There's a whole new world[60] out there of psychic and spiritual awakening just waiting for you to discover it. What are you waiting for?

LOOKING AHEAD

Opening the third eye and the blissful awareness of losing and regaining your identity in the universe may not happen immediately. It may take many attempts, but don't be despondent if you haven't glimpsed this transcendent state yet. Trust that you will when the time is right for you and keep working through the rituals in this book, as every time you perform a ritual you open yourself up spiritually to the universe. The Heart rituals follow on next and they will help you connect to the most powerful spiritual energy of all – love.

60 Theresa Cheung, *The Element Encyclopedias of the Psychic World: 20,000 dreams and birthdays*, HarperCollins, 2005-2007

Heart
RITUALS

Rituals for a more loving and fulfilled YOU

Life begins when your heart starts beating and ends when it stops. But your heart doesn't only keep your body and brain alive. It is also your emotional home and in many ancient spiritual traditions is considered to be the source of true power and understanding. In essence, your heart connects and unites your mind, body and spirit. Everything depends on and centres around your heart.

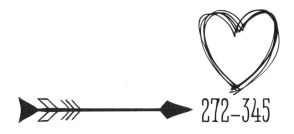

272-345

EVIDENCE-BASED FOUNDATIONS

Research confirms ancient wisdom that your heart is far more than a physical organ. It is the seat of your feelings and has a power and a wisdom of its own. Studies from the Institute of HeartMath[1] show that when you experience feelings of love, peace, creativity and joy, your heart beats in a calmer, gentler way. The HeartMath team have even coined a term for this and it's called "heart coherence", a state of existence in which your body and mind are in perfect harmony. HeartMath studies show that feelings of anger, stress and fear have the opposite effect on your heart rate. Other research on the negative effects of stress on your heart health certainly backs this up. So, when you are able to connect with your heart fully and experience feelings of happiness and peace, you are physically, mentally and spiritually at your peak.

The exciting news is that researchers have identified the key things you can do to keep your heart happy and in a state of "coherence". Here you will find these activities presented in a series of rituals designed to be performed one a day over a period of 74 days. The rituals fall naturally into three heartfelt groups: Examining Your Heart, Talking to Your Heart and Using Your Heart. The reasons why each ritual makes your heart smile will be backed up with evidence wherever possible but, as the heart is a mystery, some things about the power of the heart can never be fully explained. Your heart is defined by the most mysterious and wonderful force in the world – love.

HOW HEART RITUALS CAN HELP YOU

For your heart, thoughts and words have no power unless they are made real by actions. Rituals are therefore perfect. They are personally meaningful actions that immediately and directly reconnect your body, mind and spirit to the simple, clear and loving voice of your heart. If you want happier relationships with others, yourself and the universe, this section of the book is definitely for you. It will help you make a sacred commitment to your heart to always listen to it. This section is

THE RITUAL YEARBOOK

also recommended if you are grieving the loss of a loved one or have recently ended a relationship, as it contains rituals to heal a broken heart. Whether these help heal your relationships with others or with yourself, understanding the reasons why each ritual can lighten your heart and then performing it with mindful intention and gratitude for the present moment (so it is ritualized), will significantly increase your chances of heartfelt happiness and fulfilment.

EXAMINING YOUR HEART RITUAL #272: HAND ON HEART

Hear what your heart is saying

The first three or so weeks of Heart rituals are all designed to help you get to know your own heart better. Every day our hearts are trying to talk to us, but all too often the messages they send us are not heard in our busy lives. You need silence to hear your heart speak. Your heart knows[2] what is good and right for you, so if you are too busy for some quiet heartfelt time, you need to make it a priority.

Your ritual today is simple. Find some peace and quiet, and when you feel calm enough, **ritualize** the moment by gently placing both your hands on your heart. After a while you will feel it beating. Tune into that heart beat and breathe deeply. Close your eyes and listen to the rhythm of your heart and what it is whispering to you. You may hear nothing at first but if you repeat this ritual often, your heart will start to speak to you – not with words or thoughts but with intuition or a feeling about what is best and right for you.

1 www.heartmath.org
2 Baptist de Pape, *The Power of the Heart: Finding your true purpose in life*, Simon & Schuster, 2014

EXAMINING YOUR HEART RITUAL
#273: HEART REACTION
Ask your heart what it thinks before you decide

Your heart senses what is right for you before you do. The research[3] is preliminary but one of the most powerful ways your body talks to you is through your heartbeat.

Heart Ritual 272 encouraged you to listen to your heart, and your ritual today takes this a stage further by encouraging you to consciously tune into your heartbeat before you make a decision. It doesn't matter what that decision is, or whether it is big or small, just take a few moments to check in with your heartbeat first by taking your pulse.

Ritualize by being fully aware of the reason you are doing this, which is to check in with the wisdom of your heart. To take your pulse, simply turn one hand over, so it is palm-side up. Then, use the other hand to place two fingertips gently in the groove on the forearm, down from the fold of the wrist and about an inch (2.5cm) along from the base of the thumb. You should feel the pulsation of your heart beat. Notice whether your pulse is steady and calm or fast and racing? Is your heart trying to tell you something important? Ignore what your thoughts are saying and listen instead to the inside story of your heart. Is your heart instinctively saying "yes" or "no"?

3 www.deanradin.com/evidence/Mossbridge 2012Presentiment.pdf

EXAMINING YOUR HEART RITUAL #274: THINGS YOU LOVE TO DO

Explore what you adore

What we love fundamentally shapes our hearts.[4] Your ritual today is to focus not just on who or what you love but on what things you love to do. Find a few moments of peace and quiet and write down ten things that you absolutely adore to do. It can be as simple as walking beside a beach or eating chocolate while watching a "rom com", or as specialist as playing a musical instrument. It doesn't matter what it is, just write it down. Nobody is going to read this list but you. Examine your heart carefully as you do this self-awareness ritual. **Ritualize** by only writing down the things that genuinely make your heart sing. If you can't think of ten things, write down five.

Then, when you have written down the activities you love, study that list. Meditate on it. You have written down a piece of your heart.

Cherish it.

4 James Smith, *You Are What You Love: The spiritual power of habit*, Brazos, 2016

EXAMINING YOUR HEART RITUAL
#275: LABEL THAT FEELING

Put your feelings into words

Feeling happy all the time isn't possible or even helpful, as negative emotions are there for a reason. They can give us a helpful reality check or teach us something about ourselves, other people or a situation we are in. Suppressing negative emotions isn't good news for our personal growth.

Research[5] has shown that when you feel sad, anxious, fearful, angry or just low and unmotivated for no reason, there is something you can do to ease those feelings and that is to put them into words. Labelling your emotions is the best way to deal with them. For your ritual today, when you notice yourself feeling less happy than you'd like to be, sum up your emotional state in a word or two – for example, "feel sad". **Ritualize** by writing this down or say it aloud. Understand the importance of naming your feelings to help you work through them. There doesn't have to be a reason why or any lengthy explanation, just label those feelings. Your heart can hear you. It will understand.

5 www.ncbi.nlm.nih.gov/pubmed/17576282

EXAMINING YOUR HEART RITUAL #276: CONNECT WITH YOUR HEART

Set a daily reminder to check in with your heart

Your intuition[6] speaks to you through your body, your dreams and also your feelings. Your heart is your emotional centre. So, if you want to immediately tune into your inner wisdom, your heart is the place to look.

The more you make connecting with your heart a daily ritual, the more natural it will feel and the more intuitive you will become. The heart rituals you've done so far have encouraged you to tune into your heart, but don't get impatient if you struggle to hear its voice. You just need to keep practising every day. Our brains have become dominant in decision-making over the years, so it will take time to approach life in a more heartfelt way. It's worth the effort, though. Your heart truly is the best mentor and friend you will ever have. Your ritual today is to make a promise to yourself to never leave your heart out of the decision-making process again. **Ritualize** by setting an alert on your phone for the same time daily – mid-morning is ideal – when the word "heart" or a heart sign pops up on your screen to remind you to always include your emotional centre in everything you say, decide and do.

6 Bolte, A., *et al.*: 'Emotion and intuition: Effects of positive and negative mood on implicit judgments of semantic coherence', *Psychological Science*, Sep 2003, 14 (5), pp. 416-21

EXAMINING YOUR HEART RITUAL
#277: TAKE YOUR HEART FOR A WALK

Create an opening for your heart to talk to you

Your ritual today is to take your heart for a walk for around 20 minutes, not for exercise but to distract your body and mind with the movement, so you can create an opening for your heart to share some of its wisdom. **Ritualize** by walking mindfully[7] at a pace that suits you. You can walk slow or you can walk fast, it doesn't matter.

As you walk just be fully present in the moment. Notice your breathing and how your body feels as it walks. When you have established a peaceful rhythm, bring all your focus onto your heart. Feel it beating powerfully in your chest as you walk. You may just want to enjoy this moment of heartfelt connection or you may wish to ask your heart if it has anything to tell you. The choice is always yours.

7 www.telegraph.co.uk/health-fitness/mind/mindful-movement-walking-way-better-state-mind/

EXAMINING YOUR HEART RITUAL
#278: OPEN YOUR HANDS
Share your heart with your hands

The way we express love to others is often through our hands - through a hand shake, a reassuring pat on the shoulder, holding hands or clapping our hands to express delight. Our hands give us the ability to help and support others and can also express so much about what is in our heart through our gestures when we talk. Energy healers and healing-touch therapists[8] use their hands to transmit healing energy to their patients.

Hands connect us to our hearts because they help us share feelings of love and joy, so your ritual today involves your hands. First, look at the backs of your hands. Gently rub them. Then, rest your hands on your thighs and gently turn your hands over to reveal your palms. Study the lines - unless you are a palm-reading expert you probably don't spend much time getting to know the gripping story of your life written in your palms. You don't need to know the meaning of the lines, just send love and gratitude to your hands and the gifts they bring you. **Ritualize** by visualizing love energy flowing back and forth between your heart and your hands as a sparkling white and pink cord, pulsating with life.

8 Baldwin, A. L., 'Reiki: The scientific evidence', Fall, 2011, pp. 29–31
J. Motz, *Hands of Life*, Bantam Books, 1998

EXAMINING YOUR HEART RITUAL
#279: THE POWER OF TOUCH
Hug the people you care about

Couples[9] who regularly touch or hug each other have stronger relationships. Hugging can also boost heart health. Obviously, you can't just go around touching people without their permission, but when it is acceptable and appropriate touch or hug people more. The simple act of touching releases a hormone called oxytocin, or the love hormone.

Your ritual today is to ensure you give someone important to you a proper hug, at least 20 seconds long. Your heart will thank you for it. **Ritualize** your hug by reminding yourself how therapeutic touch is not just for your heart, but also for the heart of the person you are hugging. If you are not in a position to give someone a hug, then be sure to shake hands, pat someone on the back or book yourself in for a massage, as research[10] shows massage can be as beneficial as a hug.

9 www.ncbi.nlm.nih.gov/pmc/articles/PMC4323947/
10 www.prevention.com/life/a20461789/how-massage-helps-with-depression-and-anxiety/

EXAMINING YOUR HEART RITUAL
#280: TEXT LESS
Speak to and visit people more

Human beings need to feel validation, acceptance and love from others. Your heart needs other people to thrive. It has been proved[11] that when people are in stressful situations, a visit in person or receiving a phone call is far more therapeutic than a text. In fact, their bodies and their hearts respond to receiving a text in the same way as if they have no support at all.

We live in a world of constant mindless texting today. Phone calls have become increasingly rare. Your ritual today is to ensure that instead of texting someone, you call them or better still visit them instead. **Ritualize** by noticing and resisting your urge to text, and consciously and mindfully making the decision to call or visit them instead. Understand why choosing to talk is such an important ritual both for your heart and that of the person you are reaching out to.

11 www.psychologytoday.com/gb/blog/love-and-gratitude/201607/talking-instead-texting-can-save-relationships

EXAMINING YOUR HEART RITUAL
#281: BREATHE WITH YOUR HEART

Connect with your heart in the present

Your heart is only concerned with the power and potential of the present moment.[12] Most of us are disconnected from our hearts because we are consumed by thoughts of tomorrow or haunted by regrets from the past. The solution is simple: take a few moments to connect with your heart in the present moment.

Life is a series of "nows". Today's ritual is one that will make you aware of your heart in the present, in the right now, which is the only place for you to connect successfully with your heart. Close your eyes and with your left hand touch your heart area. **Ritualize** by taking a deep breath in and out and becoming mindfully aware of your breathing in the present moment. Then gently shift your focus from breathing with your lungs to imagining you are breathing in and out with your heart. Give yourself as long as you need to imagine this and with each in-breath imagine you are breathing in love, peace and joy, and with each out-breath you are breathing out fear, stress and anxiety. Breathe in the love deeply and exhale the stress completely. Imagine your heart growing stronger as it fills up with love and joy, and visualize how this heart-breathing ritual makes your heart feel warm and glowing. When you can feel that inner warmth igniting your heart, open your eyes and continue your day fully present and always connected to heart wisdom.

12 www.heartmath.org/articles-of-the-heart/the-math-of-heartmath/heart-focused-breathing/

EXAMINING YOUR HEART RITUAL
#282: REBORN WITH HEART

Open your heart to goodness and beauty

An open-hearted positive approach[13] to life sees beauty, goodness and love in everyone and everything. Although this is a joyful way to live, it isn't always easy as the world can be a dark place at times. We may never know the reason why bad things happen but daily rituals can help you find your own meaning.

Your ritual today is designed to help you live your life with a more open heart. Find a place where you can lie down and close your eyes. Curl yourself into a tight ball with your knees pulled into your chest. When you are in this foetal position, contract all your muscles and hold this contracted position for as long as possible. Focus on the deep symbolic meaning of what you are doing. Then, relax all your muscles, and **ritualize** by gradually uncurling yourself from the foetal position and luxuriating in an enormous full body stretch. Let your heart open and make room for all the goodness and beauty that it can let in. Pull yourself gently into a sitting position, open your eyes and observe everything around you as if it was the first time you had ever seen them. Notice the beauty that you may have missed before you were reborn with an open heart. Carry that enhanced perception of beauty with you into your daily life.

13 www.ncbi.nlm.nih.gov/pmc/articles/PMC3122271/

EXAMINING YOUR HEART RITUAL
#283: NOTES FOR YOUR HEART
Music is literature for your heart

Music touches your heart when words can't. Studies[14] show that listening to sad music has the opposite effect and can bring healing and inspiration. So, your ritual today is to listen to at least one of the following pieces of mellow classical music.

★ Samuel Barber's *Adagio for Strings*
★ Rachmaninoff's *Piano Concerto No. 2 (Second Movement)*
★ *Nimrod* from Elgar's *Enigma Variations*

Don't be tempted to skip this ritual if you are already familiar with these famous pieces or they are not your typical choices of music. Close your eyes and **ritualize** by rubbing your heart area with your hand as you listen. Hear the sound with your ears, but listen with your heart. Allow yourself to feel whatever the music inspires within you. Let the healing sound remind you of the remarkable healing powers within your own heart.

14 www.medicaldaily.com/breakup-songs-play-sad-happy-music-healing-process-371584

EXAMINING YOUR HEART RITUAL
#284: HEART MEDICINE

Music can evoke emotion and help heal your pain

Yesterday's ritual encouraged you to listen to emotionally-healing classical music. Today your ritual is to do the same as you did yesterday, but with one piece of popular music. Again, listen to the music with your heart and your ears. Here are some suggestions.

★ "My Heart Will Go On" by Celine Dion
★ "I Can't Make You Love Me" by Bonnie Raitt
★ "The Winner Takes It All" by Abba
★ "Everybody Hurts" by R.E.M.

Ritualize by holding your hand on your heart and reminding yourself that music speaks what can't be expressed. It helps heal your heart and make it whole, because when you listen to it you can empathize with the words, music and the person who wrote and/or performs it. You don't feel alone.

EXAMINING YOUR HEART RITUAL
#285: HEART BEATS

Let your heart go with the beat

Emoting can be healing and cathartic, but it has an expiry date. Your heart also wants you to move on. Research[15] shows that listening to upbeat music can help give you a positive twist on difficult situations. Today's ritual acknowledges that experiencing painful emotions can make you stronger, not weaker, and encourages you to listen to music expressing that. Try one of the following:

★ "You'll Be In My Heart" by Phil Collins
★ "I Will Survive" by Gloria Gaynor
★ "So What" by Pink
★ "Better In Time" by Leona Lewis

Ritualize by nodding your head to the beat and feeling your heart grow wiser and stronger with every beat.

15 www.healthline.com/health-news/mental-listening-to-music-lifts-or-reinforces-mood-051713#1

EXAMINING YOUR HEART RITUAL
#286: HEARTFELT MOVIES

Lose your heart in a film

Movie therapy[16] is watching films made for TV and cinema for therapeutic reasons. An increasing number of therapists are seeing that movies have value and can change the way people think and feel. Your ritual today is to indulge in some movie therapy. Choose one of the following films, put your feet up and lose yourself in it. Even if you have watched all these movies before, there is always something new and inspiring for your heart to discover and feel when you watch them again and again.

* ★ *Love Actually*
* ★ *Titanic*
* ★ *Forest Gump*
* ★ *Billy Elliot*
* ★ *Ghost*

Ritualize as you watch by reminding yourself that you are watching a heartfelt movie that has a message about resilience, empathy, compassion and the power of love.

---

16 www.webmd.com/mental-health/features/movie-therapy-using-movies-for-mental-health#1

EXAMINING YOUR HEART RITUAL
#287: WHAT IS LOVE?
Understanding the power of love

Today's ritual encourages you to discover the power and wonder of love within your own heart. You are probably familiar with these verses[17] because they are so often used at weddings. Your ritual today is to silently read the following words:

Love is patient, love is kind. It does not envy, it does not boast, it is not proud. It does not dishonour others, it is not self-seeking, it is not easily angered, it keeps no record of wrongs. Love does not delight in evil but rejoices with the truth. It always protects, always trusts, always hopes, always perseveres.

Ritualize by reading the words out loud and noticing how more personal and relevant the words sound when you understand that the definition of love can be you.

I am patient, I am kind. I do not envy. I do not boast, I am not proud. I am not rude, I am not self-seeking. I am not easily angered. I keep no record of wrongs. I do not delight in evil but rejoice in the truth. I always protect, always trust, always hope, always persevere.

17 1 Corinthians 13: 4-7

EXAMINING YOUR HEART RITUAL #288: THE ROAD TO COMPASSION

Let your heart be kind

There is evidence[18] to suggest that compassion can keep your heart beating for longer. Compassion starts with self-care. The kinder you are to yourself the more at peace your heart will be. When your heart has found peace with itself, feelings of compassion for others and the planet will come naturally to you.

Compassion is often the result of having gone through hard times ourselves. Through them we learn that the only way to change the world for the better is to be kinder to one another. Your ritual today will help you nurture and grow the seed of compassion, which is loving kindness.

Ritualize by once again placing your hand on your precious heart and say out loud with mindful intention, "I am healthy. I am happy. I am protected. I am at peace." Next, think of someone important to you and say out loud, "May you be healthy. May you be happy. May you be protected. May you be at peace." Then, repeat this for someone you know but are not close to. After that, say these words for someone who challenges you or you don't have an easy relationship with. Then, last, but by no means least, repeat this ritual for everyone on the planet using the words, "May you all be healthy."

18 https://psycnet.apa.org/record/2011-17888-001

EXAMINING YOUR HEART RITUAL #289: BECOME A COMPASSION CHAMPION

Commit to silent acts of kindness

Being kind to others is most rewarding[19] when it doesn't feel like an obligation or something you do to make yourself feel good.

Yesterday's ritual encouraged you to nurture within your heart feelings of compassion for yourself and then to extend those loving feelings towards others without them knowing. Today's ritual inspires you to take your compassion in the most empowering direction. **Ritualize** by making sure at some point today you do something kind for someone else but without them knowing it is you. For example, tidy up the office for your colleagues or donate some groceries to the local homeless shelter. The ideal is to do your act of kindness anonymously but, if that is difficult, do it without expectation of a personal thank you or anything in return.

Understand the significance of your actions. You are showing the universe that you are on the path to discovering true inner peace because you are helping others simply for the joy of helping. Let your act of true and authentic compassion today inspire you to further acts of secret compassion. Channel your inner Batman or Wonder Woman. The power of these superheroes often lies in their hidden identity.

19 https://greatergood.berkeley.edu/article/item/three_insights_from_the_cutting_edge_of_compassion_research

EXAMINING YOUR HEART RITUAL
#290: UNIVERSAL HEART

Transform the mundane into the sacred

Rituals transform the mundane into the sacred.[20] For this ritual you need a flower or a picture of a flower to heighten your heart's perceptions – ideally a single rose but any beautiful flower you can find is perfect. Study it carefully. Lose yourself in the brilliant detail and connect to the infinite beauty of that flower. Then, when it is time to eat your evening meal, before you begin, shift your focus from the mundane to the sacred by recalling the details of that flower in your mind.

Ritualize by opening your heart to its beauty as you recall your flower and connect to that beauty. Then, give thanks to the universe for the sustenance that food gives your body and the nourishment and heightened perception the image of the flower in your mind gives to your heart. Push a forkful of food to one side of your plate and mentally offer that portion as an offering to the universe and all its wonder and beauty, living inside and around you. Mindfully eat your meal.

· · · · · · · · · · · · ·
20 https://upliftconnect.com/sacred-rituals/

EXAMINING YOUR HEART RITUAL
#291: OPEN YOUR HEART
Yoga for your heart

Many of the heart rituals so far have focused on your emotional health, but don't neglect the importance of keeping your heart physically healthy, too. Yoga has been shown[21] to improve the physical health of your heart, as well as your emotional health. In yoga the heart is the centre of compassion.

Today's ritual is a yoga pose that can improve blood and oxygen flow to your heart and also open your heart space. It's called the Triangle pose because that is the shape formed by your trunk when you do it. **Ritualize** by breathing slowly and deeply, and focusing your full attention on your heart space and how it feels. Simply stand upright with your feet slightly more than shoulder-width apart. Then, lift both arms sideways and bend over gently to the right until you can hold your right ankle with your right hand. Don't twist your body. If you can't reach your ankle, hold your shin or thigh. Do this for at least 20 seconds and feel your heart space opening.

21 www.ncbi.nlm.nih.gov/pmc/articles/PMC3193654/

EXAMINING YOUR HEART RITUAL
#292: OPEN YOUR HEART AGAIN
Find time to restore your heart

Today's ritual offers you another heart-opening yoga pose, known as Corpse pose. For this you will need a thick towel or a blanket. Fold the towel and put it on the floor. Lie down so that the towel is under your lower back, shoulder blades and head, but not the rest of your body. Recline comfortably. Rotate your arms outward so the palms are facing the ceiling. Close your eyes, let go, breathe and feel your heart expanding. **Ritualize** by breathing deeply and focusing your full attention on the present moment as you become aware of the space opening up in your heart.

An alternative if you don't want to lie down, is simply to stand tall, clasp your hands behind your back and raise them slightly, puffing your chest and your heart within it, forward.

EXAMINING YOUR HEART RITUAL
#293: HEART IN MOTION
Reach for the sky

The ancient Chinese exercise of Tai Chi[22] (*see also* Get Moving Power Ritual 33, pages 54-5) can improve heart health, boost mood and increase longevity. The gentle flowing circular movements of Tai Chi truly are a loving and calming caress for your body, mind, spirit and heart. Today's ritual is a simple exercise called Touch the Sky, which will hopefully inspire you to research more about Tai Chi or sign up for a class. **Ritualize** as you perform this exercise by breathing slowly and deeply, and focusing only on the movement of your arms and hands.

To begin, sit up straight in a comfortable chair. Place your hands on your thighs with your palms facing upward and your fingertips pointing inward toward each other. Then, inhale and raise your hands in front of your chest and as you do slowly turn your palms outwards. Continue the slow-motion movement by lifting your hands above your head. (This is not a stretching exercise so don't feel you need to reach far with your arms.) Keep your elbows relaxed and slightly bent. Exhale and relax your arms, and gently lower them to your sides, returning your hands to the starting position with your palms turned inward. Repeat five times. You are aiming for continuous slow-motion movement, inhaling slowly as you lift your arms over your head and exhaling deeply as you lower them.

22 www.webmd.com/heart-disease/heart-failure/news/20110425/tai-chi-benefits-heart-patients

EXAMINING YOUR HEART RITUAL
#294: THINK WITH YOUR HEART
Reconcile your head and your heart

In Chinese medicine the words for "thought" and "love" both have the word "heart" in them. In Japanese tradition there are two words for the heart, one for the physical organ and another for the "mind of the heart". Modern research[23] is proving the wisdom of these ancient traditions and showing that when it comes to making decisions, harnessing the power of your emotions is crucial.

Your heart is your internal guide and we would all feel happier and more fulfilled if we thought not just with our heads but also with our hearts. Today's ritual is a reminder to always check in with your emotions every time you make a decision. Listen to what your mind is saying and take note of all the rational arguments, but then give yourself a few quiet moments alone to hear the voice of your heart. **Ritualize** by writing down what comes to you from your heart. Let the words flow. Use sentences like, "I have a feeling that ..." or "I sense ..." or "My heart is telling me...".

Remember, both your thoughts and your feelings can be wrong. The idea behind this ritual is to help you reconcile your head with your heart by giving your feelings as much consideration as your thoughts. The two do not need to be mutually exclusive. You are in charge of both your thoughts and your feelings, and by focusing on your values and what matters most to you, you can find ways to make them work together.

23 www.elitedaily.com/life/scientifically-think-heart-not-brain/917698

TALKING TO YOUR HEART RITUAL
#295: CONNECT WITH YOURSELF
You are not what you feel

The previous rituals have encouraged you to listen to what your heart says and now it is time for you to speak and connect to your heart. To strengthen your heart connection you have to acknowledge, understand and express your emotions. Your heart is an organ of feeling. If it can't feel it may be beating, but it is not alive. As we get older a lot of us suppress our emotions, in particular the messy and challenging ones, but every emotion we have is there to teach us something and even if we don't understand why we are feeling a certain way, just paying attention to that feeling and acknowledging it can increase our emotional intelligence.[24]

Your ritual today encourages you to notice negative feelings and put your hand on your heart to acknowledge you hear what it is saying. **Ritualize** by saying out loud, "I am not angry (or sad or fearful, etc.), I am *feeling* angry (or sad or fearful, etc.)". Remind yourself that feeling something does not define you. Emotions do not own you. They can't make you do anything negative or destructive. You are in control of them. They are just passing through. So feel them; learn from them;

then move on with gratitude for the lessons and healing wisdom all your emotions bring.

24 Daniel Goleman, *Emotional Intelligence: Why it matters more than IQ*, Bantam, 2006
25 https://mic.com/articles/103490/why-we-should-all-be-reading-more-poetry#.t2F4EYG5g
https://www.sciencedirect.com/science/article/abs/pii/S0197455610001140
https://poetrytherapy.org/index.php/journal-of-poetry-therapy/

TALKING TO YOUR HEART RITUAL
#296: LOVE SCRIPTS DAY 1

Meditate on words written for your heart

Your heart needs to feel. If you routinely stifle your feelings, your heart will suffer and your life will lack colour. Poetry is the language of feeling. It allows you to experience both positive and negative emotions. Art in all its forms can open hearts, but poetry in particular is believed to have great cathartic benefits. Indeed, research[25] has shown that regularly reading poetry can encourage you to self-reflect and boosts mood.

Incorporating more poetry into your life will strengthen your heart connection. Most of us stopped reading poetry when we left school and consider it an acquired taste. Today's ritual hopes to bring some of the joy of pondering the deeper meaning of a few lines of immortal poetry back into your life. **Ritualize** by reciting the words and connecting to their meaning not with your mind but with your heart. Indeed, you may find some of the words can't be interpreted logically and can only be understood by your heart.

Your ritual poetry appreciation lines for today are:

> *"To see a world in a grain of sand*
> *And a heaven in a wild flower*
> *Hold infinity in the palm of your hand*
> *And eternity in an hour."*
>
> WILLIAM BLAKE

Memorize the words if you can. Research the poem and if you find an opportunity to quote or discuss its meaning in a conversation with others (or yourself) during the day, feel free to do so. Perhaps this ritual will inspire you to seek out poetry to appreciate on a regular basis. But whether it does or not, it will give you pause for thought and hopefully fill your heart with newfound insights, deeper meaning and joy. See the world as a poet would – with your heart rather than your eyes.

TALKING TO YOUR HEART RITUAL
#297: LOVE SCRIPTS DAY 2

Have the courage to feel

Your ritual today – and for the next three days – follows exactly the same guidelines as yesterday, but with different poetry scripts to ponder.
Let your heart rather than your mind interpret the meaning that feels right for you. There is no right or wrong interpretation with poetry. What matters is what the words inspire in you. Whatever speaks to you personally is what is important here.

For the next few days of rituals after you have thought about the lines of poetry given – and perhaps even memorized them – stand up, take a few breaths and then **ritualize** by saying them out loud with as much expression as you can. Speak clearly, projecting your voice as if you were speaking to an audience. Let your voice tell a story.

> *" Do not stand at my grave and weep*
> *I am not there. I do not sleep.*
> *I am a thousand winds that blow. "*
>
> MARY FRYE

If you feel joy and inspiration reading these words, celebrate that. If you feel sadness or other emotions, don't be afraid. Have the courage to feel them. Crying is cathartic.[26] If you are concerned you will feel overwhelmed or blown away by your emotions once you open yourself up to them, remind yourself that you and you alone are in control of them. Just because you feel an emotion, it doesn't mean you are that emotion.

A lot of us try to protect our hearts from painful feelings, but your heart is meant to feel not just happiness but a wide range of emotions, including

26 https://psychcentral.com/blog/
7-good-reasons-to-cry-the-healing-
property-of-tears/
www.researchgate.net/
publication/230794248_When_is_
Crying_Cathartic_An_International_Study

sadness. Think of your heart as a muscle, the more you use it the fitter and more intelligent it gets. A broken heart is not a weakened heart but a heart that can heal and regenerate stronger, wiser and more powerful than before.

TALKING TO YOUR HEART RITUAL
#298: LOVE SCRIPTS DAY 3

Poetry can tell the story of your heart

Simply contemplating this question can bring you closer to your heart. **Ritualize** by saying it out loud with as much expression as you can.

"Tell me, what is it you plan to do with your one wild and precious life?"
MARY OLIVER

TALKING TO YOUR HEART RITUAL
#299: LOVE SCRIPTS DAY 4

Welcome poetry into your heart and your life

Do these words speak to your heart? **Ritualize** by saying them out loud with as much expression as you can.

"Did you waste the day, or lose it, was it well or sorely spent? Did you leave a trail of kindness or a scar of discontent?"
EDGAR GUEST

HEART RITUALS

TALKING TO YOUR HEART RITUAL
#300: LOVE SCRIPTS DAY 5

Let poetry into your heart so it can empower your life

You have a right to be here on this beautiful planet living a fulfilling and meaningful life. **Ritualize** by saying the words out loud with as much expression as you can.

> *"Go placidly amid the noise and haste and remember what peace there may be in silence…You are a child of the universe, no less than the trees and the stars; you have a right to be here. And whether or not it is clear to you, no doubt the universe is unfolding as it should."*
>
> MAX EHRMANN

TALKING TO YOUR HEART RITUAL
#301: LOVE SCRIPTS DAY 6

When your heart speaks, listen

Today's ritual - and the rituals for the following two days - follow the same guidelines as the previous few days, but instead of poetry you are going to spend your day pondering the emotional meaning of profound quotes, beginning with this one:

> *"The best and most beautiful things in the world cannot be seen or even touched – they must be felt with the heart."*
>
> HELEN KELLER

THE RITUAL YEARBOOK

As before, **ritualize** by saying the quote out loud and understanding it with your heart rather than your mind. Feel free to do some of your own research around the quote and use it or discuss it in your daily conversations with yourself and others if you can.

TALKING TO YOUR HEART RITUAL
#302: LOVE SCRIPTS DAY 7

The power to see clearly is within your heart

Your heart knows what is right and true for you. Follow it. **Ritualize** by saying the words out loud with as much expression as you can.

"It is only with the heart that one can see rightly; what is essential is invisible to the human eye.

ANTOINE DE SAINT EXUPERY

"A person who is disconnected from their heart is not living."

PAULO COELHO

"How many undervalue the power of simplicity but it is the real key to the heart."

WILLIAM WORDSWORTH

HEART RITUALS

331

TALKING TO YOUR HEART RITUAL
#303: HEART SPEAK

Let inspiring words motivate you to take action

Whenever you feel demotivated or lacking in motivation, talk to your heart and ask it to help you reconnect with your deepest emotions – they are the sacred energy behind all your rituals. They empower you to think and talk less and to act.

Your ritual today is to let the following two quotes sink into your heart and motivate you to live your life with true purpose. **Ritualize** by reading the quotes out loud first and then commit them both to memory.

" Actions speak louder than words."
ABRAHAM LINCOLN

"Change starts with you."
GANDHI

TALKING TO YOUR HEART RITUAL
#304: BRAVEHEART
Protect your heart and keep it strong

Today's ritual will help you understand that you are in charge of protecting your heart whenever it feels vulnerable. You can control your emotions.[27] An open and loving heart is not a heart that is held hostage to your emotions, it's a heart that is honest and feels things deeply but on *your* terms.

Your ritual today is to begin and end your day with a heart protection ritual. Find a piece of paper and draw a heart shape on it. Write your name inside it. Then, draw a protective bubble or force field around the heart, making sure there are no gaps. **Ritualize** by visualizing that this is your own heart with a protective bubble around it. Feel the strength and energy of that force field and know that you - and only you - are in charge of your emotions and you - and only you - can protect your heart. You are only going to allow love and positive things in. Negativity just can't break through the force field. Repeat this ritual whenever you feel your emotions getting the better of you or when you are around people who drain you or make you lose heart.

27 Dickenson, B., 'You're More in Control of Your Emotions Than You Think (Says New Brain Science)', February 17, 2017, retrieved from www.elle.com/life-love/a42863/how-emotions-are-made/ Interdisciplinary Affective Science Laboratory, *Research*, retrieved April 19, 2017, from www.affective-science.org/research.shtml

TALKING TO YOUR HEART RITUAL
#305: TAKE HEART
Set healthy boundaries

An open and loving heart is a truly beautiful thing. But if you don't set personal boundaries with other people and in your relationships, your heart will feel depleted. Unclear personal boundaries cause stress, anger and resentment because you are giving away your personal or heart energy unconsciously. The stress, anger and resentment aren't the real problem here, it's that you have weak and unprotected personal boundaries.[28]

Today's ritual encourages you to check in with your heart whenever you are around people. **Ritualize** by tapping your heart area and asking it how it feels. Imagine your heart is like a car with warning lights. Your feelings are those warning lights and if they are ones of anger, fatigue, resentment or anxiety, this is a warning that your personal boundaries or energy field have been invaded. You are giving your heart energy away and taking on board things that are not yours. It's time for you to know your limits, so make self-care a priority, clearly communicate your boundaries, needs and priorities, and ground yourself by repeating yesterday's Braveheart ritual.

28 https://psychcentral.com/lib/10-way-to-build-and-preserve-better-boundaries/

TALKING TO YOUR HEART RITUAL
#306: PARENT YOURSELF
See yourself through the eyes of a loving carer

For most of us the parent-child relationship is the first bond our heart has. It sets the scene or example for all the rest. If you had a difficult childhood in which you didn't feel your needs were met, this can lead to problems with your sense of self and with forming healthy relationships with others. It's never easy but you don't have to continue to have your heart and life defined by traumas from your past.

Today's ritual requires you to parent yourself. The moment you wake up in the morning, speak to yourself the way a loving parent would with words of gentle but firm encouragement and guidance. **Ritualize** by telling yourself out loud that you are special and deserve to be loved simply for being *you*. Think of all the things you love about yourself and focus on those. Commit to being there 24/7, supporting and encouraging yourself in the way a loving parent unconditionally nurtures and supports their child. If for whatever reason you don't feel worthy, know that you can recover from an ingrained belief that you are unworthy. Throughout the day continue to speak to yourself as if you were your number one fan. Cheer yourself on from the side-lines. Be there for yourself, always.

TALKING TO YOUR HEART RITUAL
#307: WRITING FOR YOUR HEART DAY 1

Record positive things you enjoy about yourself

Study[29] after study has shown the benefits of journalling to boost mood and self-esteem, and your heart loves you to keep a diary, too. Your heart also grows stronger when you cultivate an attitude of gratitude.[30]

Your ritual today is to combine both these personal transformation tools and start a gratitude journal, but not to record the people or things in your life that you are grateful for. In this journal all the entries are about you and what you enjoy most about yourself. Devote five minutes at the end of your day to recording things that you are grateful for about yourself. **Ritualize** by reminding yourself as you write that what you are doing is not self-centred but an act of self-love. Your heart grows stronger every time you note what you love about yourself. Start this evening by writing one paragraph that describes your personality in a positive way. Imagine you were introducing your character in a novel and you are the hero of the story. Forget about spelling and grammar, just let the words flow.

29 www.cambridge.org/core/journals/advances-in-psychiatric-treatment/article/emotional-and-physical-health-benefits-of-expressive-writing/ED2976A61F5DE56B46F07A1CE9EA9F9F
www.forbes.com/sites/nomanazish/2017/12/29/five-legit-reasons-to-keep-a-journal-in-2018/
30 https://greatergood.berkeley.edu/article/item/tips_for_keeping_a_gratitude_journal
https://psychcentral.com/lib/the-health-benefits-of-journaling/

TALKING TO YOUR HEART RITUAL
#308: WRITING FOR YOUR HEART DAY 2

Who are you?

Your ritual today - and for the next five days - is to continue writing good things about yourself for at least five minutes a day. Remember the focus is to consciously write about yourself in an honest but positive way. For this week any self-criticism isn't going to be expressed in writing. **Ritualize** your journalling by understanding why it is so important for you to write about yourself in a glowing way. You are empowering your heart with every positive word you write. Being grateful for who you are is good for you.

It isn't as easy as you think writing relentlessly positive things about yourself, especially if you have got used to minimizing or criticizing yourself, so to help you think along the right lines start by answering the questions below.

★ What makes you unique?
★ How would your best friends describe you?

TALKING TO YOUR HEART RITUAL
#309: WRITING FOR YOUR HEART DAY 3

Getting to know you

Your heart ritual today is to continue to express gratitude for who you are in writing. **Ritualize** by consciously focusing only on what is positive and interesting about yourself as you write. Use the following theme to inspire your self-gratitude journal entry today.

★ Make a list of five of your best character traits.
★ Choose one trait and write about how you express that trait in your daily life.

TALKING TO YOUR HEART RITUAL
#310: WRITING FOR YOUR HEART DAY 4

Congratulate yourself today

Your heart ritual today is to continue to express gratitude for who you are in writing. **Ritualize** by consciously focusing only on what is positive and interesting about yourself as you write. Use the following theme to inspire your self-gratitude journal entry today. It's one you need to do at the end of the day.

★ Write down at least five things about today that you want to compliment yourself about. (They can be as simple as having eaten a healthy breakfast or not having lost your temper.)
★ Explain why these things are so positive – no matter how trivial you feel your self-compliments are.

TALKING TO YOUR HEART RITUAL #311: WRITING FOR YOUR HEART DAY 5

Make yourself proud

Your heart ritual today is to continue to write about yourself in a positive light. **Ritualize** by consciously highlighting only the positive in yourself as you write. Use the following theme to inspire your self-gratitude journal entry today.

★ Write down at least five things you have done at any time of your life that you are proud of. (They don't have to be anything major and can be from any time in your life.)
★ Explain why you are proud of yourself for doing those things.

TALKING TO YOUR HEART RITUAL #312: WRITING FOR YOUR HEART DAY 6

Finding hidden depths

Continuing your week of self-gratitude journalling, your ritual today is to do some research and write your findings in your journal. **Ritualize** by focusing on only recording the positive about yourself. Research the following and write down all the good things you discover about yourself:

★ The (historical and spiritual) meanings of your first name.
★ The good things that happened in the world on the day you were born.
★ Positive traits associated with your sun sign (doesn't matter whether or not you believe in astrology, just have some fun researching here).

TALKING TO YOUR HEART RITUAL #313: WRITING FOR YOUR HEART DAY 7

Show me the love

Complete your week of journalling with this writing ritual. **Ritualize** by reminding yourself of the importance of self-gratitude for your heart to thrive. Every time you are grateful for the person you are, endorphins are released and your self-esteem soars. Answer the following two questions and remember you can only answer in positive terms about yourself:

★ What would the "childhood you" love about who you are today?
★ What did you do for your body, mind and heart this week that showed yourself true love?

TALKING TO YOUR HEART RITUAL #314: SURPRISE YOUR HEART

Fear and love cannot coexist in your heart

Love inspires and nourishes your heart. Fear has the opposite impact. It drains your heart and breeds inaction, negativity and anxiety.

Your ritual today is to fight fear whenever it strikes by doing the unexpected.[31] As soon as you feel fear, instead of letting it take root and fester as it normally would, **ritualize** by taking some deep breaths. As you breathe deeply, promise yourself you will not react to fear in the way you normally would. Instead, you are going to sing "Humpty Dumpty Sat on the Wall". Understand that fear can't cope with you doing something unexpected, so it will be destabilized. Then, connect to your heart and listen to what it is saying.

31 www.nhs.uk/conditions/stress-anxiety-depression/overcoming-fears/

TALKING TO YOUR HEART RITUAL
#315: POSITIVE ANCHORING, PART 1
Create your own luck

Positive anchoring[32] is a therapeutic technique from neurolinguistic programming (NLP) that can inspire feelings of love, trust, safety and security. Like yesterday's ritual, it can help you overcome heart-draining fear.

   This positive anchoring ritual is one you need to perform over the course of two days. It's an incredibly powerful one, so well worth the effort. Today, your ritual is to organize an experience that warms your heart and makes you feel comforted – for example, walking in the woods or spending time with loved ones or pets, or simply reading a beloved book. Then, while you are in that experience, become mindful of your positive emotions and choose a small object from your surroundings. It could be a feather, a leaf, a bookmark, a napkin or anything meaningful to you. **Ritualize** by "impregnating" your emotions onto that object. Then, put that personal object under your pillow when you go to sleep at night.

32 https://chopra.com/articles/from-chaos-to-calm-in-an-instant-how-to-create-a-positive-anchor

TALKING TO YOUR HEART RITUAL
#316: POSITIVE ANCHORING, PART 2

Carry your talisman with you

Today's ritual follows on from yesterday's. When you wake up in the morning, take your personal object from under your pillow, kiss it and put it in your purse, wallet or pocket or a bag you always carry, so it is close to you at all times. It is now your personal talisman or good-luck charm.

Whenever you face a stressful or difficult time today or in coming days, find your talisman and hold it close to your heart. **Ritualize** by feeling once again the warm and loving feelings that you impregnated it with like a perfume. In time, you may not need to physically touch your talisman, just the thought of it will be enough to bring you feelings of calm, security and love.

TALKING TO YOUR HEART RITUAL
#317: BE DIVINE
Unburden your heart

"To err is human, to forgive is divine", is a wise old saying and, like many wise old sayings, it is profoundly true. Only a heart that is at peace has the power to forgive.

Forgiveness is emotionally healing,[33] so your ritual today is all about letting go of personal grudges and bitterness. It links closely to Spirit Ritual 211 (see page 244), but takes things one step further. For this ritual you are going to write or type a short forgiveness letter to someone in your life who has hurt or upset you. **Ritualize** by connecting with the loving compassion in your heart as you write and understand that hurt people often hurt others. Remind yourself that forgiving is not forgetting or being a push over. It is simply letting go of the burden that feelings of resentment place on your heart and putting the focus on your own wellbeing. When you have written or typed your letter, send it to that person using your thoughts and feelings, but do not actually send it.

Your act of forgiveness has lightened your heart. It's time now for you to move forward and fill your heart with love and peace.

33 www.mayoclinic.org/healthy-lifestyle/adult-health/in-depth/forgiveness/art-20047692

TALKING TO YOUR HEART RITUAL
#318: RENEW YOUR HEART
Become a person of heart

Love is not outside you, it's within you. Today's ritual is a powerful one. It will help you connect to the love that has always been and always will be in your heart.

Turn your bath or shower today into a heart ritual by playing beautiful music, lighting candles and using herbal products. Rosehips and lavender are ideal but choose what feels right for you. You may also wish to place a rose quartz crystal close by, as rose quartz is associated with self-love and compassion. Then, when you have washed and pampered yourself in this sacred atmosphere, say out loud the following words and **ritualize** by placing your hand on your heart as you speak, "From this day on I am kind in my thoughts, words and actions to both myself and others. My heart is renewed. I am a person of true heart."

USING YOUR HEART RITUAL
#319: ASK ONE QUESTION
Search for your answer to one simple question

Now that you are performing daily rituals to connect with your heart, it's time for you to really use your heart, starting with feeling gratitude, which is like Prozac for your heart. The problem is, when you feel heavy-hearted, you may not think you have anything to feel grateful for. Thankfully, that doesn't matter. Research by neuroscientists[34] has shown that simply reminding yourself of the importance of gratitude and then expressing it improves emotional resilience.

Your ritual today is not just to search for something you are grateful for, but to express that gratitude in real life with words and actions. Feeling gratitude and not expressing it is like buying someone a present but not giving it to them. **Ritualize** by making a point of thanking someone in person, making eye contact with them as you do so, or sending someone a thank-you note. Remind yourself that even if you don't feel grateful, your heart grows stronger each time you express your gratitude through your actions.

34 Alex Korb, *The Upward Spiral: Using neuroscience to reverse the course of depression, one small action at a time*, New Harbinger, 2015

USING YOUR HEART RITUAL
#320: MAKE MORE DECISIONS
Give your heart more choices

Your heart loves you to make choices, the more the better. This is because making a decision[35] can give you tremendous satisfaction, as well as a feeling of being more in control. Indecision has the opposite effect.

Your ritual today is designed to encourage you to regard all the decisions you make today, and every day, as choices rather than things you "have to do" or believe you "should" or "ought to" do. **Ritualize** by reminding yourself that whenever "shoulds" and "have-tos" decrease your motivation, everything you do in your life is a choice. You may think you don't have a choice but in reality you do. For example, you may feel like you have to work today and this attitude will cause stress. But you can reframe that by telling yourself that you are choosing to go to work today because your career is important to you and so is the salary it pays you. In much the same way, if you exercise because you feel you ought to, you won't get the same mood boost as telling yourself that you are choosing to exercise because you know it is good for your health.

Your heart glows and thrives every time you make choices that are good for you, so see your life as a series of positive choices, not an endless list of "shoulds" and "ought tos".

· · · · · · · · · · ·

35 www.telegraph.co.uk/news/science/science-news/6557517/Pursuit-of-pleasure-drives-human-decisions.html

USING YOUR HEART RITUAL
#321: TRUST EXERCISE

Establish a trusting bond between yourself and your heart

Self-doubt[36] disconnects us from our feelings and our intuition. Our heart has our back but so often we don't believe it when it speaks to us.

If you've ever done one of those team-building exercises when you lean backward and just have to hope your partner will catch you before you hit the floor, you will know how powerful such an exercise is in encouraging bonding. You will also know how disappointing the exercise is when you don't have the trust to let yourself just fall. One of the reasons for this may be that you don't know the person you are working with well enough, or you have issues with trust. Today's ritual asks you to tune into your heart with the aim of understanding both your heart and yourself better, so you can begin to establish an unbreakable bond of trust. Find somewhere quiet. Place your hands over your heart and close your eyes. **Ritualize** by breathing deeply and becoming aware of your heartbeat. When you feel calm and fully present, ask your heart this question: "Do I trust my own heart?"

Then, open your eyes and write down whatever answer comes to you. Study that answer and tune into the feelings your answer inspires. Do you trust the answer? Now think of a time when you did trust or believe in yourself and write down how that felt. Do the same for a time when you lacked self-belief and record how that felt. This ritual is one you may have to repeat until you can clearly identify what it truly feels like when you believe in and trust yourself.

36 https://journals.sagepub.com/doi/abs/10.1111/1467-9280.01456

USING YOUR HEART RITUAL
#322: CHANGE YOUR LOVE DIRECTION

Love with all your heart

Happy and fulfilled people live lives that are motivated by love, but it's not the kind of passionate, heady love we see in the movies. It's sustainable love. Many of us seek love and meaning in short-term infatuations or material things. What we don't realize is that these solutions are always temporary.

Sustainable love[37] requires self-restraint, commitment, courage and honesty. Your ritual today will encourage you to love with all your heart. Read out loud to yourself the following Bible quotation from 1 Corinthians, 13:1, "If I speak in the language of humans and angels but have not love, I am but a noisy gong and a clashing cymbal."

Ritualize by reflecting on what these profound words mean to you as you say them. Think of those times in your life when you have sought highs and thrills from an infatuation or the purchase of a material object and how that high or thrill never lasted. Then, think of the meaningful relationships in your life, those relationships you have where people accept and connect with you honestly. Reflect also on the things in your life that give you a lasting feeling of pride and satisfaction rather than a short-term fix. Notice that sustainable love may feel mundane or hard work in comparison to the excitement of temporary love, but it is where the most reward lies. Ask yourself where you have been directing your energy all your life. Are you a clashing cymbal or is your life given meaning by the enduring love in your heart?

37 Fowers, B., 'Positive illusions about marriage among married and single individuals', *Journal of Family Psychology*, 15, pp. 95-109

USING YOUR HEART RITUAL
#323: PEOPLE POWER
Spend time with people who "get you"

Everyone is their own person, but we are more affected by our relationships than we think.[38] Your ritual today encourages you to become fully aware of just how much your relationships are impacting your emotional wellbeing.

Take a few quiet moments and write down the names of the five people you currently spend the most time with. **Ritualize** this activity by noticing the feelings you have when you write down each name. Is the feeling uplifting or is it draining? If it is draining, your heart is calling out to you to make important changes in your social life. Then, write down the names of five people you feel closest to because they understand you. Study that list because you are looking at people who touch your heart.

Do the two lists match? Are you spending your time with people who support and nourish you or people who drain you? If the latter, it's time to take action.

38 www.hsph.harvard.edu/news/hsph-in-the-news/widowhood-effect-greatest-first-three-months/

USING YOUR HEART RITUAL
#324: AFFIRM YOURSELF WITH A KISS

Begin your journey to greater self-love

Your heart needs meaningful relationships but the most important one you will ever have is the one you have with yourself. You simply can't have lasting, meaningful relationships with others if you don't love yourself first.

However, loving yourself is not as simple or as easy as it sounds. You need to understand, accept and be at peace with who you are and this is why rituals are so powerful because one of the foundation stones of rituals is self-care.[39]

At some point today give yourself a ritual kiss on the back of one of your wrists. **Ritualize** your self-kiss by reminding yourself that this is a symbolic sign that the relationship you have with yourself is crucial for your happiness and success in life. You are telling yourself that you value and nurture yourself with this kiss. You are affirming yourself and becoming your own best friend. If you feel uncomfortable doing this ritual, ask yourself instead if you really are your own best friend. If the answer is "no", then commit to becoming that best friend today.

39 https://digest.bps.org.uk/2013/03/18/rituals-bring-comfort-even-for-non-believers/

USING YOUR HEART RITUAL
#325: THREE SIMPLE WORDS

Know your value

Trying to please other people or live up to their expectations can crush your self-esteem because you are not being true to yourself, or who you really are. Low self-esteem is strongly linked to anxiety, stress and depression. Your heart knows what is true for you. It suffers when your self-worth is so low that you feel the need to prioritize pleasing others.

Today's ritual is a simple one. You are just going to say out loud the following three words: "I am worthy." It is important to say them out loud so that your heart and mind can hear them. **Ritualize** by monitoring how you feel when you say these words. You will probably notice resistance at first. Keep repeating the phrase out loud until your resistance to hearing yourself say this starts to fade and you start to feel you believe it.

USING YOUR HEART RITUAL #326: MARRY ME

Start your day with a proposal

Loving yourself[40] is the foundation stone of a healthy, happy and fulfilled life.

Today's ritual encourages you to start your morning with a self-love visualization ritual. As soon as you wake up imagine you are a being of sparkling light. Think of all the things you are grateful for about yourself. You may want to include your open-mindedness as this ritual is going to ask you to do something right "out there". You are going to marry yourself! **Ritualize** by noticing how odd this idea feels at first and then reflecting on why in fact it makes perfect sense. After all, you are the most important person in your life and you are going to be with yourself for the rest of your life, so you may as well celebrate your love for yourself. Indeed, today's ritual could be the most important one you ever do. Here's a suggestion for a self-love vow you may want to say today and every day when you get up.

" From this day forward, I pledge to wake up every day filled with light and love for myself. I will ask myself what I need and give myself everything I have. I will take care of myself both when times are good and when times are challenging. I will honour myself and always love and honour the wisdom of my own heart."

40 www.newscientist.com/ article/dn19575-love-yourself-to stay-healthy/
www.sciencedirect.com/ science/article/abs/pii/S009265 6610000929?via%3Dihub

USING YOUR HEART RITUAL
#327: DRESS UP
Wear clothes that make your heart smile

What you wear[41] can make you feel more confident, so take time to plan your outfit today. Wear clothes that make you look and feel good. This sounds so simple and obvious, but many of us don't pay really enough attention to the clothes we wear and the impact this has on the way we feel about ourselves. Dressing well is not vanity. It is taking care of yourself.

The colour of your clothes is of particular importance and colour therapists would agree. Black is sophisticated and always a great favourite, but your heart responds more to all the colours of the rainbow. Your ritual today is to ensure your outfit has plenty of colour. **Ritualize** by choosing colours to wear that reflect what is in your heart and what you want to express to the world. To get you thinking along the right lines, here's a guide:

★ Red is for passion and desire
★ Orange is for creativity and success
★ Yellow is for energy, learning and laughter
★ Green is for new beginnings, healing and nature
★ Blue is for communication and inner peace
★ Black is for mystery and what is hidden
★ Purple is for intuition and spiritual growth
★ Pink is for love and compassion
★ White is for innocence, peace and calm

41 www.scientificamerican.com/article/dress-for-success-how-clothes-influence-our-performance/

THE RITUAL YEARBOOK

USING YOUR HEART RITUAL
#328: BE HUMAN
Ditch self-criticism

Your heart suffers if you are self-critical. Self-acceptance[42] is the key to a happy and fulfilled life. Loving yourself with all your heart involves accepting who you are, warts and all.

Today's ritual will help you accept that you have faults, weaknesses and issues. You are not perfect and never will be. If you wear a ring, whenever you hear yourself being self-critical today, **ritualize** by taking that ring and putting it on another finger. If you don't wear a ring, put a rubber band on your wrist and change it from wrist to wrist. Each time you move the ring or rubber band forgive yourself and remind yourself that nobody is perfect and, if you do make a mistake, it's not a big deal unless you keep repeating it. Mistakes are what being human is all about. Mistakes are opportunities to learn and grow. Ask yourself what you can learn from them and then move on. Truly commit to regulating your self-criticism. Notice how the constant changing of ring or rubber band gets really annoying.

Note: If you don't wear a ring or have a rubber band, find something else as your reminder. For example, taking your shoe off and putting it on again or switching your phone on and off each time self-criticism threatens to demotivate you.

· · · · · · · · · · ·

42 www.sciencedaily. com/releases/2014/ 03/140307111016.htm

USING YOUR HEART RITUAL
#329: MAKE IT PERSONAL
Create meaningful connections with others

If you had all the money and opportunities to do anything you wanted and you were the only person on the planet, would you feel motivated to do anything at all? Probably not. The most important relationship is the one we have with ourselves, but we are social creatures. We need other people in our lives to give us a sense of belonging and connection.

Research[43] shows that a lack of meaningful connections with others isn't good news for your heart. Your ritual today puts the spotlight on a key relationship in your life. It can be a partner, family member, friend, colleague or someone who you interact with on a regular basis. All you need to do is think of a personalized way to greet that person that you are going to use every time you see them. For example, you could create a special handshake or unique way to high five or hug this person every time you meet them. **Ritualize** your greeting by making it clear to yourself and this person that this greeting is just between the two of you. If you already have a secret language with a loved one, savour those relationship rituals and understand why they matter so much. Making another person feel special to you using the glue of rituals strengthens the heart connection between you.

43 http://time.com/5212558/loneliness-social-isolation-heart-health/

USING YOUR HEART RITUAL
#330: FROM ME TO YOU
Be open and honest with each other

Rituals help nurture authentic heart connections between people. That's why from today and for the next few days your daily rituals will be centred around ones that research[44] shows can strengthen bonds with loved ones, family and close friends. Do be aware however that although relationships contribute significantly to your happiness, you can still be complete by yourself.

Your relationship-building ritual today is to be completely open with someone who means something to you. A lot of people are in relationships and still feel lonely. Set aside some time to have a meaningful conversation. During that conversation reveal some of your innermost thoughts. Don't hold back. **Ritualize** by being fully present as you share your heart and be fully aware of the meaning of what you are doing. Talk to each other and not about each other. An honest[45] and loving heart is the foundation of every strong relationship.

Note: If you are at a stage in your life when for whatever reason you don't feel particularly close to anyone, these relationship-building rituals also apply to the relationship you have with yourself, which determines the quality of your other relationships. Remember the golden rule: *People don't treat you how you treat them, they treat you how you treat yourself.* Rituals help you take better care of yourself and when you do that all your relationships improve. You can't give others what you don't already have yourself.

· · · · · · · · · · · · ·

44 Dr David Niven, *The 100 Simple Secrets of Great Relationships: What scientists have learned and how you can use it*, HarperCollins, 2006
45 https://journals.sagepub.com/doi/abs/10.1177/0265407586031001

USING YOUR HEART RITUAL #331: LET THEM BE

Accept others without trying to change them

The biggest problem with relationships is loving someone for who we want them to be, rather than who they actually are. Appreciating others during their low points[46] and letting go of the need to criticize or blame plays a huge part in building successful relationships.

If you've ever watched the movie of *Bridget Jones's Diary*, you may recall that tender scene when Darcy tells Bridget he likes her just the way she is and how those few words have a transformative impact on her confidence. Your relationship-building ritual today is to tell someone close to you that you like, love or appreciate them just the way they are. **Ritualize** by reminding yourself that to be fully accepted by someone without wanting them to change for you is the definition of true love and friendship.

---

46 www.mentalhelp.net/blogs/whose-fault-is-it-how-blame-sabotages-relationships/

THE RITUAL YEARBOOK

USING YOUR HEART RITUAL
#332: PAY ATTENTION PLEASE
Learn something new about someone you think you know

At the start of every new relationship you want to know everything you can find out about the other person. But as time passes there is a tendency to be less curious and this inattention[47] can cause relationship problems.

Your ritual today is to make a point of asking someone important in your life at least three different questions. **Ritualize** by listening attentively to what they say and reminding yourself that just as you are forever evolving, so are they. It's impossible to know everything about a person, however much we think we know them. You are keeping your relationships fresh with your questions and the gift of your full attention as you listen to their answers.

47 www.tandfonline. com/doi/abs/10.1080/ 00926239908404010

USING YOUR HEART RITUAL
#333: FIVE SECONDS

Share intimate moments

Emotional intimacy is enhanced by hugging, kissing, touching and eye contact. As time passes in relationships, physical closeness can decrease just as mental intimacy can. Lack of physical closeness and connection can create emotional distance. It's time to kiss[48] and make up.

Today's ritual is to ensure you make time to be physically intimate or close to someone special. Kiss, hug, shake hands or stare with your full attention into the eyes of someone special for a minimum of five seconds. **Ritualize** by counting in your head slowly to five when you kiss, hug, or gaze into their eyes. This may sound odd, but five seconds is the minimum length of time required to establish feelings of greater intimacy. Let this ritual inspire you to be more physically intimate with loved ones every day.

48 S. Kirschenbaum, *The Science of Kissing*, Grand Central, 2011

USING YOUR HEART RITUAL #334: FACE OFF
Send each other selfies

The reason most of us seek out relationships with other people is that we want to know we mean something to someone else. There's no better way to let someone know you are thinking of them and you hope they are thinking about you than to send them a photo of yourself or a selfie. Small thoughtful acts[49] like this are what matter most in relationships.

Your ritual today is to share a photo of yourself with someone special to you. Ideally, this should be someone who you would like to see more of but their work or life commitments mean that time together is limited. **Ritualize** by reminding yourself as you take the photo that it is just for them and *only* them, so don't post this special selfie on social media. It will give them a lift because you matter to them. Ask them to send you a photo in return

49 Appleton, C., *et al.*: 'Partners in passage: The experience of marriage in mid-life', *Journal of Phenomenological Psychology* 32: 41-70 (2001)

USING YOUR HEART RITUAL
#335: EAT WITHOUT SCREENS

Don't take your phone to lunch

Have you ever been to a restaurant or coffee shop and seen a couple silently staring at their phones? Have you ever had a conversation abruptly terminated because the other person stops to answer a call or text? It doesn't make you feel very important does it? Technology is connecting people online but in person it can tear them apart.[50]

Make a point today of switching your phone to silent when you are having a meal or drink with someone. The same applies to all the conversations you have. Don't let your phone pull you away from connecting to the person standing or sitting right in front of you. **Ritualize** by reminding yourself that in this present moment what matters most is human, rather than digital, interaction. There is plenty of time when you are by yourself to answer texts or scroll your newsfeed. When you are with people be *with* people.

50 https://psychcentral.com/blog/4-ways-technology-may-be-ruining-your-relationship/

THE RITUAL YEARBOOK

USING YOUR HEART RITUAL
#336: SHARED EXCITEMENT
Replace the predictable with novelty

When people do exciting things together,[51] they tend to bond faster. At the beginning of relationships, most of us make an effort to do fun, new things together but over time novelty is replaced by the predictable. Time to turn things around.

Make time to do something new or exhilarating with someone in your life who matters to you. Ditch being predictable. If you can't do it today, then schedule a future date. It can be any exciting activity, such as kayaking or bungee-jumping; or an entirely new experience for you both, such as signing up to do voluntary work together; or it can be something you have always wanted to do but never found the time, such as simply lying down to gaze at the stars. **Ritualize** your activity by paying full attention to how novelty energizes your relationship.

51 www.theatlantic.com/health/archive/2014/10/the-importance-of-sharing-experiences/381493/

USING YOUR HEART RITUAL
#337: LIGHT A CANDLE
Bring some magic into everyday interactions

If you lead a hectic and busy life, it can be so easy to take the people who truly matter to you for granted. Pausing for just a few moments to connect with your heart and remind others that they are sacred to you can make all the difference. Research[52] shows that fulfilling relationships grow stronger when there are shared rituals.

Today's ritual draws inspiration from one of the most ancient rituals in the world – lighting a candle to make a moment feel sacred. But this time you are lighting a candle to express to someone how special they are to you. **Ritualize** by thinking about how important the person is to you as you light the candle. Then, take a photo of the candle and send it to them with a message saying they light up your life. In this way you don't just make them feel special, you bring an element of sacredness into your relationship.

52 Dr David Niven, *The 100 Simple Secrets of Great Relationships: What scientists have learned and how you can use it*, Harper Collins, 2006

USING YOUR HEART RITUAL
#338: LOOK ANOTHER WAY
Wait a few seconds before disagreeing with someone

Rituals help you make a sacred commitment to your heart. Ensuring your emotional needs are met becomes a justified priority but, like everything in life, there is a balance. It is important that loving self-care doesn't turn into narcissism.[53]

Although you are important, everything is not always about you. You can't always expect admiration or people to share your views. At some point today when you find yourself disagreeing with someone, wait a few seconds before you reply with your established point of view. Consciously try to put yourself into their mindset. You can also do this ritual when you listen to or read an opinion you disagree with online or via the media. **Ritualize** by reminding yourself that there is some truth in every person's point of view, and understanding this, without necessarily prescribing to it, makes other people respond more positively to you.

Note: Jane Austen's *Pride and Prejudice* is well worth re-reading or watching to reinforce this ritual.

- - - - - - - - - - -

53 www.psychologytoday.com/us/blog/the-pathways-experience/201808/narcissism-the-potus-and-us

USING YOUR HEART RITUAL
#339: ON THE DARK SIDE
Identify the toxic people in your life

Believing that deep down there is always something good to find in other people is a heartfelt way to live. However, there is a small percentage of people to whom this spiritual ideal does not apply. These are people with undiagnosed personality disorders, the most common of which is narcissistic personality disorder or NPD.[54] People with NPD are highly manipulative, self-absorbed and only "loving" when you are useful to them.

Today's ritual is designed to help you identify toxic people in your life. Set aside a few moments to research "narcissistic personality disorder" online and **ritualize** by writing down what you discover about toxic narcissism. Then, apply the information to your personal relationships. Does anyone you know lack empathy but need your constant attention and admiration? Are they "charming" but their actions do not match their words? Are they never there for you but you are always there for them? If you know someone like that, withdraw your emotional investment in them immediately because relationships with toxic people go from bad to worse however much love and energy you pour into them. If you don't know anyone like that, count your blessings but use your newfound awareness of this disorder in the future.

Note: Not all narcissists are flamboyant egotists. Some are covert and hide behind a false mask of humility. If someone jumps into your life and sounds too good to be true, chances are they are toxic. This is all beginning to sound dark but the intention is not to alarm, rather to help you understand you can't do anything to make a relationship with a narcissist mutual. Your heart will thank you for cutting off all future contact with toxic people.

54 Melanie Tonia Evans, *You Can Thrive after Narcissistic Abuse*, Watkins, 2018
www.sciencedaily.com/terms/narcissistic_personality_disorder.htm

USING YOUR HEART RITUAL
#340: MENDING YOUR HEART

Heal and grow stronger from emotional pain

There comes a time in every person's life when they encounter heartbreak of some kind. It could be due to a relationship breaking up, a loved one dying or a disappointment. Whatever it is, pain is felt in your heart and it can sometimes seem like that pain will never end.

Today's ritual acknowledges the importance of expressing your emotions if you are grieving[55] for someone or something. You need a pen and paper and a tomato or a strawberry. The idea is to help you express your pain safely, but at the same time set the intention for opening up space in your heart to heal and move forward.

Find some time when you can be alone and undisturbed. The tomato or strawberry is going to represent your heart. Hold the fruit and cry at it, yell at it or caress it. Whatever you are feeling, express it. Then, **ritualize** by writing the following on your piece of paper, "My heart heals and grows stronger from this experience. I am open to love from within and all around me." Feel empowered as you write. Next, take the fruit and wrap the paper around it. Now bury that paper and fruit somewhere and visualize the fruit decomposing and the earth reclaiming your grief.

55 www.funeralzone.co.uk/blog/5-ways-to-express-your-feelings-when-grieving

USING YOUR HEART RITUAL
#341: A TIME AND A SEASON
The only thing that never changes is change

Today's ritual, like yesterday's, is designed to help you cope with and heal from emotional pain. It is a ritual you can experiment with today or whenever your heart feels heavy. Simply say out loud, "This too shall pass."

Ritualize by focusing on the profound wisdom of these wise words as you say them. There is a time and a season for everyone and everything, including your feelings, and the way you feel right now will change. Nothing stays the same. You will not always feel like this. This doesn't mean you will forget or never feel pain and grief again. The idea that time heals all wounds is a myth. Grief is a journey and that journey is unique for everyone.[56] However, in time your emotional perceptions will shift and your heart will absorb, adapt and evolve.

Remind yourself, too, when performing this ritual that there is nothing wrong with heartbreak. You are a human being with a loving heart, and hearts are meant to feel. We learn and grow from all our emotions. Feeling grief means you are alive. Some people are meant to live on in your heart and not your life.

Note: The best way to shift your perceptions is to take positive action. Rituals are positive actions and the Closing Rituals section of this book will offer ways to help you heal emotional pain.

56 Julia Samuel, *Grief Works: Stories of life, death and surviving*, Penguin, 2017

HEART POWER RITUAL
#342: COLOURING-IN TIME

Tune into your heart

If your heart is filled with healthy self-love, all your actions will be inspired by compassion and kindness. You respect yourself and others respect you in return. Those who don't respond to your loving heart will naturally fade out of your life. There is clarity and inner peace.

Self-love is crucial for a happy and fulfilled life but this doesn't happen naturally. Just as you need to exercise your muscles, you also need to practise the art of self-love and connect with your heart every day. Daily rituals are the perfect way as they are acts of ultimate self-love.

The last four rituals in this Heart section are powerful visual reminders that actions, not thoughts, change your life and nourish your heart because within you is all the happiness, creativity and beauty you will ever need. They draw their inspiration from art itself. For the next four days you will be given a shape rich in deep meaning that only your heart can understand fully. You may want to colour it in as you reflect on that meaning. Colouring elicits a similar relaxed mindset to meditation,[57] so it can help you switch off your thoughts and focus mindfully on the present moment. If you don't want to colour in, tracing or drawing the shape on a blank piece of paper can have the same therapeutic effect.

Before you begin, **ritualize** the present moment by breathing slowly and deeply and focusing all your creative energy on the shape. Nothing can boost the energy of self-love more than tapping into your creativity.

To follow are a few pointers about the symbolic meaning of each shape and you can research online about their symbolism, but don't overload yourself with facts. Simply gaze at the shapes, absorb their energy, colour them in or draw them yourself. Lose yourself in them and, as you do, hear the clear, calm

57 www.medicaldaily.com/therapeutic-science-adult-coloring-books-how-childhood-pastime-helps-adults-356280

voice of your heart speaking to you through them. What creativity have they inspired in your heart? What does your heart want you to do?

SHAPE SHIFTING:
THE YIN-YANG SYMBOL

The yin-yang is an ancient Chinese symbol[58] depicting the existence of opposites in the universe. The belief is that we all contain *yin* (the feminine, shadows, mystery) and *yang* (the masculine, brightness, growth) within our hearts and lives, and the secret to happiness is to find a balance between the two.

58 Robert Wang, *Yin Yang: The way of heaven and earth in Chinese culture*, Cambridge University Press, 2012

HEART POWER RITUAL
#343: WALKING THE LABYRINTH

Find your own way

A labyrinth is not to be confused with a maze. You won't find dead ends or false tracks as you would in a maze. There is only one path to the centre and back out and this path is called the one line or unicursal. Having said that, the path does twist and turn and sometimes seem to head in the opposite direction you hope to go in, before reaching the centre.

You are probably thinking that a labyrinth sounds a lot like the journey through life from birth to death and you would be right there. It has tremendous symbolic power and not surprisingly is a spiritual symbol found in many ancient cultures. The term has its origins in ancient Greece. Walking the labyrinth was a popular ritual and labyrinths built for that purpose can be found all over the world in churches and places of worship. The idea is to walk the labyrinth with slow, intentional steps in absolute quiet. As you walk, you bring to mind a question or a prayer. Then, when you reach the centre, you listen for an answer and take that insight away with you back into your everyday life. On your way in and out you will find yourself nearing the centre and then heading away from it. You may encounter other people briefly on parts of your journey as they silently walk their own path, symbolizing the many twists and turns and encounters of real life.

Nowadays the image of a labyrinth remains one of great power. That's why your ritual today is to set aside some time to focus your intention on the labyrinth drawing (*see* page 372). Trace the journey to the centre, which represents your heart. When you reach the centre, what question do you want to ask your heart? **Ritualize** by using your finger to trace your journey. If you feel inspired you may wish to colour in the various different paths to your heart. All the time, focus on the journey to the centre of your heart and what this inspires in you.

Note: If you would like to find a labyrinth to walk physically, check out https://labyrinthlocator.com where you can locate labyrinths all over the world. You may also like to create your own labyrinth using cardboard, pens and paper, or set one up with rocks, stones and sand in your garden.[59]

59 Lauren Artress, *Walking a Sacred Path: Rediscovering the labyrinth as a spiritual practice*, Riverhead, 2006

THE RITUAL YEARBOOK

HEART POWER RITUAL
#344: MANDALAS FOR YOUR HEART

Rediscovering wholeness from within

The word "mandala" simply means "circle". The circle is a universal symbol of wholeness and completeness, and a mandala drawing represents our relationship with infinity, within and beyond ourselves. Many ancient spiritual traditions used the mandala for meditation and inner guidance. It is believed to have originated from the Hindu tradition, but is most often associated with Buddhism. Today it is used as a personal transformation and growth tool by many therapists. The insights that emerge from working with it are believed to come directly from your heart or authentic self.

Typically, a mandala is a colourful design that shows the never-ending potential of both your life and the universe you are a part of. It is a pictorial representation of the journey of your life and what path you should be on. The design should be as appealing to you as possible, so that it completely absorbs your creative focus and allows you to gain insight from within.

Your ritual today is to focus on and draw, write or colour in the mandala drawing (*see* page 374) or, better still, create your own mandala. The internet has lots of inspiration for mandala designs. **Ritualize** by setting your intention to connect with the intuitive wisdom of your heart and then concentrate only on the mandala and the unique design you are creating within it. If your mind wanders (and it will) simply bring your focus back to the drawing. Take deep breaths and relax. Allow the mandala and the intention you are imprinting in it to absorb your attention entirely. Lose yourself in it and notice the intuitive feelings and clarity your heart reveals to you. Notice every detail about it. Feel the mandala come alive with your heartfelt intention.

Note:[60] Creating your own unique mandala allows you to choose the meaning behind its design. As you draw and colour it in, use whatever shapes, colours, words and symbols feel intuitively right to you. Let the drawing, writing and colouring connect you to the creative energy of love. Connect with your heart's wisdom and enjoy the task. Don't judge or criticize what you produce, create it with lightness of heart and feel it come alive. When you have finished your mandala, put it somewhere where you can see it and be inspired by it every day.

60 Susanne Fincher, *The Mandala Workbook: A creative guide for self-exploration, balance and wellbeing,* Shambhala, 2009

HEART RITUAL
#345: PURE OF HEART

Know the power of your own heart

"We shall not cease from exploration
And the end of all our exploring
Will be to arrive where we started
And know the place for the first time."

T. S. ELLIOT

Every ritual in this section of the book has been designed not just to help you understand and reconnect with your heart on a daily basis, but also to protect, honour and celebrate it. Now that you have greater insight into its power[61] to guide and inspire your life, today's ritual encourages you to think about your heart in the way an artist would. Choose colours that you intuitively feel express what is inside your own heart. If you would like some guidelines on colours, see Ritual 327 on page 354 but, remember, it's what each colour means to you that matters the most.

You can colour in the heart symbol on the next page or draw your own heart shape on a blank piece of paper and colour it in. **Ritualize** by losing yourself in this creative task, feeling your heart come alive as you colour in the shape. Ponder why you have chosen specific colours – you don't have to stick to just one, so express yourself.

Remember, it's impossible to feel happy and at peace all the time. This life can be messy, but just as an artist can create a picture that is both beautiful and conflicted, you can also create a picture of your heart that is beautiful to look at.

61 Baptist de Pape, *The Power of the Heart*, Schuster, 2014

LOOKING FORWARD

If you haven't worked through all the other sections of this book yet, please do so now before moving on with your final rituals. This is because they are Closing rites, designed to help you embrace the end of your ritual year. Nothing is forever but endings can be profoundly beautiful when they are ritualized. Rituals help you to let go of the past and things that are no longer meant for you with grace, and open your heart to new beginnings.

THE RITUAL YEARBOOK

Closing RITUALS

Bringing your sacred year to a conclusion

You may have noticed that for each day of your ritual year the word **ritualize** has been highlighted to emphasize the importance of assigning personal meaning to each ritual. If you don't ascribe personal meaning to a ritual, it is simply something you do, an action or a mindless habit. It's the personal meaning that gives daily rituals power to change your life for the better because that meaning connects you to your own infinite potential as well as something higher or greater than yourself. You won't find the word ritualize highlighted anymore in this final section, as hopefully the point has been made. You don't need reminding that every action, everything you do, truly has sacred potential.

346-365

Many of us don't like goodbyes or endings, but this section will show you how to ritualize and celebrate them. Whether it be the passing of the year, the end of a relationship, stage or time, the loss of a loved one or even coming to terms with the fact that your own life must one day end, rituals help you understand that every ending offers the opportunity for a new beginning. They also help you understand that whenever bad or challenging things happen or we feel we have lost something we value, these things don't happen to us, they happen *for* us. Everything that happens to us helps us learn and grow and evolve into a better version of ourselves.

Whether you believe in destiny or not, rituals can help you embrace change, let go of the past, live joyfully in the present and look forward to a future where great and beautiful things await.

FINAL THOUGHTS

Remember, these Closing rituals should only be performed in the final three weeks of your sacred year, as they consolidate material from all the previous rituals. Be aware that the first three rituals are for days of the year on which you typically celebrate endings or look forward to new beginnings - your birthday, an anniversary and holidays - but they can also be performed on any day of the year, if you so choose. Rituals 349 to 360 should be done in daylight, while 361 to 365 are best in the evening when darkness falls and your day draws to a close.

CLOSING RITUAL
#346: HAPPY DAYS

Celebrate the gifts every year brings you

You may have got to the age and stage in your life when you are happy to let your birthday pass without a fuss, or you may still make a point of celebrating the day you were born. Whatever the case, your ritual today will transform your attitude toward your birthday.

You will need a pack of small candles for this ritual. Each candle represents a decade of your life, so pick out the number of candles you need for that. If you are in the first year of a new decade that counts as a candle – for example, if you are 41 you need five candles. Then, light each candle for each decade you have been alive and reflect on that decade as you light each candle, before moving onto the next. If you have photos or memories from that decade, use the time to review them. Feel gratitude and love for the memories and gifts each decade of your life has brought you. Celebrate the person you were and are.

When it comes to the decade you are currently in, light that candle with feelings of excitement and joy for what lies ahead. Feel deep gratitude[1] for the gift of every birthday you have ever had and the ones you have yet to come. Then, think of a small, inexpensive gift you want to buy yourself. Write down what that gift is. In the next few days purchase it, wrap it and put it aside for opening on your actual birthday.

You will love it because it is a gift to you chosen by your authentic self.

1 www.psychologytoday.com/gb/blog/mindful-anger/201807/science-proves-gratitude-is-key-well-being

CLOSING RITUAL
#347: MAKE TODAY COUNT

Celebrate and be there for yourself every day

Today's ritual can be performed on an anniversary, but it is not exclusive to anniversaries or special days. It is a simple reminder that each day is a miracle. Each day is a fresh start and you are born again. Today is not ordinary, it is utterly unique and can never ever be repeated. When you wake up this morning, look at yourself in the mirror, smile and say out loud: "Is today going to be the best day of my life?"

Asking yourself this question[2] will energize your brain and change your perspective about the day ahead. Remember, questions are always more motivating than answers. Asking yourself this helps you understand that the day ahead is what you make of it. You will look for ways to live to the fullest.

If your motivation to make your day count ebbs, take inspiration from Steve Jobs. When I was 17, I read a quote that went something like, "If you live each day as if it were your last, someday you'll most certainly be right." Jobs went on to state that this really made an impression on him and for the rest of his life he would look in the mirror every morning and ask himself if today was the last day of the rest of his life, would he be doing what he was about to do today. If the answer was "no" for too many days in a row, Jobs knew he had to change something.

2 Senay, I., *et al.*: 'Motivating goal directed behaviour through introspective self-talk: The role of the interrogative form of a simple future tense', *Psychological Science*, April 2010; 21 (4), pp. 499–504

CLOSING RITUAL #348: DISAPPEAR

Treat yourself to time out

Your ritual today is to plan a day when you can quite literally disappear, break from your usual routine and spend time alone. There is tremendous benefit[3] to regular time out by yourself. If an entire day just isn't feasible, plan for a few hours or even an hour when you aren't accountable to anyone or anything. Mark that day or time in your diary. Tell people you will be away then and can't be reached until the time you say you will arrive back. Stick to that schedule.

People who have your best interests at heart will understand your need to do things alone. Just make sure what you do during your time-out ritual is something that enriches you in a positive way. It might be as simple as a spa day or a trip to the cinema by yourself. It doesn't matter what it is. The important thing is during that time you break your routine and treat yourself to the pleasure of your own company, so you can return to your life refreshed and re-energized.

Note: Holidays are ideal times to reinforce the significance and meaning of rituals in our lives. If you are planning an extended holiday, you may want to use it as an opportunity to revisit some of the Power rituals in this book. If you have a day off, seize the opportunity to reinforce the 21 Foundation rituals.

---

3 www.forbes.com/sites/amymorin/2017/08/05/7-science-backed-reasons-you-should-spend-more-time-alone/

CLOSING RITUAL
#349: SAIL AWAY

Shed past identities with grace and gratitude

Experts[4] believe it is important to say a formal goodbye when we leave things behind that were once central to our identity, for example when we leave a job or university, or a significant relationship ends.

The process of shedding roles can be messy and sometimes take years to come to terms with. One of the reasons it can take so long is that we don't have rituals in place to help us let go and release the past with grace, and look forward to the future with hope rather than fear. For this ritual, you need to head outside and find a leaf or a twig. Imagine that the leaf or twig is your past identity. Then, take it to a nearby stream or river or any source of running water, mindfully drop it in and watch it - and your past self - drift away.

4 https://exploringyourmind.com/everything-must-farewell-ritual/

CLOSING RITUAL
#350: UNDER AND OVER
See things a different way

Yesterday's ritual encouraged you to let go. This isn't always easy if there are unresolved tensions and feelings such as regret, anger or guilt. This is especially the case when we don't feel we know why a relationship ended. We can also have unresolved feelings when senseless things like accidents or natural disasters happen. There seems to be no meaning or purpose behind it all.

Rituals can help us find inner peace. Studies[5] also show that metaphors can bring understanding when other explanations fail. Today's ritual combines the power of ritual with the power of a profound metaphor. Think of something in your life that you struggle to come to terms with. (If you can't think of anything, the news is awash with stories to make your heart feel heavy.) Close your eyes and breathe deeply and slowly. When you feel calm and centred, visualize a beautiful tapestry. (If you need inspiration search online for some famous tapestries.) Then, imagine the underside of the tapestry. It will be a chaos of messy knots and loose ends. Looking at that underside you would have absolutely no idea that it could create the beautiful image on the topside. Let this metaphor inspire you every time your life feels senseless. It can remind you that perhaps – just perhaps – there is a bigger picture and you can find meaning in the chaos.

---

5 https://psychcentral.com/news/2015/03/13/metaphors-help-us-understand-others-thoughts-and-feelings/82281.html

CLOSING RITUAL
#351: VIOLET IS THE NAME

Let the colour purple be your guide

According to colour therapy[6] violet and all shades of purple are the colours most strongly associated with connecting to the highest and best form of yourself. Violet is believed to help people forgive themselves and others, and let go of feelings of sadness, guilt and regret.

Your ritual today is to open your eyes and your heart to the colour purple. If you have purple items of clothing or jewellery, wear them. Light purple candles. Type in a purple font or use purple pens. Rub a couple of drops of violet essential oil on your hands. Print out a picture of the violet-coloured lotus, which is a symbol for the crown chakra or energy centre in Hindu and yogic traditions, and put it on your wall or make the lotus your screen saver. (The crown chakra is located at the top of your head and is associated with renewal and transcendence.)

It doesn't matter how you decide to use purple today, find a way to incorporate more of this healing colour into your life and allow purple visual reminders to open up a connection within your heart to the wise and peaceful part of yourself. Take a few moments to visualize purple light radiating from the top of your head and, as you do, set your intention to release negativity and heal any open emotional wounds.

From now on let any sighting of the colour purple be a spiritual calling card reminding you of the importance of forgiveness, letting go and connecting to your own inner beauty.

6 https://onlinelibrary.wiley.com/doi/abs/10.1002/col.20597

CLOSING RITUAL
#352: BE CERTAIN

Say "Amen" when you complete a task

Today's ritual encourages you to let go with grace and certainty. In the Christian tradition the word "Amen" is usually spoken after a prayer or creed. In Pagan tradition, people typically say "so mote it be" after a spell. Other religions and traditions have similar words that they typically use to express ratification, agreement and closure.[7]

"Amen" is derived from a Hebrew word meaning "truth" or "certainty". Your ritual today is to say out loud "Amen" or "so mote it be", or to choose any word or phrase that signifies satisfied agreement, when you complete each one of your daily rituals. Say it out loud with joyous enthusiasm or say it with a silent but determined whisper. Choose what feels right to you. You may also wish to start saying it when you complete everyday tasks, like washing up or cleaning the shower.

Notice how powerful words of closure bring an element of the sacred into your daily life and a sense of completion and satisfaction that might have been missing before.

7 www.dictionary.com/e/amen/

CLOSING RITUAL
#353: ASK MORE QUESTIONS

Great answers are inspired by great questions

Asking questions rather than finding answers is often the catalyst for letting go of life experiences that no longer serve or fulfil you. Today's ritual encourages you to keep your mind as curious as possible. Set aside a few minutes and write down your answers to the following "big", soul-searching questions:

★ What do I believe in? Why do I believe in it?
★ Why am I here?
★ Why is there suffering in the world?

Big questions force you to consider why you do what you do and why you choose to do it. Never stop asking yourself questions that seem impossible to answer, because the power is in the question and not the answer. Think of it this way. A woman screams in pain when she gives birth to a baby. We understand why she is in pain, so we accept her screaming. Imagine if we knew why there was suffering. We would probably accept suffering as normal and ask no more questions. We would live in a world without empathy and compassion.

In the words of Tony Robbins,[8] "If you want big answers, ask yourself big questions." Big questions prompt you to come up with your own big answers – answers that can change your life.

8 Anthony Robbins, *Awaken the Giant Within*, Simon & Schuster, 2001

CLOSING RITUAL #354: IS THIS TRUE?

Purge negative thinking

Your ritual today will help you let go of negative thinking for good. Sometimes a negative thought or belief can take firm hold. It ruminates in our heads and our hearts. We can't resolve it and lose focus and self-belief. Whenever you catch yourself thinking negatively, stop what you are doing. Sit down and ask yourself this one question, "Is what I am now thinking true?"

Write down the answer that immediately comes to mind and ensure it explains how you know it to be true. Write about how you typically react when you have this negative thought. In other words, what does it make you do? Finish by writing about how your life would be right now if you didn't have this negative thought.[9]

Now read through your answer and try to identify how your thoughts about someone or something are the cause of your pain, rather than the people and events themselves. In short, *they* are not stopping you letting go and moving forward with your life, it's your thinking that is. And what's the best way to counteract negative thinking? Positive action using the power of daily rituals, of course!

Note: Today is a good day to simply read the Mind section of this book.

---

9 This ritual is inspired by 'The Work', recommended in Byron Katie's *Loving What Is: Four questions that can change your life*, Rider, 2002

CLOSING RITUAL
#355: EXIT STRATEGIES

Cast away the old to make room for the new

Endings tend to be messy if we don't mark them in our lives properly with rituals. Yet typically we have no problem going to bed at night and letting the day go. Your ritual today is to apply a similar graceful and natural exit strategy to all areas in your life, particularly any that are holding you back or weighing you down with emotional baggage. This could be a relationship, a job or simply letting a phase in your life go. Light a candle and follow these steps:

★ Appreciate and feel gratitude for what is ending, even if you have conflicting emotions about it.
★ Ask what the ending has taught you about yourself or your life.
★ Let go of what is holding you back in the same way you let go of each day when it ends.
★ Open yourself up to the gifts of the future with your sacred awareness that every exit is also a new entry. Visualize yourself walking through a black door and closing it behind you.
★ Blow out your candle and imagine yourself walking toward another door – a brightly coloured one – and opening it with excitement to see what lies beyond.

THE RITUAL YEARBOOK

CLOSING RITUAL
#356: THE POWER OF WORDS
Consciously shift your language

Sometimes it is not what we do but what we say that holds us back and stops us letting go of negativity. Words flow out of our mouths every single day and we don't often pay much attention to them, but experts[10] believe language – like actions – can change your brain. It seems that the constant repetition of words can influence the expression of genes that govern your health and wellbeing.

Your ritual today encourages you to let go of negative words. Before you are about to say a swear word or any negative word, clap your hands or click your fingers. Think of an alternative, positive word that can motivate you instead and consciously use that. Remind yourself how a subtle shift in language can help you release negativity and positively impact your emotions. Encourage yourself to use more power words, like "peace" and "love". Congratulate yourself every time you hear yourself saying power words, because each time you use them you are walking away from negativity toward a brighter and happier future.

Note: Today is a good day to simply read the Success section of this book.

10 Dr Andrew Newberg, *Words Can Change Your Brain*, Avery, 2012

CLOSING RITUAL
#357: ANYWHERE CLEAN

Pick up litter

Cleaning is a proven[11] stress reliever. It can also be a potent ritual to help you let go of what is holding you back, not just physically but emotionally. If you've ever done a spring-clean of your living area, you will know how cathartic this feels. But spring-cleaning doesn't have to be limited to the season or to your home. Whatever time of the year it is for you, decluttering can lighten your heart and your life, but today you are going to take tidying up to the next level.

Your ritual today is to pick up at least three pieces of litter and put them in a bin. Obviously make sure the litter is safe to pick up and afterwards be sure to wash your hands. Monitor how doing this makes you feel. At first you may notice a resistance or an attitude of "this is not my responsibility", but try to consciously override that. Think of the litter as emotional debris. It's time to clean up. Not only will this help you resolve emotional tension, it will also serve the public good. Indeed, today's ritual may even inspire you to commit to picking up litter on a regular basis or perhaps you may want to join a public litter-picking group for a park or a beach. Research[12] shows that this isn't a pointless exercise. It gives litter pickers a sense of purpose and protects the environment.

Note: Today is a good day to simply read the Foundation section of this book.

11 www.prevention.com/health/mental-health/a26010541/marie-kondo-tidying-up-health-benefits/
12 www.unenvironment.org/news-and-stories/story/picking-litter-pointless-exercise-or-powerful-tool-battle-beat-plastic
13 www.mentalhealth.org.uk/publications/doing-good-does-you-good

CLOSING RITUAL
#358: BE OF SERVICE
Reach out to help others today

One of the best ways forward when things are ending in your life and you feel lost or directionless is to offer your services to others less fortunate than you. This may feel counterintuitive and the very last thing you want to do, but supporting others takes you right out of your head, straight to your heart and spirit.

Research[13] supports findings that sometimes it truly is better to give than to receive. Your ritual today is to find a way you can help someone less fortunate than you. This could be by buying a homeless person a cup of tea, volunteering in a soup kitchen, joining a volunteer helpline or simply by visiting an elderly person in your neighbourhood who lives alone to see if they need any help. It doesn't matter what you do as long as you reach out to someone going through a harder time than you. If you are feeling low, join a support group of other people who are also feeling low and listen to their stories so you can offer your advice. Chances are you will find someone who has been through far worse than you. In this way your service to others will put any feelings of negativity or loss you have in perspective and help promote feelings of gratitude for the things in your life that you take for granted.

If you feel that helping others isn't worth the effort because the world is an unfair place and you will not make a difference, learn this famous story by heart, so you can quote and share it with others.

An elderly man was walking along the beach at sunset when he noticed a young boy close to the water. The boy kept bending down and picking up things and throwing them into the sea. He walked closer and noticed that the boy was picking up starfish that had been washed up on the beach and were dying from lack of oxygen, and

was throwing them back into the waves. The man told the child to stop. He explained that it was impossible to save all the starfish and this kind of thing was happening on hundreds of beaches all along the coast. "You can't possibly make a difference" he explained. The boy smiled, bent down and picked up another starfish, and as he threw it back into the sea, he replied, "Made a difference to that one."

THE RITUAL YEARBOOK

CLOSING RITUAL
#359: MEANINGFUL GOODBYES

Infuse your farewells with meaning

Every day we find ourselves saying goodbye to the people in our lives, as they go about their business. We barely give it a second thought. It could be a quick hug but more likely it is a casual, "See you later", a short and simple "Bye" or a nod of the head. Or we could do nothing at all as we rush through our busy lives. Without sounding morbid there is no guarantee that you will see someone again when you say goodbye to them. Of course, the chances that you will are overwhelming but, just for today, be conscious of how you say goodbye to everyone you interact with, not just those you meet in person but those you message online as well.

Your ritual today is to pay close attention to all your goodbyes[14] and infuse them with sacred meaning. If you can, touch the person physically by shaking their hand or giving them a hug or a kiss, to remind them how special they are to you. Also think of meaningful ways to say goodbye when you are messaging or texting. If you prefer to stick to a simple "Bye", be sure to take a few moments to send loving energy to the departing person. Make all your goodbyes count.

14 www.psychologytoday.com/gb/blog/transitions-through-life/201804/say-goodbye-create-ritual

CLOSING RITUAL
#360: OVER THE SHOULDER

Moving through your grief

Your final daytime closing ritual focuses on the hardest emotion to let go of all – grief. It is a very painful and life-changing experience and, contrary to what many people think, you don't ever get over the loss of someone close. Time does *not* completely heal or make you no longer miss them. You find ways to adapt to the loss and keep the spirit of that person alive within you.

Rituals have been shown[15] to help alleviate grief following the loss of a loved one, both in the immediate aftermath as well as in the days, months and years afterwards. The same research also showed that it didn't matter what the ritual was as long as it was personal and had meaning. Loss of control is a common feeling when you are grieving and rituals can help bring back a sense of control and calm.

You need salt to perform this powerful closing ritual. Salt has been considered lucky or protective for centuries. Sprinkle some into your hand. Look at the salt and think of someone you have loved and lost. Then, head outside and find a place where you can throw the salt over your left shoulder.[16] As you throw it, tell yourself that this age-old superstition isn't a cure-all, but it will help you ward off the pain of grief and bring you and your loved one in spirit some comfort and strength.

· · · · · · · · · · · · ·

15 https://dash.harvard.edu/bitstream/handle/1/10683152/norton%20gino_rituals-and-grief.pdf?sequence=1
16 www.express.co.uk/life-style/science-technology/433862/Knocking-on-wood-and-throwing-salt-over-your-shoulder-can-reverse-bad-luck-says-study

·
·
·
·

THE RITUAL YEARBOOK

CLOSING RITUAL
#361: THANKS FOR THE LIGHT
Gaze at the beauty of the setting sun

There is nothing more breath-taking than watching the sun set. It can open up a deep connection with nature and also remind you that endings are natural and can be truly beautiful. Wherever you live in the world and whatever your horizon is, you can create a sunset ritual. Simply find a place where you can sit and gaze at the sun going down. Focus on your breathing and feel gratitude for your life on earth.

If possible, watch the remains of the day slip away in total silence and only speak when the sun has gone down. Close your ritual with a smile that celebrates your certainty that the sun will rise again tomorrow. If you haven't got time today, schedule another evening for this ritual and seek out beautiful pictures of the setting sun to fill you with awe.

Note: Today is a good day to simply read the Body section of this book.

CLOSING RITUAL
#362: GRACEFUL ENDINGS
Light at the end of your day

Endings, whether it be a relationship, a job, or a phase in your life, are a perfectly natural and essential part of life, just as night is a natural and essential end to the day. The problem is many of us struggle to cope with endings.

Today's ritual will reinforce the point that endings are natural new beginnings. At the end of your day, light a candle and burn a little sage if you have some. Sage is the herb associated with wisdom and graceful endings. Get a pen and paper and write down what you appreciated about your day. As you write, remind yourself that you will never ever see today again. Once you go to bed and fall asleep, it will be gone for ever. If time is a teacher, what have you learned from today? If you don't think you have learned much, visualize yourself tomorrow and what you will be doing. Feel excitement for the potential waiting for you there. Promise yourself that you will learn something new about yourself tomorrow.

Then, blow out your candle to mark the end of your day with gratitude and grace, knowing you have left your day behind and acknowledged its significance. Your day is over and all is well. Tomorrow is another day.

CLOSING RITUAL
#363: SEAL THE EMOTIONAL GENIE

To ease heartache, store things in a box

We all need to find ways to work through heartache and find emotional closure in a way that empowers rather than diminishes us. One particularly helpful way[17] to find closure is to put things associated with your emotional upset in a box.

Your ritual this evening is to spend some time thinking about someone or something in your life, present or past, that has caused you emotional pain. Get a pen and paper and for ten minutes write about your experience and what you learned from it. Pour out your heart. Then seal your notes in an envelope. If you prefer, you can find a small box or container to put your notes in alongside photos or personal items associated with your painful experience. As you perform this ritual, feel in your heart how these actions are helping you to find closure.

17 https://journals.sagepub.com/doi/pdf/10.1177/0956797610376653

CLOSING RITUAL
#364: CLOSING POSITION
Bow your head and look up

The ancient Hindu word *Namaste*[18] is more than a way to signal the beginning and end of a yoga class; it is both a loving greeting and a peaceful farewell that can deepen spiritual connection. The word has many interpretations, but in general it means "I bow to you" or "From the light of my spirit to the light of your spirit" and it expresses an intention to connect to your higher self and the higher selves of others.

Your ritual today is to say *Namaste* out loud at both the beginning and the end of your day. Both times when you say it hold your hands in the prayer position close to your heart and bow your head. In the morning say it with the intention of connecting to the best version of yourself and the best version of all the people you are going to interact with. Take the idea of *Namaste* into your day to see if it inspires all your interactions.

In the evening say it as a peaceful, loving and grateful farewell to your day and all that was beautiful and good in it. Using the same word to greet and end your day will once again remind you that endings and beginnings are as one.

Note: Today is a good day to simply read the Heart section of this book.

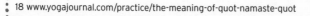

18 www.yogajournal.com/practice/the-meaning-of-quot-namaste-quot

CLOSING RITUAL
#365: GOODNIGHT
Living without regret

CONGRATULATIONS! You have reached the end of your ritual year! It isn't an ending, it's a new beginning. It's the start of another 365 days of rituals. Moving forward, use all that you have learned to help you see sacred potential in everything that you do. Rituals are the life-changing power of "I do". They transform you into a person of action – a person the universe can finally believe in. Exciting times lie ahead for you.

Your year-end ritual today is to find that piece of paper you put in an envelope at the beginning of your year (*see* Introduction, page 12. Read that letter from your past self to your present self. Do you still have the same feelings now? Have you evolved? Celebrate your successes. If you feel there is still a way to go, remember that a meaningful life is a never-ending journey and not a destination. Happiness is not always the place where the greatest progress is made. Just as exercise stresses your body to make it stronger, setbacks challenge you to evolve into a better version of yourself. As long as you are learning and evolving you are living a life of meaning.

NO REGRETS

There is an ancient belief that suggests when you die the first person you meet in heaven is the highest version of yourself. Your best self is the infinitely wise part of you that understands true happiness and fulfilment can never be found in externals, other people or material things. It can only ever be found within. Your authentic self is the part of you that knows the power of your daily actions and how ritualizing them can help you create a life that is both good for you and an inspiration to others.

All the rituals in this book can help you evolve so you can experience the bliss of meeting your best self in this life rather than the next. Then, when the time eventually comes for your last goodnight, you will have only peace, love and gratitude in your heart. You will have lived what is the best and most rewarding life of all – a life of absolutely no regrets.

CONTACT THE AUTHOR

If you have any questions or insights to share, feel free to get in touch with me at angeltalk710@aol.com or via www.theresacheung.com. I'd love to hear from you. Let me know, too, if there is one ritual from this book that you feel has had the greatest impact on your life. (If you are struggling to choose, consider what ritual you would recommend to your 16-year-old self.) Be sure to take advantage of the free ritual tracker available at my website on the ritual page to help you commit to your daily rituals and stay energized, productive and living your amazing life full of purpose.

SIMPLE BUT POWERFUL REMINDERS

★ Actions speak louder than thoughts, feelings or words.
★ Rituals are the life-changing power of "I do".